An Alien in a Strange Land

An Alien in a Strange Land

Theology in the Life of William Stringfellow

ANTHONY DANCER

with a foreword by Rowan Williams

CASCADE *Books* · Eugene, Oregon

AN ALIEN IN A STRANGE LAND
Theology in the Life of William Stringfellow

Cascade Publications
An Imprint of Wipf and Stock Publishers
199 W. 8th Ave., Suite 3
Eugene, OR 97401

www. wipfandstock.com

ISBN 13: 978-1-59752-906-8

Cataloging-in-Publication data:

Dancer, Anthony, 1967–

    An alien in a strange land : theology in the life of William Stringfellow / Anthony Dancer ; foreword by Rowan Williams.

    xiv + 272 p. ; 23 cm. Includes bibliographical citations and index.

    ISBN 13: 978-1-59752-906-8

    1. Stringfellow, William. 2. Christian biography. I. Williams, Rowan, 1950–. II. Title.

BX4827.S7954 D19 2011

Contents

Foreword by Rowan Williams • *vii*

Acknowledgments • *ix*

Introduction • *xi*

1   Outlook and Orientation • 1

PART ONE: Location—The Law and the Church

2   Social Context I • 15

3   The Empirical Imperative: Law, Politics, and Vocation • 36

PART TWO: Movement—Faith and Politics

4   Social Context II • 99

5   Resisting Religion: The Vocation of the Church • 125

6   Radicalizing Agency: Encounters Pro and Con • 166

7   Moving in Freedom amidst Death and Life • 206

8   Conclusion • 244

Bibliography • 253

Name Index • 269

I've said to Bill uneasily:
dreams in that house are like a hot pot
constantly stirred, fumes intense, voices
grandiloquent. What gives?
Bill paused between beats, like the sea.
Like the sea, he's no explainer, but pure depth.
He's not on earth to unravel dreams—
to precipitate them rather, like a slowly turned
vintage vat. Drink then, and dream on.

—Daniel Berrigan, *Block Island*, 2.

Foreword

WILLIAM STRINGFELLOW IS ONE of those people who is impossible to classify easily, and who is an equally unsettling figure for partisans of all complexions. A passionate radical, committed to the poor and to a variety of "progressive" causes, he was a scathing critic of the reduction of Christianity to social service. A persistent proclaimer of the absolute authority of the Bible, he was perpetually in conflict with fundamentalists and deeply hostile to what he regarded as defensive, moralistic, or pietist readings. Identified by the greatest Protestant theologian of the twentieth century as the man that America should be listening to, he never held an academic post or indeed any significant public role.

But Karl Barth's praise for him as the voice America needed to hear was and is well-founded. Stringfellow had an unfailing eye for that confusion of loyalty to the state or the social order with fidelity to Christ that appears so regularly in modern European and American Christianity, and he was able, with the same energy and clarity as Barth himself, to insist that "religion," as a specialism or a hobby or a secluded and secure subdivision of social activity, was the prime enemy of "biblical" existence, of the faith that lives under the annihilating and recreating Word of God. As the title of Tony Dancer's excellent study suggests, he accepted (though not easily) the reproach and marginality this involved, and lived and wrote with a degree of solitary integrity that is very rare.

He was not without flaws, and Dancer lets us see some of them. The merciless concentration of Stringfellow's prose can sometimes come across simply as tense, grating, and even pompous. His personal tensions and disagreements were often wrapped in the rhetoric of high principle, as if there were one and only one utterly correct way of responding to specific problems; his break with the East Harlem Protestant Parish is a painful illustration of this. His judgement of people was sometimes erratic. He could be bitterly critical of some for what seem like disproportionate reasons and surprisingly indulgent to others who look less serious, honest, or intelligent (I confess to the uncomfortable feeling that, despite his realistic portrayal of the man's weaknesses, he was rather soft on the sad self-dramatizings of Bishop James Pike). But he was a man who indisputably faced and carried the cost of his relentless honesty with enormous courage and style. And the written legacy, complex and forbiddingly intense as much of it is, remains one of the great deposits of twentieth-century English-language theology, deplorably neglected by most and badly in need of the sympathetic tracking of its developments and location against its background that Tony Dancer offers here.

This is an invaluable foundation for the full biography that is still to be written, utilizing abundant archival material and private testimony to very good effect. But it is also a picture of one man's theological pilgrimage set against the backdrop of post-war America and sketching the trends of the age, in society and church, with great skill and perceptiveness. At a time when the marriage of religiosity and fearfully defensive nationalism is as much in evidence as it ever was, and when the churches are showing an exceptional talent for throwing away any residual credibility by the bitterness of their internal quarrels, Stringfellow's uncompromising witness to the biblical imperatives is water in a dry land. He still summons believers to say no, in Jesus Christ, to the power of death, as expressed in oppression, religious anxiety, moralizing superiority, and to say yes to the new creation, life in the "holy nation" which is called out as a sign to all human social existence of what God makes possible. I hope this book will send many back to Stringfellow's own unique and disturbing work, so that the churches may again be challenged to be what they actually are for the sake of the world's healing.

Rowan Williams
February 2010

Acknowledgments

THIS BOOK BEGAN AS a thesis in 1998. It has come a long way since then. For that, my thanks are due to a number of people.

My supervisors, Chris Rowland and John Webster, have both been exceptional, and I am indebted to their assistance and patience, and their ability to just be there for me when I needed it. Their positive outlook on the research sustained me. I am especially grateful for their willingness to read and comment upon the work in its many draft forms—at times it was well above and beyond the call of duty. There is little doubt it would not have found its present form without them. I am also indebted to Alan Brinkley, who was so generous with his time and expertise, introduced me to the history of the period and guided my search. Also, thanks to John D'Emilio for taking the time to answer my questions, and making suggestions on where to look.

Similarly, I am indebted to Bill Wylie-Kellermann, whose friendship, encouragement, and insight have done much to maintain me on an even keel.

My thanks to the AHRB for their funding, and to The Queen's College for providing the financial support necessary to allow me to attend the archives at Cornell. Whilst at Cornell I was fortunate enough to be able to make contact with Jack Lewis, and my thanks are due to him for insights into both the Christian Faith and Life Community and Stringfellow, much of which sadly never made its way into the final version of this book.

Thanks are also due to my board for providing me with time off to complete work on this manuscript and ready it for publication, and a scholarship from the St John's College trust board that thankfully assisted me during this period.

Introduction

WILLIAM STRINGFELLOW WAS THE kind of oddity that doesn't come along every day. He spoke truth to power, whether either party was fully ready for such a conversation, as so often they were not. His was a voice from the margins, honed on the street, eloquent and incisive. His was a very human, fragile, passionate life attempting to live in freedom and obedience to God, against the tyranny of empire. He spoke as much with his life as he did his writing. Although reprints of Stringfellow's books in recent years provide easier access to much of his published writing, there remains no sustained treatment of and engagement with Stringfellow at a biographical level. There are many reasons for this, and although this is no biography it does contain within it a sustained engagement with his life. It is only by engaging his theology through biography that we can begin more fully and comprehensively to appreciate Stringfellow's significance to us today, particularly as we seek to discern what it means to be human and faithful amidst our rapidly changing social context. Theology, as Stringfellow realized only too well, is a fundamentally practical, political, and missional discipline orientated around, and orientating, our life in the world.

The first chapter introduces Stringfellow and establishes the research methodology employed herein. The relationship of Stringfellow's life and his theology is such that in seeking to understand the latter it is necessary to enquire into the former. This research therefore takes the form of *biographical theology*: a critical examination of Stringfellow's lifework that explores the way in which his commitment to politics and faith informed his vocational (and therefore theological) formation and articulation to the point at which his moral theology becomes most fully immersed in the politics of the Bible. This commitment to politics and faith make personal and social context, private and political life, crucial to the formation of his life and theology, and therefore this book places Stringfellow's lifework within his socio-political context.

Chapter 2 examines the socio-political context of the 1950s, in relation to which Stringfellow essentially sought to locate himself. These were crucial years for America, dominated by the themes of threat (Cold War and communism) and prosperity (economic growth); excess and fear amidst a culture of consumption provided the framework for cultural identity.

Chapter 3 goes on to examine Stringfellow's engagement with both the law and the church during this period and pays particular attention to his decision for both faith and law: on both counts a conversion experience was to prove paradigmatic for his later work. This chapter also draws upon his experiences in the ecumenical movement, the law, and later in Harlem. The themes of reconciliation and authenticity emerge to the fore, and the politics of ecumenism—the political dimension of unity—has a high profile. Paying particular attention to examining the emergence of this politicization, it examines his time in Europe, before discussing his commitment to the Bible and the layperson. Attention is also given to his emerging understanding of the Christian life as worship, and the consequences this has for his understanding of the law and the church. Finally, it examines his lifework as he encounters the East Harlem Protestant Parish and poverty, and discovers the concrete reality of the power of death in the principalities and powers. The empirical imperative that dominates his lifework is here a desire for political and personal authenticity.

Following this, chapter 4 explores some of the salient features of the sociopolitical landscape of the 1960s. It shows how this period was one of hopeful democracy, in which movements of dissent and protest began to emerge; it was a time of radical protest and liberal government, and yet by the beginning of the 1970s the nation had become polarized. It explores how, whilst the "threat" of communism persisted, and in fact took very real and manifest form, liberal politics dominated government in the form of the Great Society, and politics and law were seen as morally determinate. Issues of rights came to the fore, mostly on the back of successful civil rights legislation, and left wing politics found a voice on the campuses of America's colleges through the movement of the new left.

Next, attention is given to Stringfellow's lifework during this period, in which he confronted what he saw as the state's bullish attitude of invincibility, along with religion's apostasy. The dominant theme of his public and private encounters throughout the 1960s and beyond was his commitment to articulating the relevance and importance of the politics of the Bible for living in freedom from the power of death. Emphasis is given to the way it was ultimately, however, less an act of criticism and more an act of restoring hope.

Therefore, chapter 5 explores how he called the church to account through his polemical writing, confronting religion in America, and identifying the complicity of White Anglo-Saxon Protestants in the maintenance of the state and their betrayal of the gospel. It also examines the hope which he extended by exploring what he believed the ministry and mission of the authentic church of Christ might look like: the centrality of the Bible, the restoration of the roles of priests and people, the seminary underground, and the character of the Christian life which this fosters.

Chapter 6 moves on to examine three radicalizing encounters that transformed his lifework: his meeting with Karl Barth (who advocated America should listen to this man), his rejection at an ecumenical conference on Religion and Race (at which he declared the answer to the racial crisis is baptism), and his meeting and falling in love with Anthony Towne (through which he discovered and experienced love and acceptance at a personal level). It discusses how these events radicalized his lifework in relation to biblical politics.

Following these discussions, chapter 7 examines their effects upon his lifework by examining his prophetic confrontation with Johnson's Great Society. This represents not so much a radical departure as a radical reorientation in relation to the power of death. The Great Society was the political hallowed ground of the mid-1960s, and Stringfellow's confrontation draws upon the resources of his lifework to date. Particular attention is given to his criticisms of race and poverty, given their prominence in his lifework. It goes on to show how, following these criticisms, Stringfellow once again offers hope, this time detailing what he terms the *ethics of reconciliation*—a demand not for novelty, but orthodoxy for *life*. It therefore looks at his incarnational christological ethic, which requires a revolution in the way in which America conceives of Jesus Christ: it is biblical politics—reconciliation of creation to God in Christ, fostering *realism, inconsistency, radicalism,* and *intercession.*

Finally, this book explores his own experience of life-threatening illness and personal confrontation of death. It discusses the way in which this was at once both a personal and public encounter, upon which he brought biblical politics to bear in resistance and advocacy. It then goes on to discuss the way in which this fostered a further and final point of radicalization in his lifework leading directly up to the production of *An Ethic for Christians and Other Aliens in a Strange Land*: the emergence of semiotic creativity, in which Babylon and Jerusalem confront one another.

The chapters of this book weave our way through a foundational part of his life and work. His lifework teaches us about hope. It is deeply political and intensely personal. It is vulnerable, human, inconsistent, and not without mistakes. It is woven together at the edges of society, pulling together the varied threads of experience and encounter. There is both a sweetness and a lament in the weaving that teach us something profound about being biblical people.

This book is dedicated to all who walk this path. Most especially, it is dedicated to Hera.

Finally, there is a saying in Maori: *E kore te kumara e korero mo tona ake reka* (The *kumara* never tells of its own sweetness). A traditional staple food for Maori, it is left for those who delight in the *kumara* and feed off it to speak on its behalf. So it is with Stringfellow. I am proud to have the responsibility to speak of such sweetness, and hope it may enrich lives.

Outlook and Orientation

INTRODUCTION

THROUGHOUT HIS ADULT LIFE Stringfellow's commitment was to politics on the one hand, and the Christian faith on the other; they were the "twin pillars" of his life and work. It was a commitment which meant that the horizon of his theological landscape was occupied most prominently by his personal and social context; the private and political life. Together the twin concerns of this commitment provide the framework through which our discussion takes place: they are the lens through which we make our examination. However, Stringfellow's life-long preoccupation with the Christian life in the world (the empirical imperative) can often cloud the reader's ability to see the subtle, significant, and strong ecclesiology which is operative in his thinking (indeed, his ecclesiology is often masked by his empirical imperative). One of the things this book does is make this ecclesiology more easily visible to those who would read Stringfellow.

Stringfellow's view of politics and faith are expressed most clearly, in some ways most elaborately, in his theological works. This book therefore examines the life-work of William Stringfellow leading up to the emergence of his moral theology in perhaps his most well known book, *An Ethic for Christians and Other Aliens in a Strange Land*, which is something of a watershed in his life and work. Consequently, it looks at the development of his understanding of both politics and faith in relation to his life and his social context, and traces the emergence of what he called "biblical politics," which is at the heart of his moral theology.

BIOGRAPHICAL SKETCH

William Stringfellow's writing spans four decades, and his life just two more, cut short by a severe medical condition that plagued him for many years. His was a life in which the threat of death was always present; a life not so much haunted as hunted by death. This situation is not without some irony, for it was precisely his experience of this physical suffering that enabled him to write in a way that was at once original and orthodox, yielding a theology that was both prophetic and unparalleled: an unshrinking demand for Christians to live in a fashion that embodied the politics of the Bible amidst a fallen world. Stringfellow himself would be wary of making such a claim. He would not have seen his life ironically, but rather simply as witness to the Word of God, in which he experienced the reality of the pervasiveness of death in the human personal and political condition. Certainly, this is how he portrayed it in his writings. This reconciliation of personal and political realities naturally finds focus in his writing in a manner which engages biblical exegesis on both political and personal levels, as he listened to and lived in the world.

Stringfellow was born in 1928 in Rhode Island, and grew up in a working class family in New England. His father worked as a hosiery knitter, but was often out of work during and after the Great Depression. However, it seems that as a child Stringfellow was not really aware of his family's poverty, and even as a young man he didn't quite fit. He writes: "At a time in life when (I suppose) I should have been obsessed with football, sex, or pop music, as my peers seemed to be, I was very bothered about the identity of Jesus Christ" (Schoonover, 1985:12).

Through dint of hard work and commitment Stringfellow won a scholarship to attend Bates college in 1945, majoring in politics and economics. It was an environment in which he flourished, especially in the areas of politics and religion, and his involvement with the Student Christian Movement (SCM) during this time led to his becoming something of a "professional Christian." At that time the SCM was an incubator of biblical thinking; the atmosphere alive with discussions of politics, biblical theology, Christian vocation, and lay theology. It was an environment which provided Stringfellow with opportunities, tools, and resources to thrive. His time at college was a period which marked the beginning of what was to become a short, yet controversial public life as a lawyer, theologian, and prophetic-critic of political society.

Even as he left college in 1949, Stringfellow was differentiated from his peers by his unswerving commitment to the importance and centrality of politics *and* faith to the Christian life, for it was a commitment few shared at that time.[1] In 1950 he went overseas to study at the London School of Economics for a year, and to engage in student Christian work around Europe. No sooner did he return to the United States than he was drafted into the army, and in 1951 was stationed in Germany as a NATO soldier.[2] He disliked his time as a soldier intensely, but engaged it fully and critically.

Following his discharge, he trained as a lawyer at Harvard Law School (1953–1956), and afterwards moved to the East Harlem district of New York City until 1962. Here he worked in the East Harlem Protestant Parish before setting up his own law practice representing the poor, outcast, and marginalized. It is through this experience that he came to see the reality of the principalities and powers: a prominent organizing theme in his theology. Throughout this time he kept up a rigorous schedule of writing and national and international speaking engagements, while remaining involved in the formation of a number of significant new initiatives in law and politics, and continued his commitment to the World Council of Churches (WCC) Faith and Order Commission.

Perhaps the most-cited event in Stringfellow's life during the early 1960s was his participation in a question and answer session with Karl Barth at Chicago University in 1962, and the subsequent privately organized social engagements Stringfellow and Barth enjoyed together. The frequency with which this event is referenced by those writing about Stringfellow is perhaps not surprising, for it was during this conference that Barth encouraged America to listen to Stringfellow and his theology. Barth had renounced criticizing America, but the message was clear: they were kindred minds, they read the same Bible.

Serious and persistent illness plagued Stringfellow, and his hectic life in New York along with his punishing schedule only contributed to his ill health. In order to change the pace of his life, he moved with

---

1. It is primarily through his reading at college, but mostly his travels to Europe, that Stringfellow was to discover others united in the same commitment, and from whom he was to draw inspiration.

2. Stringfellow served as an Army Supply clerk at the rank of sergeant.

Anthony Towne to Block Island, Rhode Island in 1967.[3] However, in 1968 his illnesses finally culminated in a lifethreatening operation in which his pancreas and spleen were removed. By this point, Stringfellow writes, "the issue had become, not whether I would live or die, but when death would succeed" (Stringfellow, 1970e:71). To everyone's amazement, including his own, Stringfellow survived. But his life was not the same. The operation made him a surgical diabetic, rendering him subject, in practical terms, to the observance of a strict medical regime, serving as death's acolytes.[4] The solitude of this new home afforded him an environment to recuperate, reflect, and work. Here he continued to write and involve himself in the local community (serving as Second Warden in the city government for a time), the World Council of Churches, a number of student Christian movements, especially the World Student Christian Federation, and he continued to address audiences throughout the country (and beyond). It was here on Block Island that he harbored Daniel Berrigan, then a fugitive from the Federal Bureau of Investigation, and with him was indicted.

His abiding theological concern was with politics and faith, especially in relation to vocation, and ethics—a concern arising out of and grounded in the Word of God. These are the themes he explored in a radically contextual way throughout his life. One of Stringfellow's other passions was the circus; such was its strength that at one point, during the summer of 1966, he and Anthony toured with a circus in New England for three months (Stringfellow, 1970e:168), and he subsequently wrote about the circus as a parable of the Kingdom of God.

The effects of this surgical operation, which saved this somewhat eclectic and charismatic life in 1968, finally took it in 1985.

WHO DO OTHERS SAY THAT I AM?

Descriptions of Stringfellow abound. The most succinct description is perhaps one that Stringfellow himself uses to describe the Christian

3. Stringfellow described Towne as his "sweet companion for seventeen years" (Stringfellow, 1982b:115): a description the publishers tried to remove lest it be misunderstood. Ironically, this was the closest Stringfellow ever came to "coming out" as homosexual. Privately, he had fewer problems expressing his love to Towne (Stringfellow, 1963i; Towne, 1963b).

4. This regime necessitated the consumption of animal enzymes to aid in the digestion of his food. However, despite consuming well in excess of 5,000 kilocalories a day, the weight loss was dramatic and went largely unabated.

life; he was "a parable before the powers."[5] Alongside this, he has been described variously as a prophet, a theologian, an agitator, an advocate, a lawyer, a lay theologian, a social critic, a politician, a connoisseur of the circus, an interlocutor with Barth, ruthless, difficult, unreliable, a man faithful in friendship and obedient in his faith, an original and con-frontational thinker, egocentric, and as a man of hope. This descriptive abundance is born out of attempts to identify the central characteristic of his life and work and to use it as the universal descriptor, or theme, for any subsequent understanding of Stringfellow's life and work. However, I suggest that all of these descriptions, in and of themselves, are incom-plete and inadequate.

Such multifarious descriptions appear to abound for two reasons: the first is that people don't know how to engage and make sense of his life and theology without a unifying theme; the second is that the sheer number and diversity of these descriptions reflect aspects of the highly eclectic character of his life and his theology.

Most people who encounter Stringfellow do so through his pub-lished writings. However, when faced with the task of describing his writing to newcomers, one discovers quickly the many ways it defies description. The result is often that of being drawn, by its narrative "force," to deploy Stringfellow to describe himself: it often appears easier for writer and reader alike to present Stringfellow's writing rather than describe and examine it.

Stanley Hauerwas and Jeff Powell have asserted that Stringfellow "didn't quite fit," being neither a theologian nor a lawyer as we convention-ally understand either (Hauerwas and Powell, 1995:31). This statement betrays precisely the frustration and difficulty of describing Stringfellow. They identify the problem with trying to assess Stringfellow's theological contribution and impact: if he doesn't fit how do we then speak of him in order to evaluate, assess, apply, and if applicable, categorize his work? Unfortunately, while perhaps attractive, Hauerwas and Powell's rhetoric is ultimately quite unhelpful and plays directly into the hands of those in both "professions" of theology and law with which Stringfellow was engaged. Rather than "not fitting," more correctly Stringfellow could be understood in many ways to be archetypal of both these "professions." Accordingly, it is not Stringfellow who didn't fit, but rather the prevailing

---

5. Bill Wylie-Kellermann (1997) describes him in just this way.

categories which do not fit him. The professions of law and theology simply could not account for his lifework.

An example illustrates this. One frequent approach has been to describe Stringfellow as a theologian *and* social critic,[6] both elements being seen as characteristic of his writing. Such a description is an attempt to speak of the clearly critical edge and insightful diagnoses which permeate his writing, often aimed at the church and the state. Such a critical edge is not all that surprising when one considers Stringfellow was writing in one of the most politically turbulent periods of recent American history, characterized by protest and a search for personal and political authenticity—authenticity sought most often from a politically radical standpoint.

This description is symbolic of the problems people encounter when they try to speak about or assess Stringfellow's work, and the way they struggle to make sense of a strong sense of dialectic in his writing, mistakenly confusing it with what one might call the external "tension" of theology and politics. This apparent tension is what emerges between critique of the contemporary context, be it ecclesial or sociopolitical, on the one hand, and the hopeful narrative of the alternate reality of the Kingdom of God on the other: the tension between the gospel's "No!" and the "Yes!" On more than one occasion he makes it clear that the problem of separation of theology and social action/criticism is actually an illustration of precisely the issue at stake and the problem he believes he is addressing. In Stringfellow's lifework, apparent logical opposition is actually held together in harmony through biblical politics.[7]

The primary problem with this "social critic" characterization lies in the way it is posed alongside the description of Stringfellow as a theologian. In so doing, it fails to fully appreciate the thoroughly theological status of Stringfellow's critical writing: the separation suggested simply

6. This description can be found in Slocum (1997).

7. See, for example, Stringfellow (1969d:15–16). For Stringfellow this tension is nothing other than the identification and denouncement of the power of death (the Fall) in the light of the redeeming gospel of Christ, in which humanity and the whole world are reconciled to God and freed from death's power, through the witness to, and ongoing enactment of, the politics of the Bible (and its semiotic creativity). As Dalferth puts it: "semiotic creativity, not the discovery of truth, is the key to translatability; and translatability, not identity, is what we need to harmonize our perspectives" (Dalferth,1988:148). Emphasizing this harmony between perspectives, he came to regard " this world in the fullness of its fallen estate as *simultaneously* disclosing the ecumenical, militant, triumphant presence of God" (Stringfellow, 1973b:41).

does not exist in his life and work.[8] The word "social" is inappropriate for it understands his critical comments precisely within, or internal to, the framework of that which he is being critical of (i.e., fallen creation and its various idols); it absorbs his critical rhetoric and seeks to conform its meaning to the epistemological self-understanding of the (essentially) fallen structure of the world. The word "critic" is inappropriate for adequately presenting the positive force of his writing and the *hope* it exudes; critique is the origin, not the end he seeks to convey.

Stringfellow was no more a "social critic" than a "social activist": he was a Christian, engaged (theologically) in the world through faith. It appears it is the characterization, rather than Stringfellow or his writing, which most often doesn't seem to "fit." "My sole intention," wrote Stringfellow in the preface to *Conscience and Obedience*, "is to affirm a biblical hope which comprehends politics and which transcends politics" (Stringfellow, 1977a:9). It should not therefore surprise us that "social critic" was a characterization Stringfellow saw fit to distance himself from.

> These are theological comments, not social criticism or political analyses, although biblically it is impossible to separate theology from these other matters. These essays make no pretense to being either wholly consistent or utterly coherent; they embody an attempt to respond in terms of the versatility of Christ's gospel to particular aspects of the American social crisis. (Stringfellow,1966c:vii)

It often appears the characterization of him as, for example, a "social critic," is problematic because it seeks to define him primarily from the perspective of the ordinary—defining him in relation to the world, not the Word. Far from proving to be his undoing, this failure to fit into any prevailing categories of theology, law, or social criticism is a helpful hermeneutical and epistemological clue to trying to read and understand Stringfellow. One can see this perhaps most clearly in the published texts themselves, in which his language and vision are not limited by this world. They are not in bondage to the power of death which he wrote so much about, but set free in the "world of the Bible" which is also our world; a word set free in, by, and through the Word.

---

8. It also would appear to confess a belief in the apparent disjunction of both roles in the wider world, again indicating a predisposition towards defining him in terms of the wider world (the external perspective upon faith), and trying to make him fit.

ECLECTIC, CONTEXTUAL, ALLURING

In this diffuseness of designations we begin to see not only part of the cause of the problems that confront the researcher, but also a key to Stringfellow's significance, namely, his commitment to the Bible and his eclectic nature, his intense proximity and commitment to context, and the way in which he engages the latter through the former. It is precisely these designations which at once provide us with the key to Stringfellow's significance and the difficulty in speaking about him.

Whilst some designations may be of more benefit than others, there is no single way of examining his lifework. Published and unpublished material tell of myriad layers of context and theme all concerned with living the Christian life in obedience to the authority of the risen Lord. Finding a way to interpret the available material such that the contextual and thematic voices are symphonic, rather than mere cacophony, is the considerable task that faces the researcher.

As all our work is historically conditioned any theologian's understanding of another's work must take into account their context. This is particularly true for any researcher approaching Stringfellow's life and work. Often, a theologian's own awareness of context is limited to an awareness of intellectual history—a direct consequence of theology's relatively recent preoccupation with functioning predominantly at a level removed from the practice of faith. The work of William Stringfellow provides a notable exception; for him, context of whatever sort was central to the theological enterprise in which he engaged, and an essential theological resource. In fact the primary motivator of his work was the context of the practice of faith, or to put another way, the place in which he found himself standing—and that was, as we shall see, often a tough place to be. Andrew McThenia described precisely this problem in a collection of papers on Stringfellow:

> It was predicted at the time of his death that within a few years Stringfellow's life and theology would become the source of numerous dissertations. That apparently has not happened. And I have a hunch about why it has not. That which is attractive to and the object of study by the academy is that which can be analyzed by means of the tools accepted in most precincts of the academy— the tools of social science. And science deals most effectively with that which is knowable in an objective sense, that which is subject to generalisation and can be replicated. Stringfellow will not fit

under a microscope very well. He probably cannot be explained. He certainly cannot be replicated . . . So much of Stringfellow's writing was autobiographical, and any attempt to distill it is to rob it of its power. (McThenia, 1995a:13)

This major problem of how to engage with and write about Stringfellow and critically assess his significance (how to put him under the microscope and examine and assess him without robbing him and his work of precisely that power which makes him worthy of study in the first place) is one I have had to deal with writing this book. That this introduction has been in part biographical is some indication of the way Stringfellow's import is generally interpreted: there is little separation between his life and his work.

How then do we examine Stringfellow's lifework? Generally responses to such a question yield answers that suggest we read him confessionally on his own terms, and there is much merit in this approach, for this was a man for whom theology, literally, was his life.[9] In his work, Stringfellow presents a carefully managed orchestration and presentation of his life, his context, and his encounter with the Bible in relation to issues and contexts, problems and solutions, insights and reflections. He lays this presentation before us in such a way that he hopes our view of the world and what is important might begin to converge with his own: his work is an existential witness, a biographical form of evangelism. This presentation takes the form of a narrative which, whilst conveying authority, is not so much forceful as invitational: an invitation to see the world the way Stringfellow did is constantly being extended to the reader through the use of various polemic devices. Authoritative power is lent to Stringfellow's orchestration by virtue of his stylistic convergence with much biblical witness, and it therefore functions as *persuasive* power—it seeks to persuade the reader through its polemical rhetoric. In other words, it functions as *witness*. If we are going to examine and assess the impact and significance of Stringfellow adequately, we need at once to be drawn in by, and yet to some extent evade, that persuasive charm and the narrative-reality it construes.[10]

9. Such responses can be seen in some of the contributions to McThenia (1995a); Slocum (1997).

10. Wylie-Kellermann also suggests that the narrative of Stringfellow's polemic echoes the power of the Gospels to re-engage the powers through their retelling. Thus, the narrative's power becomes itself actively resistant to the powers. "Stringfellow saw

Others, especially those engaged in academic research, believe they require a more critical and objective approach, and to these ends Stringfellow is problematic. While reading Stringfellow as he wished to be read and critiquing his work on its own merit is necessary for understanding and examining the character of his theology, there is a demand for more. We need at once to accept his own self-description, and yet also look behind and in front of it: where did it come from? What and who influenced him? Was there a long gestation for his theology? Are there significant points in its formation? Why does he opt for the contexts he does? Why does his theology seem so similar to other European theologians—at once familiar and yet foreign? How did he come to such a radical understanding of faith and politics? How did he understand being a lawyer in relation to theology? What was his driving force? Unfortunately, this critical-objective approach frequently falls foul of the problems indicated by McThenia, but could potentially shed significant light on Stringfellow's work, if only it could be harnessed alongside the first, more confessional approach.

Therefore, although there are inherent difficulties with this critical-perspective approach to Stringfellow, it should not be discounted, but embraced along side confession. The merit of the confessional perspective to our work and theology—essentially that it unfolds "the internal perspective [on faith] in such a way that it reconstructs the external perspective within the perspective of faith," and is stronger than a theology which does not (Dalferth,1988:56)—cannot be disregarded. For the researcher of Stringfellow, some means by which these methods can be united is required.

How then, for the purposes of this research, do we read William Stringfellow? How does one orientate oneself in relation to his theology (his lifework) in order to critically assess and better understand it? The approach I have chosen is that of biography, for it holds together the tensions so far discussed, whilst providing an original outlook on Stringfellow's lifework.

---

the narrative of his own self-accounting as yet another engagement which carried the struggle a step further, affecting again the exposure of the powers. This is biblically apropos. A gospel, for example, is the good news of Jesus' open confrontation with the rulers and authorities, which is itself—in the retelling of proclamation—a frontal assault on their rule" (Wylie-Kellermann, 1997:3–4).

In his own writing, Stringfellow was quite explicit about his commitment not only to biography but also to understanding biography as theology. Biography unifies Stringfellow's work and his own life, and his commitment to biography has direct consequences for his use of scripture. Consequently, aspects of his life and work, and their conjunction, must form the basis of any research into his theology. This reflects his commitment to the Christian life as a parable-like witness. Stringfellow locates its importance in the following way:

> *Any* biography and *every* biography, is inherently theological in the sense that it contains already—literally by virtue of the Incarnation—the news of the gospel whether or not anyone discerns that. *We* are each one of us parables . . . What I am discussing is how the living Word of God is implicated in the actual life of this world. (original emphasis Stringfellow, 1982b:20)

Understanding theology as biography renders experience as a significant, if not *the* significant, resource for theology. However, for Stringfellow this experience is one of the Word encountering us in the world, rather than purely our experience of the world and of God: the initiative rests with the Trinity (sustaining us as we inhabit/embody restored creation). This is, by his own admission, nothing other than the doctrine of revelation. Stringfellow referred to the event and process of being aware of *this* significance of one's biography as *vocation*. So conceived, vocation does not merely describe or explain the Word's encounter with us in the world; it is its conscious embodiment in history and in hope.

For Stringfellow, the biographical nature of theology places Christological and pneumatological anthropology at the very heart of his theological enterprise; it is the story of inhabiting restored creation. Consequently, he is primarily and essentially a *practical theologian*, concerned with the radical lifelong explication and exploration of the Christian life as ministry and mission—the lifelong process of orientating ourselves in relation to God, the world, and others.

PROCEEDING

The relationship of Stringfellow's life and his theology is such that in seeking to understand the latter we must also enquire into the former; the two cannot be separated in any meaningful way. What follows is therefore biographical theology: a critical exploration and examination of Stringfellow's lifework which explores the way in which Stringfellow's commitment to politics and faith informed his vocational (and therefore theological) formation and articulation to the point at which his moral theology becomes most fully immersed in the politics of the Bible.

In dealing with the material biographically, I have made the decision to organize it in a predominantly chronological manner, wherever possible. To this end the research has two parts. Part one explores the period leading up to the end of the 1950s, and examines the emergence of themes and concerns which lay the foundation for Stringfellow's later theology: *locating* Stringfellow's lifework, and the places from which his theology emerged. Part two traces the continued development of what becomes his moral theology through the 1960s leading up to its initial explicitly formalized (most fully radicalized) presentation in *Ethic for Christians and Other Aliens in a Strange Land*: it looks at the *movement* in his lifework to this moment. The empirical nature of Stringfellow's lifework is such that each part in turn contains a distinct chapter which provides the sociopolitical context in whose light Stringfellow's life-work must be understood.

PART ONE

Location—The Law and the Church

Social Context I

INTRODUCTION

THE POST-WAR YEARS WERE a crucial era not just for Stringfellow, but
for America generally. Stringfellow's passion for politics meant that
he was fully conversant with the culture of which he was a part, and he
understood clearly the issues at stake, their relationship to one another,
and their gravity. Therefore, before we look at Stringfellow's engagement
with the 1950s we must first immerse ourselves in it, in order to understand something of the social, political, and economic context in which
he lived and worked, and to better discern the underlying currents that
he addressed.

THREAT AND PROSPERITY: THE HISTORICAL SETTING

The scene is 1950s America—the incubator of modern Western culture.
American citizens are filled with optimism for the future. Cultural icons
abounded, for it was the decade that brought us such things as Formica,
Barbie dolls, hula hoops, junk mail, processed food, credit cards, modern
advertising, household gadgets, rock and roll, supermarkets, McDonald's,
IBM, polio vaccine and other medical breakthroughs, the suburbs, and
the emergence of the term "teenager" (and its cultural embodiment).
Stringfellow had just returned home from Europe, buoyed up by his
studies at the London School of Economics, and by what he had seen
and experienced in his travels around Europe, including meeting and
speaking with Tito, Muslim leaders, Soviet students, a variety of cooperatives, and the community at Iona.[1]

1. Stringfellow (1950c) provides details of just some of Stringfellow's speaking engagements as World Student Christian Federation/United Student Christian

The 1950s context out of which Stringfellow emerged is perhaps one of the most politically and economically dramatic in American history, crowded with the contradictions and complexities that transformed America into the country that we know today. Violence and conflict have played a significant role in America's formation; the Revolution and the Civil War provide perhaps the two best examples of this. However, if the America of the history books was forged in the crucible of conflict, then modern America was forged, to a greater extent, in the post-war crucible of the 1950s: a crucible of optimism and fear.[2] It was a decade characterized by both the mass consumption of goods at a level hitherto unheard of, and a fear of being consumed by communism—the ideology which was perceived to threaten this new world order and the "economic liberty" it appeared to bestow. During this period America saw the realms of science fiction transformed into the happenings and expectations of everyday life. With them, the consumption ethic was born into American culture.

Prior to these events America was quite simply a very different place. Many things characterize the face of the 1950s, but two of the most significant upon both post-war America and Stringfellow's formation and writing were the Cold War and the post-war economic boom (and all that this entailed).[3] Together, they are the essence of the political

---

Council "Special Visitor" in Europe and the Middle East in 1950. It includes venues such as Iona, Finland (including observation of cooperatives), France, the Baltic States, Czechoslovakia, Prague (meeting with Soviet dominated world student organization), Belgium, Israel, Egypt (with Christian and Muslim leaders), Greece, and Yugoslavia (including an interview with Tito), and would have meant that Stringfellow was on the road from June 25 to December 21, 1950. All this took place amidst the turbulent political climate of the era (Stringfellow, 1950c).

2. Optimism and fear have been forever present in America's historical formation and were present at the time of the Civil War and the Revolution (War of Independence). However, the way in which "optimism" was expressed in the 1950s is, according to Patterson (1996), quite unique, and the boom of which it was a part radically altered the landscape of America's geo-economic and political landscape.

3. James Patterson's highly regarded account of American history for the period 1945–1974 is particularly insightful and authoritative (Patterson, 1996), synthesizing a great deal of historical material. Accompanied by very helpful discussions with Professor Alan Brinkley, History Professor at Columbia University, it has formed the basis for much of my knowledge for this research. It is a huge area of historical research. Other useful studies of this period include: Chafe (1991); Diggins (1988); Leuchtenburg (1983); Janowitz (1978); Wolfe (1991); Gaddis (1982); Polenberg (1980); Wuthnow (1988).

economy that Stringfellow inhabited. These factors, more than any others, also provide the catalyst for the subsequent disillusionment which led to the civil rights movement and the rise of counter-cultural dissent.

Threat

THE COLD WAR

The resolve of both the United States and the Soviet Union hardened following the end of the war, and by 1948 the Cold War was well under way, fuelled by the attempted negotiations of two nations with conflicting ideals and similar goals. The unexpected death of Roosevelt at the end of the war led to the installation of Truman as president. In the first months of his presidency, he struggled to find a way of dealing with the Soviets: inexperienced at diplomacy, he swung from acquiescence in favor of war-time cooperation (for example allowing Soviet occupation of Poland) to an iron fist of intolerance and apparent invincibility, buoyed up by the successful test of the atomic bomb. Eventually, the question of how to deal with the Soviets, and especially Stalin—the scope of whose political ambitions no one fully anticipated—was answered in the form of what was to be known as the "policy of containment." This policy was a decisive factor in the commencement of the Cold War and until the cornerstone of all subsequent American foreign policy. In addition, it shaped America's self-perception, and the world's perception of America, upon the international political scene.

However, its military interpretation, especially in the 1950s, went directly against the spirit of the Long Telegram of George Kennan, from which the policy ultimately emerged. The central premise of this policy was the assumption of Soviet rather than American responsibility for the breakdown of war-time cooperation, and that the brutal expansion of the Soviet state must be resisted and contained until its ultimate collapse, brought about by its own internal inconsistencies and oppressions. The military interpretation effectively locked the two nations into an arms race and promoted the fear of imminent destruction as the motivation for its support.

The Cold War was hostile to all things communist—the "great sinister anti-Christian movement masterminded by Satan"[4]—which posed a

---

4. Words attributed by Patterson to Billy Graham (Patterson, 1996:329), which should be contrasted to Stringfellow's own work on Christianity and Communism, to be examined in the next chapter (Stringfellow, 1947b).

threat to the newly emerging American way of life—freedom and prosperity. It was a period characterized by events such as the atomic tests at
Bikini Atoll, the (often forgotten) war in Korea and McCarthyism. It was
also a period characterized by homophobia, and for the purposes of our
discussion we need to examine this in more detail.

Sexuality and Deviation: Emergence and Organization

The apparent rise of homosexuality in post-war America was predominantly considered a sordid tale—an infection run rampant requiring the
nation to resist its onslaught. This was how the media, the government,
and consequently most people in America perceived homosexuality at
this time; although the death penalty for sodomy had been abolished, all
but two states still regarded it as a felony.[5] In order to understand what
was going on, we need to consider two things; first, how homosexuality
emerged in modern America and second, what made it appear so prolific
as the post-war era commenced. When considering these, the question
which needs to be uppermost in our minds is one of context: how did
the nation as a whole respond to homosexuality?

According to D'Emilio, the emergence of homosexual and lesbian
identity is largely due to the momentous shift to industrial capitalism and
the conditions this shift provided. Until this time the family unit had been
central to the process of production. Within this free labor system, men
and women were removed from their household economies and placed
in the marketplace, exchanging their labor for payment. Production of
commodities shifted from the home to the factory. Impersonal cities
emerged to replace the small towns with their close-knit communities
and attracted a large proportion of Americans; as much for the anonym-
ity they afforded as the opportunities they provided. In this free-market
setting, D'Emilio suggests, "sexuality moved into the realm of individual
choice, seemingly disconnected from how one organised the production
of goods necessary for survival." Here, "men and women who felt strong
erotic attraction to their own sex could begin to fashion from their feeling a personal identity and a way of life" (D'Emilio, 1983:11). Thus, by the
beginning of the twentieth century, out of socioeconomic upheaval and
subsequent changing attitudes towards sexual relationships, a subculture

---

5. Only murder, kidnapping, and rape elicited heavier sentences (D'Emilio, 1983:14),
see also Marotta (1981:15).

was born. One of the favorite gathering places for male homosexuals were YMCAs.

In the twentieth century, "regulation of homosexual behavior was left to the church and the criminal justice system" (D'Emilio, 1983:15). Indeed, as gay subculture took root in twentieth-century American cities, police invoked laws against disorderly conduct, vagrancy, public lewdness, assault, and solicitation in order to haul in their victims (D'Emilio, 1983:14).[6]

However, following the Second World War there was a resurgence of credibility in psychiatry, and psychiatric explanations, and people came to see sexual behavior as being either healthy or sick. Homosexuality fell into the latter category. Up until the 1950s, to be known as homosexual was simply to be seen as deviant. Practically, to be known publicly as being gay was, culturally, politically, and legally to be oppressed.

The war years had a remarkable affect upon homosexual life and identity. It allowed gay men to find one another without attracting attention, and oftentimes gain sympathy and acceptance from other heterosexual soldiers. With the patterns of daily life weakened, intimacy found expression, and homosexuals and their culture emerged strengthened. The changes could neither be undone nor immediately stopped by peace time, and indeed Kinsey's reports of 1948 and 1953 on male and female sexual behavior provided controversial data for the reassessment of conventional moral attitudes.

However, while the subculture emerged strengthened and increasingly exposed through the growing ease of association, American culture at large had not notably changed its attitude or outlook towards this minority group. Moreover, if it could find justification to persecute its homosexual minority, it would have little problem locating them and doing so. "Justification" arrived with the dawning of the "McCarthy era" of anticommunism and the un-American Activities Committee.

Thought of as "outcasts" by the religious consensus, homosexuals were considered sexual perverts and were viewed as unsuitable for government service: it was a life thought of as unbiblical and therefore as un-American.[7] In support of this, the Senate drew selectively upon the

6. For a fuller account of this process, see D'Emilio and Freedman (1988); D'Emilio (1983). This may go to explain to some extent Stringfellow's own involvement with the YMCA movement, especially during the 1940s and early 1950s.

7. It is worth considering the possibility that the choice of being a lawyer may well have been a reaction to this legal abuse of homosexuals for Stringfellow.

Kinsey report to argue that homosexuality was far more widespread, and therefore a far bigger problem, than anyone had so far imagined.[8]

The Government's anti-homosexual stance was reflected in wider society at this time, and was also reflected in the McCarthy communist "witch hunts."[9] National security, especially the FBI, worked flat out to try and expose homosexual activity in American society, including mail interception and entrapment.[10] Accusations of homosexuality, like those of communism, were often ill founded. They were frequently used to destroy individuals, and by political adversaries as a means of discrediting opponents. Homosexuals, like communists, were considered America's invisible threat from within, and the perceived congruence between the stereotypes of the two groups was significant: the latter poisoned peoples minds whilst the former corrupted their bodies (D'Emilio, 1983:48–49).

Scapegoating communists and homosexuals was an easy matter, undertaken throughout the 1950s and especially prominent at its outset. Treatment of homosexuals was noticeably hostile throughout this decade. It grew out of a cultural history with clearly hostile and homophobic views. The 1950s marks the first time that the phenomenon became a subject of serious and widespread public concern and discourse. According to D'Emilio, gay people in this period were shunned to the margins of society, and there, as outcasts, often internalized the negative descriptions that were thrust upon them.

Against this stream, "Donald Webster Cory"[11] published a controversial and significant book entitled *The Homosexual in America* (Cory, 1951), which applied civil rights ideas to homosexuality. Cory wrote out of personal experience as a gay man who had struggled with his homosexuality. From an early age this had led him to "empathize with others who were disadvantaged, especially the blacks he encountered in his native Brooklyn" (Marotta, 1981:6). He was inspired by Gunnar Myrdal's highly significant study of race relations (Myrdal, 1944), which put for-

8. A fuller account of the kind of oppression faced by homosexuals at this time can be found in D'Emilio (1983:40–53).

9. In fact, more people were fired from their jobs or publicly exposed for being homosexual than for being communist, despite the general categorization of this period as the era of McCarthy's "communist witchhunts."

10. The FBI held files on many people, including Stringfellow.

11. The name is a pseudonym used by this man in his gay political activity.

ward the idea that the "Negro problem" was actually just discrimination on behalf of the whites and not a "Negro problem" but a "white problem." In other words, a "majority problem," rather than a "minority problem." To him, the parallels between the way society (mis)treated blacks and the way it treated homosexuals, were clear. The book was to prove highly significant for the radical political organizing of homosexuals that was about to commence. As it developed, Stringfellow's own lifework was to resonate this view in relation to America's churches and the racial issue.

It is not so remarkable then that, amidst the stereotyping and the persecution, there was in fact some truth to the connection of homosexuality and communism, for in 1951 a group committed to homosexual emancipation with strong communist ties was founded in Los Angeles: the Mattachine Society. The leaders of this small, secret group were pioneers in conceiving homosexuals as an oppressed minority, and in so doing sought to transform feelings of shame into those of pride. The leftist leanings of the leaders of this radical group united a political commitment for social change with the emancipation of a minority group.[12] They believed political organization was the key to self-protection and social change. The group grew in popularity, and "cells" began on the East Coast, including New York City. The politics of homosexual emancipation were closely tied in with the politics of the Progressive Party presidential candidate Henry Wallace, and given the political climate and the nation's homophobic and anticommunist mood, secrecy remained of primary importance to the society. The radical leadership of the society was short lived and was replaced in 1953 with one that gave rise to a greater emphasis upon "education, public reform, and help . . . [which] would bring about the recognition of basic similarity, equality of treatment, and integration that were tantamount to social progress" (Marotta, 1981:11). In the years to come the Mattachine Society sought legitimacy.[13]

12. The leftist leanings, especially towards communism, were not shared by the members of the society at large, who felt that the society should never be identified with any "ism" (Marotta, 1981:11).

13. While there is no direct evidence linking Stringfellow to this movement at this time, it seems reasonable to assume that its radicalizing force would in some way have influenced him as a young gay man just starting law school. Later as a lawyer Stringfellow was to represent members of the Mattachine Society through the George Henry Foundation, and was also to address their gatherings (Stringfellow, 1965a).

> Again and again, they minimized the differences between het-
> erosexuals and homosexuals, attempted to isolate the "deviant"
> members of the gay community from its "respectable" middle-
> class elements, stressed the responsibility of lesbians and gay
> men for their second-class status, and urged self-reformation.
> (D'Emilio, 1983:113)

In all this it is incongruous that while sex remained a great taboo, and
sexuality an area of great unrest, violence flourished and was encouraged by the nation at large.[14] The "biblical morality" which pervaded the
culture of America seemed to extend to sexual morality, but not to peace
and justice. It was not until the 1960s that homosexual emancipation
was to re-emerge, this time as a rights issue, concerned with such issues
as justice.

Prosperity: The Consuming Decade

Economic and political backing for military interpretation of the policy
of containment of the Cold War was widespread, augmented no doubt by
the extraordinary economic boom of the domestic economy.[15] Prosperity
in the United States soared to unparalleled heights in the years following
World War II. The United States emerged from the war "immeasurably
stronger, both absolutely and relatively, from the carnage. In a new balance of power it was a colossus on the international stage" (Patterson,
1996:82).

In this strength, consumption became the means and measure of
achievement. Unprecedented and accelerated economic growth was
supported by significant spending on research and development, which
in turn helped encourage advances in science and technology, growth of
electronic, tobacco, and aircraft industries, soft-drink and food process-
ing companies, and chemical, plastics, and pharmaceutical companies.
This growth was fostered by federal agencies and private producers, who
between them energetically encouraged people to spend their money
(e.g., government provision of low-interest loans to facilitate home-buy-

14. This is relevant to our discussions on Stringfellow, for his criticism was of violence not sexuality—and as we shall see in chapter 6, when he does point to sex being
wrong it is because of the failure for one to love and honor the other—in other words
the way sex becomes a violent act. Thus, he inverts society's criticism.

15. For a full account of the origins of the Cold War, along with how America was
perceived around the world, see Patterson (1996:82–136).

ing and suburban expansion). Installment plans were offered by retailers and manufacturers alike to entice prospective consumers, and in 1950 the modern credit card (Diner's Club) made its historic arrival.

In fact, credit cards and advertising between them spurred a massive increase in borrowing, with private indebtedness more than doubling during the decade.[16] Advertising was, according to Patterson, one of the "most celebrated growth areas of the 1950s" (Patterson, 1996:315). While advertising had been present before the 1950s, it had never before attained such celebrity; as the driving force behind consumer culture, it progressively assaulted the values of thrift and saving of the Depression era. Older people, their values having been shaped by the Great Depression, looked in astonishment at the willingness of people to go into debt over such frivolous items as household gadgets, large new cars, swimming pools, travel, eating out, and binges at the new "supermarkets." With the assistance of credit and low-interest loans, advertising encouraged a new generation to develop "ever-rising expectations about the Good Life" (Patterson, 1996:315).

In the society emerging in the 1950s, the means to purchase cars, homes, or other conveniences provided people with an enhanced sense of dignity and a sense of themselves as both citizens and individuals. During this period of growth America's prosperity soared to new heights and created an ever-widening economic crevice between its citizens and those of the rest of the world. Nothing, it appeared, was beyond the reach of American's economic and technological advancement—such was its optimism in the age of the "atomic revolution."[17]

As Patterson indicates, whilst representing just 7 percent of the world's population, America possessed 42 percent of the world's income, and its manufacturing output accounted for half the total global output, producing 57 percent of the world's steel, 62 percent of its oil, and 80 percent of its cars.[18]

16. From $104.8 billion to $263.3 billion. However, private debt including corporate debt actually rose from $264.4 billion in 1950 to $566.1 billion in 1960 (Patterson, 1996:315).

17. This phrase was *National Geographic's* characterization of the age and highlighted the high profile, and naively optimistic welcome things atomic received from the general public at this time. Naivety was prevalent regarding the dangers of radioactivity: at the time it appeared to make science fiction science fact, and thus to capture the spirit of the age.

18. Median family income by 1960 was $5,620, and during the 1950s the GNP rose by 37% as a whole, to $487.7 billion. This is why it was deemed a "boom decade."

> Per capita income in the United States in mid-1949, at $1,450, was much higher than in the next most prosperous group of nations. . . at between $700 and $900. . . Urban Americans at that time consumed more than 3,000 calories in food per day. . . This caloric intake was around 50 percent higher than that of other people in much of western Europe. (Patterson, 1996:61–2)

The strength of these statistics in the post-war world resulted in America's being greeted and perceived warmly on the international stage. American citizenship was well publicized and for obvious reasons was highly desirable. However, despite this excellent self-publicity, becoming an American at this time was by no means an easy task, for the social stability of the economic boom was ensured through the enforcement of strict immigration laws.

Already we need to bear in mind that Stringfellow's choices (e.g., moving to Harlem and setting up a free law practice) stood in dissent from the cultural norm of the economic boom, and the experience of hope and expectation which that boom sustained. As we shall see later, this economic boom itself played a significant part in his discovering the principalities and powers. However, the buoyant economy was accompanied by developments on many fronts, most echoing or contributing to the sentiment of hope and expectation that prevailed. Advances in medicine and science, an emphasis upon cultural consensus, the role of religion, suburbanization, and the rise of icons and expectations contributed to this, whilst the persistence of poverty was optimistically confronted by elaborate programs of urban renewal. In order to better understand Stringfellow's context at this time, we need to pay attention to these now.

MEDICINE AND SCIENCE

Scientists, doctors, and medical researchers rose in public view to near omnipotent status on the back of such discoveries and developments as the atom, penicillin and streptomycin, and the introduction of vaccines which reduced the incidence and mortality of a raft of diseases including polio. Sales of newly developed tranquilizers boomed.

However, with the advances so the cost of medical care rose, resulting in large sectors of American society being alienated and excluded

---

Unemployment was remarkably low at 4.1–4.4% between 1955 and 1957 (Patterson, 1996:450–51).

from these advances; no sooner had medicine and science delivered promise of a "healthier" life, than that promise was taken away from many of those who would have benefited the most—the poor and marginalized. This division occurred predominantly along racial lines. While millions could not afford access to these developments, the expanding middle class enrolled in health plans, benefited from easier access to care, and grew increasingly enamored with the medical profession. Doctors attained lofty (idolized) heights of prestige and cultural status during this time on the back of the public's faith in medicine and the capacity of science to save the world from ill.[19] On the face of it, the hope which engulfed this generation was well placed. Yet it was a faith blindly placed; blind, for example, to the conflict of doctors promoting smoking through advertising, while medical research at the time clearly indicated the hazards of tobacco.

Doctors could save the world, technology could make the world a better place, the military would defend everyone from foreign (communist) aggression, and all one had to do was sit back, consume, and enjoy the benefits the boom afforded. Moreover, soaring prosperity signified to many the success of the American way of life and God's blessing upon it, thereby necessitating the failure of other (communist) societies.

CLASS AND ETHNICITY

This was a period which heralded "a world of relative social calm and consensus" (Patterson, 1996:321); it placed an emphasis upon unity and tranquility that sought to differentiate the prosperous and seemingly harmonious America from the disquiet and presumably conflict-ridden Soviet Union and other communist societies. This was to be a dominant theme in American self-perception, continuing to the present day. It was, in short, America's differentiation and identification grounded in the rhetoric of harmony and unity, and occurred prominently on two fronts: class and ethnicity.

Many Americans believed that in the 1950s ethnic consciousness was declining, and they pointed to numerous statistics to support their

19. The introduction of the poliomyelitis vaccine illustrates the kind of development that gave rise to this faith. Polio was widespread, and at the beginning of the 1950s an epidemic afflicted nearly 32,000 children, another in 1958 affected nearly 58,000 and killed 1,400. However, the vaccine was developed shortly after, and introduced through a nationwide inoculation program in 1954–1955. Within a few years, the threat of polio ceased. By 1962 there were only 910 cases.

claim. At the heart of this harmonious consensus was the naturalization of foreign immigrants. The desire for a not-too-distant time in which ethnic differences no longer mattered (a time of consensus) was expressed by writers like Will Herberg, in his widely acclaimed study of American religion and ethnicity (Herberg, 1955). Herberg was impressed by what he perceived as the apparent ability of the "melting pot" of America to assimilate people into an "American Way of Life." He suggested that ethnic loyalties (e.g., what one eats, who one marries, where one lives, how one votes) were rapidly weakening, whilst racial and religious identifications remained strong. It was an argument that seemed persuasive to what Patterson describes as the "aggressively assimilationist milieu of the mid-1950s" (Patterson, 1996:328); these were people who wanted to believe it to be true.

And it is in the light of Patterson's description that we must ask whose consensus and which social calm it was that the period ushered in? No doubt with the horrors and wounds of the Holocaust so fresh in the minds of the politicians (if not the people) of this decade, such a claim to social calm must be treated with some measure of sympathy. However, it is clear, certainly from Stringfellow's experiences, and also from our discussions of homosexuality and the Cold War, that disquiet continued unabated throughout the 1950s, and thus any notion of "consensus" betrayed an underlying reality of marginalization of various social groups on grounds of gender, sexuality, ethnicity, politics, race, and class. Later studies in the 1960s and 1970s subsequently confirmed that both ethnic differences and class distinctions refused to disappear easily; the heralded "consensus" was one brought on by the apparent bliss of middle-class consumerism.

God's Providence?

Religion in America has always functioned within a toleration-but-separation model. At this time, religious discourse tended to be a mix of optimism and apprehension. Amidst the economically heady days of the Cold War, anti-communist feeling and homophobia ran high in American culture and religion, and both the Cold War and the fear of a rise in homosexuality stimulated this growth in certain kinds of religiosity, predominantly "evangelical." It was a growth to a large extent based upon fear, for homosexuality remained covert throughout the decade.

This fear was filtered through widespread changing attitudes towards sex and sexuality.

The economic success of the United States during this period was believed by many to be a literal sign of God's favor and blessing; the growth in religious affiliation should not, therefore, come as a surprise. The cultural attribution of "God's blessing" of riches and unity upon American culture, over and against the "godless idol" of communism, was manifestly a caricature, and one that was widespread. The church was seen by most as the mediating structure which provided for nurturing and promulgating sound, broadly based cultural values upon which "decent" society depended (Mensch and Freeman, 1993:69–70).

Self-identification as Protestant, Catholic, or Jew was increasingly central to the culture, and accordingly America touted itself as the most religious in the world. The role of organized religion during this decade was seemingly a powerful one, and church building (delayed by both depression and war) was rapid and widespread, particularly in the suburbs, outpacing even consumer expenditure (Mensch and Freeman, 1993:68).

There was an ecumenical spirit at that time within Protestantism[20] promoted most enthusiastically amongst evangelicals, and evangelicalism experienced a massive rise in popularity at that time. Billy Graham,[21] a popular figure in conservative evangelicalism, preached against modern life's hedonism, materialism, and secularism. He denounced communism and demanded that it be battled at every opportunity. Millions, especially those who felt alienated from the middle classes (e.g., the poor and uneducated), were attracted to such messages.

---

20. In 1943 the National Association of Evangelicals was founded, and in 1950, the National Council of Churches. Both featured as key organizations within this emerging ecumenical spirit. The ecumenical spirit did not, generally, extend to the laity.

21. The rise of Graham's popularity was at a pace entirely befitting the boom of the 1950s. From humble beginnings in a one room office in 1950, his Evangelistic Association grew at such a rate that by 1958 it had a staff of 200 and operated out of a four-story office building, answering some 10,000 letters a week, and collecting and giving away some $2 million annually. Graham appeared on a weekly television program and offered a syndicated column which appeared in 125 newspapers. A frequent visitor to the White House, his influence was significant and far reaching. One of his more prominent warnings was that the world was coming to an end (Patterson, 1996:330).

Such a view did much to bolster the caricature that communism was evil because it was godless. It is a caricature which Stringfellow did not share.[22]

When promoting a "decent society" evangelicals rejected the otherwise prevalent social gospel movement, believing the way it tied the fulfillment of Kingdom of God with secular politics to be too strong. Instead, the promotion of "sound" *personal* values or ethics was seen as the key to general public social decency prevailing; such was the relationship of pulpit and politics in this new religion of the 1950s.

Greater ecumenism was achieved in part by distancing church members from their own denominational histories and encouraging them to rely instead upon the universality of religious experience: an emphasis drawing as much on the pragmatism of William James as the revivalism of evangelists like Dwight Moody (Noll, 1992:288–94).[23] Nineteenth-century revivalism, and the movements for moral reform it gave rise to (most noticeably, the Social Gospel movement), became the main focus of much apparently successful evangelical work throughout the century, fundamentally shaping the evangelical Christianity that was the inheritance of 1950s America. Compared to the attentions given to moral reform, Christian efforts in politics were far less well organized (Noll, 1992:299); by and large, politics was seen as a public forum "for

22. This is evidenced most succinctly in his college thesis relating communism and Christianity (Stringfellow, 1947b), see chapter 3 under the section "Reconciliaion: Emergence of Faith and Politics." In the course of writing this thesis, Stringfellow was in correspondence with the (leftist) politically liberal Commerce Secretary (and former vice President) Henry Wallace, who told Stringfellow, "This question is one of the most fundamental in the whole world today" (cited in Stringfellow, 1947b:1). Wallace was also editor of *New Republic* (which Stringfellow received), and later ran for president in 1948, but was defeated by the man who had replaced him as vice president: Harry Truman (Patterson, 1996:123–26; D'Emilio, 1983:60–61). Simply, Wallace was perhaps the most prominent and significant leftist figure in American politics at the time, and Stringfellow seemed to respect him. Generally, Wallace was critical of the bombastic imperialist language used by many prominent Americans at the time to describe America's mission in the world and its relationship to the Soviet Union. However, it appears that at times even he resorted to speaking in a *similar* language (Brinkley, 1998:108).

23. Ultimately, this reliance upon a universal "religious thing" or religious experience is influenced by Schleiermacher, but in America it can be traced from Wesley, through Jonathan Edwards, and later seen in Charles Finney's establishing of modern revivalism. Although he never got as far as writing it, at one stage in 1966 Stringfellow planned with a sense of irony to write a novel of the murder mystery genre, entitled *The Moody Murders* (Ziegler, 1966). Remarkably, the publisher failed to see the historical connection, and thought it was a splendid idea.

promoting principles of morality both Christian and American" (Noll, 1992:300).

Surprisingly, it was also a decade which saw the clear and controversial association of church and state through constitutional amendment; 1954 saw the addition of the self-identification "one nation under God" to the Pledge of Allegiance in order, Eisenhower said, to enrich a world otherwise "deadened in mind and soul to a materialistic philosophy of life." He went on to say: "Our government makes no sense unless it is founded on a deeply felt religious faith—I don't care what it is" (cited in Patterson, 1996:329).[24] By 1955, Congress had endorsed this amendment by making one of its own and adding the statement "In God We Trust" to U.S. currency. At the time, they did not see any apparent blurring of the separation of church and state through these actions, for most people believed that God "had endowed the United States with a mission to spread the sacred truths of the Declaration of Independence and the Constitution throughout the world and to destroy the diabolical dogmas of Communism" (Patterson, 1996:330). Evangelists like Billy Graham were at the forefront of this mission. It was both a vision and a mission of which Stringfellow was openly critical: a voice of dissent in the wilderness. And again, it was through reading the Bible in this context that his moral theology was to have its origins.

To sum up, the taming effect of America's toleration-but-separation model of church-state relations upon American religion was clearly evident. This approach created a situation in which religion was

> trapped, frozen, in its perpetual de facto accommodation of power. It became a social ornament and buttress, not changing people's lives, only blessing them; not telling them to do this or omit that, just congratulating them for whatever they do or do not do. Religion is invited in on sufferance, to praise our country, our rulers, our past and present, our goals and pretensions, under the polite fiction of praying for them all. The divine is subordinated to the human—God serves Caesar. This is what Americans quaintly call "freedom of religion," and what the Bible calls idolatry. (Wills, 1972:260 cited in Mensch and Freeman, 1993:69)

And amidst the religious pluralism and "ecumenical spirit," such idolatry was rife. Christianity had come to be perceived (and in some places remains) as an enclave and a place of personal and private spiri-

24. See also Mensch and Freeman (1993:69).

tual safety, detached somehow from the concerns of the "work-a-day world." Not surprisingly, it was a situation which energized Stringfellow.

MINORITY ACCESS

Whilst extensive, for many millions of marginalized people, African- and Mexican-Americans especially, the boom was effectively another country's success story. While hidden behind the rhetoric of the government and commercial interests, this was the reality Stringfellow encountered in Harlem, and to which his writing testifies. These groups constituted the 30 percent of America that remained in poverty despite (or perhaps because of) the wider economic boom. For such minorities the boom which embraced and thrived upon mass production and mass consumption, buoying up a generation's hopes and expectations for the future, was both alienating and alluring.

Predominantly, access was the thing which stood in the way of marginalized groups participating in the boom: access to education, to employment, to medicine, to consumption, to quality of life. University education was key to attaining a good income, yet few in these groups were likely to be in a position to attend college or university.[25] Education was one of the primary means by which the gap between the wealthy and the poor was sustained, and "by the mid-1950s the average earnings of young men after a few years of graduation . . . approached those of considerably older men" (Patterson, 1996:313).

Patterson goes on to say that during this period, however, education for minority children and the poor grew increasingly inferior—and that is not to say that other general education grew better, for it did not. The cost of educational democratization was an overall dumbing-down.

Simply put, more than at any other time in America, wealth became the key to participation, and production/consumption the key to wealth. The marginalized, while often used cheaply in production, were excluded from many of the benefits the boom offered.

URBAN RENEWAL AND DISPLACEMENT

Wealth and opportunity prompted geographic relocation for many people—out of the crowded and polluted cities, to (metaphorically) greener

---

25. The G.I. Bill, which granted financial assistance to demobilized servicemen, was the major source of exceptions to this general rule, and one upon which Stringfellow relied. The financial help on offer was limited.

pastures. In the exercise of "choice," the cities were left to those who had no choice. The poor (who were mostly ethnic minorities) were left to dwell in slums: something Stringfellow saw as the physical sign of the disunity of American culture.

Millions of people moved to what became known as the suburbs, leading to the steady decline of the more traditional downtown amenities and the rise of new out-of-town shopping and recreation facilities; the shopping mall was born, and drive-in's of every variety (from cinemas to restaurants) flourished. In fact, an entirely new road-based transportation network was built to cater to this suburban expansion.[26]

At this time the people who flocked to the urban centers (of which New York was one of the best examples) were mostly those fleeing farms and small towns. They were victims of rural de-population (which had been accelerated by the technological revolution that was taking place) that rendered manual labor unnecessary. These demographic changes were of great significance to the changing culture and landscape of America at this time, and also to Stringfellow's own commitment to East Harlem: slum populations grew, and the space available for accommodation shrank as it was sold off for redevelopment.

To many, the suburbs (from whom African-American's were largely excluded) signified conformity and all that was oppressive about the 1950s. These were cultural rather than economic concerns. This conformity deadened political debate and engagement; instead of politics, people's concerns lay elsewhere—with buying the right car, keeping the lawn like one's neighbors', eating the right breakfast cereal, and voting Republican (Rowland, 1956). The suburbs represented the depoliticization and desensitization of the American middle classes.

The suburbs were constituted by pretty well all of "middle America," and therefore most of the Episcopal church, of which Stringfellow was a member. Suburbia did much to cocoon its occupants and insulate them

---

26. Concerned, the government introduced a plan of "urban renewal" in which land was redeveloped by private companies who would erect better housing for low-income people. Generally, the plan was unpopular and ineffective, and resulted in the displacement of the poor ("poor-removal" or "Negro-removal"). Not surprisingly, Stringfellow was critical of this plan. The plan effectively removed low-cost housing (shunting its occupants around cities) and replaced it with expensive housing that enriched builders and landlords. By 1955 only 200,000 public housing units, rather than the targeted 810,000, had been constructed. For further discussion on urban renewal, see Jackson (1985) and Patterson (1996:335).

from the issues of the "world outside," and the church did little structurally to challenge this: the suburbs were in fact a kind of Disneyland.[27] The gaze of inhabitants of the suburbs was inward, and Americans grew less concerned with changing the world and more preoccupied with their "inner world"; like religion, psychiatry boomed during the 1950s.

Amidst the clamor and turmoil of a country emerging out of a world war and the established "threat" of a Cold War, the suburbs afforded people a feeling of safety and comfort which they craved, and anaesthetized them to the political reality which surrounded them.

> Acquiring "things" . . . was hardly new to American life in the 1950s—just easier because many more people had much more money . . . People did not surrender to the tyranny of conformity. Rather, they searched understandably for whatever enabled them and their families to feel comfortable and safe . . . Critics of affluent excess during the boom years of the mid-1950s tended sometimes to expect human beings to deny themselves material pleasures . . . Others, however, began to imagine a better society in which the best of American ideals could be put into practice. (Patterson, 1996:341–42)

And amidst all this, Stringfellow's life was one of self-induced poverty, proclaiming a very contrary message.

ICONS AND IDOLS

Given that many Americans enjoyed a greater prosperity and a higher disposable income than ever before, it may at first glance appear odd that 1955 saw the birth of the modern commercial "success story" that is McDonald's, where a family of four could eat for less than two dollars. McDonald's success seems in part attributable to two things: a burgeoning car-culture, and an idolization of new "convenience food."[28]

Idols and icons were everywhere: rock and roll singers, movie stars, gadgets, television, clothes, and of course, perhaps the most universal icon of all, the car.

---

27. Disneyland started in 1955 and was an enormously successful business, testifying as much to the affluence of consumer culture, as the appeal of repackaged-reality to the suburban masses.

28. One major thesis is of the McDonaldization of society (Ritzer, 1998, 2000), which has also been explicitly picked up by John Drane in relation to evangelistic developments in the church (Drane, 2000).

The optimistic and materialistic mood of the era was captured through design, and automotive design encapsulated this in an accessible, and apparently desirable, form. Unsurprisingly, car manufacturers profited enormously during this period, especially General Motors, which convinced people to scrap some 4.5 million cars annually and replace them with the latest models—"sleek, multi-coloured, gas-guzzling, chrome-encrusted conveyances featuring (after 1955) sweeping and non-functional tail fins . . . The designs deliberately recalled the lines of jet planes and generated a streamlined, futuristic feeling—one that was emulated in many other products, from toasters to garden furniture to new kitchens that featured all manner of sleekly crafted electrical conveniences" (Patterson, 1996:316–17).

THREAT AND PROSPERITY: ENTANGLEMENT AND EMERGENT IDENTITY

In the post-war period, Americans' material desires were fulfilled through a culture of opportunity and plenty. These desires were strengthened by the government's concentration upon the threat which communism was perceived to pose to this culture. Americans' desire for acceptance, consensus, and self-realization materialized through this economic contentment. Abundance and material satisfaction became the key to self-satisfaction and identity: it was the source of authenticity. Essentially, in this post-war culture prosperity functioned as the necessary ingredient for identity, in order that the success of capitalism over communism might emerge as the justifying Godly order, determining cultural and personal identity. Establishing difference or differentiation from aliens therefore appears crucial to the formation of identity at this time.

Yet each period in history has its discontents, and this one is no exception. By the end of the early 1960s this land of plenty had, for the newly emerging adult generation at least, turned into a land of disenchantment; the apparent failure of this prosperous culture to deliver the fulfillment it had promised led to wide-scale frustration and disillusionment by many young adults. Consequentially, the 1960s and 1970s were periods of quite dramatic personal and political challenge and change. It is a time most remembered as one in which the sweet invincibility of the state turned publicly sour and once again gave rise to the public exhibition of its darker side through, for example, the Vietnam War. The disenchantment with post-war America eventually gave rise to many radical movements and thinkers. One of the earliest was Stringfellow.

CONCLUSION

It is the staggering economic growth of the 1950s which was, according to Patterson, "the most decisive force in the shaping of attitudes and expectations of the post-war era" (Patterson, 1996:61). It shaped a generation's hopes, desires, and expectations, against a backdrop dominated by the communist "threat" and its containment through American foreign policy. Its effects were far-reaching and widespread. This culture emphasized harmony and unity as the characteristic features of God's chosen people: they had marched out of the ruins of the second world war, and entered the promised land. It stood as a nation under God, and the churches "seemed content to supply a cosmetic window dressing to the American way of life, without nerve or spirit to do more" (Mensch and Freeman, 1993:68–69).

This air of political conservatism was in fact akin to what we might now term the "feel-good factor" and prompted faith in the untold blessings and opportunities of science, technology, education, medicine, and expertise: from the harnessing of the atom and the G.I. Bill as a means of access to education, to the rapid expansion of medical experimentation and the automation of mass production and consumption and associated wealth creation (Patterson,1996:67). It also prompted the privatization of religion: faith became a de-politicized zone, along with the suburbs, and there the church reigned.

Collectively, this faith, and the accompanied ability of the economy to deliver, gave America a newfound self-confidence.[29] This self-confidence embraced and ironically represented the dream of the American way; not a story of rags to riches, but the belief in hard work as the means to social climbing, equality of all people and equality of access, and a belief that the next generation would necessarily do better than the present one. It was, in short, undiluted faith in progress, "the egalitarian ideals of the American Revolution" (Patterson, 1996:66), and the Protestant work ethic. It was an embrace which modern political-historical scholarship

29. If we compare the social psyche amidst this social and economic boom with the Great Depression which immediately preceded the war, it would not be unfair to say that, in many ways, the war provided an economic solution to the problems of pre-war America. This is a view largely supported in Brinkley (1998:94–110).

seems to indicate was at best flawed, and at worst, founded upon an illusion.

Amidst the rhetoric there were contradictions, and participation in this promised land and its varied riches (e.g., medicine, education, good housing) was conditional upon one not being in any way an "alien," whether sexually, ideologically, racially, or economically. In the America of the 1950s, the marginalized had no home and were not embraced. Non-alien status was conferred through "normality," and all such terms were defined by the ruling majority: white, middle-class Anglo-Saxon, and predominantly Protestant, males. So, for instance, normality was appropriated by virtue of access, which in turn was achieved through consumption, which was granted through wealth, which in its turn was procured through work, which was attained through good education, access to which was, by and large, determined by race (by not being a minority). Thus, what the 1950s exposed more clearly than perhaps anything else was the inverse of the identity it professed. Harmony and unity were misappropriated terms applied to these middle classes, perpetuating the myth of identity and embrace in a culture of exclusion and racism.

It was an illusion Stringfellow saw and confronted with both nerve and spirit. He did this by making a number of extraordinary "abnormal" choices, and it is Stringfellow's engagement with this context, and these choices, to which we now turn our attentions.

3

The Empirical Imperative

Law, Politics, and Vocation

IN OUR DISCUSSIONS OF the socio-political context of the 1950s some hint was given as to Stringfellow's engagement with it. It is time to flesh this out a bit more. This period of his life marks the foundation of his later life and work. This chapter explores some of the prominent happenings in the early years of Stringfellow's adult life, and in particular pays attention to his decision for both faith and law: a "conversion experience" on both counts, which was to prove fundamental to his life-work.[1] It goes on to explore the relationship of faith and politics that developed in his work, and the influence of the ecumenical movement upon it.

DECISIONS FOR FAITH AND LAW

> He became a lawyer who challenged law to be itself instead of an arbitrary abstraction or cover for chicanery. He challenged the law to be what scripture said it must become: a guide for acting fairly. (Berrigan and Berrigan,1985)

When Stringfellow went to the London School of Economics (LSE) he was passionate about politics and about having a political career; his decision to become a lawyer was taken in light of this commitment to politics, rather than in spite of it. For many in America at the end of the 1940s, the decision to become a lawyer would have been seen as an astute and expedient career choice for furtherance of political ambitions

---

1. The discussion which dominated the areas of faith and law can be found in a succinct presentation in Stringfellow (1956h).

and undertaking eventual political office. Certainly Stringfellow's decision was a political one; but perhaps all was not quite as it seemed.

Stringfellow's passion was at this stage in his life a consuming one. His political ambitions seem initially fuelled as much out of the desire to further democracy, as his single mindedness and seemingly unswerving self-assurance.[2] He wrote: "Ever since I can remember, I have been interested in politics. And long before I took God seriously, it was my aspiration to have a political career" (Stringfellow, 1948:1). So, it is clear that his political zeal predates his Christian faith, or what he refers to as "taking God seriously."[3]

It is precisely this faith which transforms his zealous ambition for political *career* into a zeal for politics as *ministry*. In other words, here in the relationship of politics and faith in his life, we find the origins of Stringfellow's transition from *career* to *vocation* which was to so inform his decision and motivation to become a lawyer.

The way in which the law and vocation came together for Stringfellow echoed the wider discussions which ensued in the establishments of the law and the church.

At this time the function and effectiveness of the law (as the final arbiter of secular society) was in dispute, called into question by a world in shock. The post-Holocaust world was still recovering from one of the most widespread and public of atrocities of the twentieth century, with its legal justification by the Nazi German government derived from natural law. While the discussions ventured into jurisprudence, essentially it remained a practical dispute, concerned with the very order and

---

2. This was an attitude often rightly perceived as arrogance. Evidence of this, particularly in the years preceding 1953, can be found in the archives in Box 1 & 2. For example, while a Rotary Scholar he was in conflict with the warden of his Rotary-supplied accommodation over the washing of socks. Stringfellow would not wash his own, but the warden expected him to. There arose a series of particularly harsh letters from Stringfellow, and when the warden would not back down, rather than just apologize and wash his own socks, Stringfellow left and had to find alternative accommodation. This dogmatic refusal to back down or admit error was to be a habit that would prove hard to break. Evidence of his self-assurance can also variously be seen in his speaking itinerary and the self-promotional material which he produced, available in Box 1 & 2.

3. The subject of his faith remains at this point "God," and it was only later to be redescribed in terms of "Jesus Christ." A significant shift in emphasis symptomatic of the developing nature of his faith.

maintenance of the fabric of society. Not surprisingly, it focused upon natural law in particular.[4]

Vidler and Whitehouse (1946) highlight the problem succinctly in a slim volume, which was to prove significant for Stringfellow's own decision to become a lawyer. In their discussion on the term "natural law," they note

> the situation is now complicated by the fact that rival parties in the contemporary world claim the term "Natural Law" for their respective theories or ideologies, even when these are inconsistent or diametrically opposed ... While many writers among the United Nations would say that the Nazis threw over the conception of a Natural Law ... Martin Bormann, head of the Nazi Party organisation, said: "We National Socialists set before ourselves the aim of living as far as possible by the light of Nature: that is to say, by the law of life. The more closely we recognise and obey the laws of Nature and of Life, the more we observe them, by so much the more do we express the will of the Almighty." (Vidler and Whitehouse, 1946:11–12)

At the outset of the 1950s the reality which the law sustained appears to have been in dispute, as was the jurisprudence sustained by natural law. It was a conversation which highlighted most succinctly and powerfully the war's legacy of the loss of absolutes and the impact of this upon humanity. The law's self understanding required a new relationship between religion, ethics, and law (Stringfellow, 1955b:1). As a young man, Stringfellow experienced this disquiet with greatest concentration during his visits to Europe and especially his time at the London School of Economics.[5] The issue of law concerned the issue of action, and for

---

4. See Mensch and Freeman (1993) for a discussion of the prominence of discussion about natural law versus legal positivism at this time. The influence of natural law extended beyond the realms of academic debate, of course. For example, Martin Luther King made appeal to it in his justification for civil rights (Branch, 1988, 740). See also Bennett, 1946; Fuller, 1949; and Niebuhr, 1936 (cited in Stringfellow, 1956a) for texts concerning natural law and jurisprudence at this time. For the coincidence of the growth of interest by Christians in the issue of law and theology at that time with the concerns about Christian vocation in secular work, see Van Dusen and Ehrenstrom, 1954.

5. Stringfellow at this time was an impressionable young man with self-determination, a good mind, and strong opinion. While at LSE Stringfellow had a chance to meet up with Vidler and discuss law and theology with him (Stringfellow, 1955a). In addition, the influence of William Temple's thought upon Stringfellow, in terms of politics and

Christians this tended most often to result in a focus upon ethics. In a culture in which religion had been firmly privatized into the realm of personal morality, and law was the arbiter of reality, this tended to result in faith being made subject to law.

The Second World War also prompted a fresh interest in the meaning of the Christian vocation in the world, emerging predominantly in the examination and questioning of the relationship of theology and theological ethics to public policy and social organization, as well as a more personal focus upon the lay person in their daily life in the work-a-day world.[6] Stringfellow's engagement with the problem emerged directly out of his commitment to and involvement with the WCC and the Faith and Order Commission.

His burgeoning faith provided the foil for his consuming, and I believe ultimately self-destructive, passion: literally and figuratively it was his redemption.[7] Over time he became aware of the way the implications of his faith extended beyond the purely academic and theoretical, into the realm of the political. The following account, originally given as a talk to Christian students while in London, tells of this realization and provides some intriguing insights into the origins of his conversion, and the seeds of his understanding of theology as a practical discipline.[8]

> There has developed for lots of reasons in my life a great interest in religion. And by the time I was in high school . . . I had begun to take God seriously. As this interest grew . . . my interest became primarily intellectual . . . Especially during my first year in college, the doctrinal aspects of Christianity were absorbing to speculate and theorize about. So I read lots of books . . . and finally it began to dawn on me that religion, while it must be intellectually respectable, must also provide the core and motivation of one's whole life . . . But though I had an honest desire to feel the reality of God's love in my own life, and to feel a personal commitment to Christ, yet I did not feel it. Now many things happened along the way which there isn't time to share with

faith, was significant at this time (see for example Temple, 1928). Temple was central to the WCC and the ecumenical movement.

6. See Van Dusen and Ehrenstrom (1954).

7. He was not so much saved from himself, as redeemed from the negative consequences of his self-destructiveness—the stubborn (perhaps righteous) anger within him.

8. When taken in the context of later developments in the 1960s, it also implicitly suggests a foundational connection between his faith and his sexuality.

you, but there came—not so very long ago—a climatic experience that is, I know, changing my life. I was blessed to share in an
unusually close friendship with another fellow—who had been
through this same sort of experience as I had with religion. Our
friendship grew very important to both of us, yet we knew that
when we left college, probably we would gradually lose contact.
(Stringfellow, 1948:1–2)[9]

This friendship appears to have been most valuable to Stringfellow at
the time and was, he says, thoroughly "God-centered." Its impact upon
political outlook was far reaching:

Because of this experience, I now look differently upon politics.
For if anything in my life is not centered upon God, and the
searching out of his will, it is destructive of this God-centered
friendship that has happened to me. Politics *must* be a ministry
for me now. (Stringfellow, 1948:2)

There is a marked and significant shift in his outlook here, from politics
as career to politics as ministry. However, despite this positive shift, his
political commitment remained at this time a commitment to the furtherance of *democratic* politics. It is a commitment to create political
people "serving Christ in their exercise of their *democratic citizenship* in
the fullest sense" (my emphasis Stringfellow, 1948:3); a commitment to
working *within* the political system. The evidence of this paper suggests
he had yet to fully discover the politics of the Bible, a discovery which
was to transform him and his political interpretation of the world yet
again. It also reveals some of the tensions already present within his life
and thinking between politics and his faith. These were tensions formed
by the journey upon which he was by now embarked, from a political
liberal with a somewhat conservative theology, to a political and theological radical. It was a journey in which politics and faith were to be
theologically unified.

This political ministry carried with it a price. With curious foresight, Stringfellow describes the cost of such ministry, and in so doing
described the path his own life was to follow.

Maybe it will mean—as it does for me—violating the strong
wishes of his parents. His only fame may be one of public persecution and vicious slander from those who fear and oppose that

9. It is possible that this relationship was with "Andy," and was both secretive and
intimate, and was one of his first homosexual relationships (Andy, 1947).

for which he stands. He must expect those whom he would serve, the people, to misunderstand and misinterpret him. He must be willing to live strenuously—and to literally shorten his life by years. (Stringfellow, 1948:4)[10]

Violating his parents' wishes, being persecuted, misunderstood and misinterpreted by those he sought to serve, while strenuously seeking to live as a faithful and literally self-sacrificial being: this is the image Stringfellow would like us to have of him, and to a large part it is an accurate picture. However, we need to ask to what extent it is description, and to what extent it is also a confession of the kind of life Stringfellow *wanted* to live (a benchmark of faithful living); to what extent is it a statement of hope or desire, as much as obedience and prophecy?[11] Either way, the description he sets forth is implicitly biographical of Jesus.

Nevertheless, Stringfellow's decision to become a lawyer reflects the way in which this journey was transforming his understanding of politics from "career" to "ministry." His decision was motivated as much by his passion and concern for politics as his burgeoning commitment to the Christian faith and SCM in which he was involved. Although the archive provides no precise indication of when Stringfellow made the decision, we can know with certainty the decision had been made by as early as 1949, during his time at the LSE, for at that time, in one of the many family newsletters written during this period, he says:

> It is my hope and intention to go to law school in the States, but it may be of interest to you to know that I am thinking seriously of spending a year in theological school first. This is not because I anticipate entering the ministry, let that be perfectly clear, but rather because it would contribute to my being a more constructive and intelligent Christian in law and in politics, where I feel that my authentic vocation lies. (Stringfellow, 1949:2)[12]

10. Compare, then, this statement with his later experience with illness and near death in the section entitled "Death and Life: Illness, Death and Resurrection" in chapter 7.

11. The idea that it was an expression of how he *wanted* to live plays a much underrated and under-assessed role, and I wonder if it might be part of what might tentatively be called the self-destructive side to his personality. It might also be an early indication of self-abandonment for the sake of the gospel. Most likely it is a combination of the two.

12. Stringfellow tells us that at the age of fourteen he decided not to become a priest (Stringfellow, 1970e:80). It was a decision which led to a passionate rejection of the "simplistic notion of decisions being mere choices between self-evident good and evil"

His letter seems to indicate that his decision to become a lawyer is not news, or at least not pressing news, in 1949: that honor is reserved for the announcement of his intentions regarding theological school. This is not a decision for "the ministry," but a decision which he believes better serves him in "his ministry"—the ministry that is politics, expressed through the concrete practice of being a lawyer.

To summarize: vocation and politics are at the heart of Stringfellow's motivation for being a lawyer and significantly the evidence from the archives places his own thinking about vocation at a point which predates the more public debates on this subject which began in the early 1950s. Stringfellow was in Europe at LSE, and then stationed in Germany in the army through to 1953. His exodus from American life, through various enterprises and taking various forms, had lasted for nearly five years;[13] he was now twenty-four years old and exuding an air of self-confident ambition which won many over in spite of his often brash style. The social context of America in the 1950s was something Stringfellow confronted upon his final return, with eyes opened as much by his experiences abroad, as by the thinking those experiences prompted. Moreover, his view changed from being defensive to being critical of the American position (Stringfellow, 1947a, 1950a). Amidst the debates on natural law (and the nature of jurisprudence), and faith and work, what transpired was an attempt by Stringfellow to seek ways of developing the latter in the light and context of the former. Gradually, through the law, politics became for Stringfellow not so much a career he embarked upon, as the means of living his vocation.[14] However, his decision to become a lawyer seems to have been most definitely a political one.

(Stringfellow, 1970e:79). Reflection upon this pattern of decision leading to understanding was to re-emerge later on in his life; see the section entitled "Death and Life: Illness, Death and Resurrection" in chapter 7.

13. 1947 saw his first trip to Europe for the World Conference of Christian Youth in Oslo, at which he first heard Martin Niemoller and Reinhold Niebuhr. This conference spawned dozens of speaking engagements for Stringfellow throughout America in the following two years, which rendered him endlessly on the road; 1949 saw him in Europe, with LSE and NATO, and in 1953 he undertook a speaking trip to India. During this trip he contracted hepatitis, which would later cause him the first pangs of an illness that was ultimately to claim his life. It is also worth considering that, as a young homosexual male growing up in a culture hostile to one's sexuality and one's politics, Europe offered a means of escape and perhaps the discovery of acceptance and/or self-acceptance. Certainly, joining the army seems to fit the pattern suggested by D'Emilio.

14. It is at this time of his visit to Europe and previously, in the context of his close friendship, that Stringfellow discovered, or rather was discovered by, God. It is at this

There is clearly much to discuss, not least with regards relating Stringfellow's own lifework throughout the 1950s with the sociopolitical context described above in chapter 2.

RECONCILIATION: EMERGENCE OF FAITH AND POLITICS

So far we have examined the aspects of the sociopolitical context of the 1950s, along with Stringfellow's decision to become a lawyer amidst the discussions on law and vocation. We shall now concentrate upon examining Stringfellow's engagement with this sociopolitical context through his lifework, particularly engaging the discussions of church and law, and Stringfellow's stance of resistance which arose in the development of his thought.

While Stringfellow benefited from a culture that gave rise to an air of self-confidence which he himself exuded, the boom of the 1950s also formed his stance of resistance and the theology which authored it. Broadly speaking, his reaction was aimed at confronting the naïve faith in progress and what is termed the "Protestant work ethic"; the place of economic abundance as the key to authenticity (since it is the abundance of Christ's love which authored his own understanding of identity or vocation); differentiation from aliens as the basis of identity; and an individualist culture driven by a culture of competition (violence).

Enduring throughout his life, the guiding concern of Stringfellow's life and theology was that of taking seriously the theological unity or reconciliation of both faith and politics to each other. He believed the two belonged together at the heart of our Christian identity, and through various ventures and experiences he sought to discern in what way they did so. This, of course, marks him out as distinct from his peers, for whom the abandonment of politics was a precursor for taking faith seriously, and vice-versa.[15] It quickly becomes clear that Stringfellow's disenchantment with America pre-dated most of his contemporaries by

point, perhaps motivated by what he saw with the Confessing Church, that he picked up his Bible, and figuratively never put it down again. This set in motion the beginnings of his own dying to career as a motivational force in his life, and therefore marks the beginning of the replacement of career with vocation or authenticity.

15. The confinement of faith to the margins of personal morality rather than public or political transformation can be seen perhaps most clearly in the Evangelical Renewal which dominated the American religious scene in the later half of the 1950s. While the renewal was writ-large amongst the churches, the dominant trend among avant-garde theologians was philosophical existentialism.

nearly a decade, and emerged out of an interplay of a variety of forces at work both in his life and world. The origins of this disenchantment can be seen in his desire to reconcile faith and politics theologically.

The emergence and solidification of his interest in faith and politics, and especially its leftist or radical overtures, reflects the radicalization of a personal worldview which until that point had been dominated by both a relatively conservative, mainstream, high-church episcopalianism, and a political view of America which, with an unabashed belief, confessed faith in the democratic process as the means to realize effective transformation. It took about a decade for the radical union of faith and politics which Stringfellow pursued to mature into something coherent.

The origins of this journey appear while Stringfellow was at Bates College in 1947,[16] and is witnessed to not only by the subjects he studied, but also by a particular paper he wrote at that time concerning Christianity and communism as they related to Soviet-American relations at the outset of the Cold War. This paper, entitled *The Relation of World Christianity to World Communism* (Stringfellow, 1947b) shows not only Stringfellow's early interested in faith and politics, but also shows his early commitment to engagement of specific political problems of the time. Amidst the emerging struggle of two global "super-powers," the use of the term "world" in Stringfellow's title was intended both to indicate the iconic and ideological nature of both Christianity and communism as they were being practiced at the time in America and the Soviet Union, and his dissent from such usage. Thus it indicates, albeit in a tentative and probing way, a genuine concern to engage the real problems of contemporary politics from a dissenting "faith perspective." The paper emerged partly out of research he undertook for the American Student Christian movement (SCM) in New England, illustrating further the extent of his commitment beyond the purely speculative or academic.[17]

The paper's conclusions center on a political emphasis of harmony, or unity. It also presents a valuable insight into the character of what

16. Here he majored in Politics and Economics. In high school, his timetable was dominated by subjects entailing various aspects of economics, politics, and history (Bates College, 1951).

17. The correspondence this project generated indicates Stringfellow's broadly leftist political leaning at that time and his commitment to the Democratic party and the political system as a means of realizing change. In Stringfellow (1956b), he makes clear his desire for election to political office as a Democrat.

often appears a highly confrontational theology, for among the papers of the late 1940s Stringfellow states clearly another motif that was to become characteristic of his theology and hermeneutics: that the theme of the Bible, and of theology, is reconciliation.[18]

Notes from a speech delivered in 1946 clearly show how, at this early stage, his theology lacked an embrace of "biblical politics." However, despite this it does indicate the early commitment to a few important themes in his lifework. Firstly, the linking of the idea of the arrival of a Christian society with people becoming more complete Christians, which echoes his later work on the vocation of the church. Also, there is consistency regarding the central place of the laity in his thinking on faith and politics. "The official leaders of the church—the clergy—are not trained to be politicians. The job is really up to us, the laymen" (Stringfellow, 1946). This latter point is an early commitment to acclaiming the amateur and recognizing the unique and distinctive role of clergy and laity.[19]

Hearing the Word

Despite its significance, Stringfellow's early commitment to uniting faith and politics is a story he refrains from telling in any of his autobiographical work. I have sought to highlight some of the more salient features of this story in our discussion here in order to identify clearly the emergence of independent thought and commitment which was to prove deeply significant for both his theology and his hermeneutics, providing the basis for his subsequent thought and action.

His commitment to faith and politics was both solidified and fostered in the years immediately following college, especially through a number of overseas visits he undertook. The first of these was as one of the American representatives at the World Conference of Christian Youth, held in Oslo during 1947. Stringfellow immersed himself in the stories and experiences of young Christians from around the world and learned some valuable lessons regarding how America was viewed by others and about the shape of Christianity in Europe at that time. In particular, he was exposed to the poverty and decay of Europe immediately following the war. It was the occasion at which, for the first time, he "felt

18. Note also the way in which the theme of reconciliation occurs around the same time as his all-important friendship.

19. See chapter 5 for further discussion of this issue.

keenly . . . the impact of life in a Christian Community" (Stringfellow, 1947c:1). He goes on:

> We had been told that there was much resentment against America because of certain of our policies. And while we were sympathetic to such reports, they were somehow impersonal and remote, and we didn"t understand the implications they had for us. Oslo changed this: or rather, Oslo has changed us . . . The tragedy of Europe's hunger stunned me one afternoon in London when I saw two boys fighting over a part of a chicken leg that had been stolen from a hotel garbage can . . . Europe is a land of hollow buildings filled with hollow people . . . It has opened my eyes to the desperate reality of the deterioration and confusion which engulfs our generation . . . It is time we in America stopped living in a soap opera world. (Stringfellow, 1947c:1–2, 4–5)

This account of his time in Oslo is important for a number of reasons. Firstly, it is *critical*: in Stringfellow's first experience of American critique by foreign nations, he found his own critical voice. The soap opera world must stop. America's immigration policies were perhaps the most criticized by others, betraying a xenophobic mood, and Stringfellow confronted them, working through the USCC and lobbying government for change.[20] The second reason is *contextual*, for his experience led him to realize the contextual nature of the criticisms he heard. In this very personal and public encounter, Stringfellow's worldview, and particularly his faith was shaken in ways that reinforced for him the important role of context in understanding.

Lastly, there is *commitment*. The criticism he encountered touched something that had previously not found such full expression. *Criticism* and *context* foster the beginnings of a kinship with the "aliens" or the marginalized he encountered, while standing in critical opposition of

---

20. This engagement found fruit later on, in 1953. The archives contain a significant amount of correspondence, two are most notable. First, a letter to John F. Kennedy, requesting a copy of report published in January that year by the President's Commission on Immigration and Naturalization Policies entitled *Whom Shall We Welcome*, and another document from McCarron-Walters Act hearings (Stringfellow, 1953b). Second, a letter from USCC itself, formulated by Stringfellow, which puts forward its position to the chair of the immigration committee (Johnson, 1953). Towards the end of the 1950s we see Stringfellow's concerns find concrete expression again, this time as a legal advocate, in the support of Joseph Sittler when he sought naturalization.

America and what it represents. It is the beginning of advocacy and resistance.[21]

Of all the speakers at the conference, perhaps most provocative was Martin Niemoller, who spoke about the Confessing Church in Germany. This event and its contents were to have a lasting impact upon Stringfellow. Its importance was solidified when he returned to the United States and began undertaking countless talks and presentations about his experience of the conference to eager audiences. At the conference, Stringfellow encountered the Word in a concrete and embodied form—the body of Christ as the Christian community. Following his experiences Stringfellow was convinced that the unity of the ecumenical movement, which was a unity that lay not in compromise or dialogue but in Christ's work for us, was the key to political stability and peace.

The importance of politics in the interpersonal realm was not lost on Stringfellow, and he realized the necessity of raising his profile for obtaining his ambition for political office, which at the time was his ambition. The conference at Oslo, and its associated speeches and publication, did much to foster this profile, and soon he won a Rotary Scholarship to attend LSE. At LSE, for the academic year 1949–50, he studied *The Relation of Modern Democratic Political Theory to Christianity* under Prof. B. Smellie. Essentially, this involved a close examination of the Malvern conference[22] and the work of William Temple. Stringfellow's decision to study Temple was not an arbitrary one, but one motivated by his commitment to the ecumenical movement. Temple, in turn, was probably an inspiration for Stringfellow's unbridled passion for ecumenism and the

21. The impact of the European post-war context upon Stringfellow's life is demonstrated in two articles: "Does the World Hate America?" (Stringfellow, 1947a) and "American Apologia" (Stringfellow, 1950a). He discovered how America was perceived by others, and how Europe still struggled to reconstruct itself and continued to bear the political and economic scars of war, while America experienced unprecedented growth and prosperity and a culture of contentment. This experience was crucial for his own formation of a critical perspective upon America as his lifework developed. It is also probable that his homosexuality fostered unacknowledged sublimated feelings of kinship or solidarity here and later.

22. The Anglican conference was held at Malvern, January 7–10, 1941, under Temple's presidency. Its findings were especially concerned with the relation of the church and economic life, and deemed the doctrine of man to be imperiled by the private ownership of industrial resources. It recommended that the Church of England should radically reform its own economic and administrative system (Cross and Livingstone, 1983:863).

unity of faith and politics. Stringfellow's support of the movement was prompted by a belief that it provided a unified egalitarian commitment to the Word of God, laity, and political transformation.

Two emerging points are telling at this time. The first is the central and pervasive role that Christ's Lordship takes in Stringfellow's thinking, and the way this leads to consideration of vocation. At this time he understood "vocation" as a person's ministry, and only later, from about 1954, was to revise and extend this to a more "existential" understanding of vocation as constituting a person's authentic identity: who they are in Christ. "Through the ecumenical movement we are brought to a recognition of the fact of the one Lord—Jesus Christ. This recognition is also the discovery of the concept of a Christian Vocation" (Stringfellow, 1950d:4). Vocation is not limited to ordination but is the enterprise of all Christian believers in all walks of life, in what Stringfellow terms our "life-work": a term which encompasses our personal life, sex life, academic pursuit and our occupation. The second point to emerge is his understanding of politics. This is the point at which we begin to see the political implications of unity and ecumenism emerging in his thought. Within this framework, the unity or peace which is sought through the political process of government is actually most authentically found in witness of the church of Christ. This is what the ecumenical movement celebrates. The unity that the world seeks is therefore found in Christ's church (the people of God), and witness to this reality occurs through our vocation. Consequently, Stringfellow believes the ecumenical movement has immense political implications "because it sharply focuses the attention of Christians on the concept of Christian vocation" (Stringfellow, 1950d:9). There seems little doubt that this progression in his thought is derived through his work on Temple at the LSE.

After the LSE, Stringfellow continued overseas, traveling throughout western and eastern Europe and speaking on behalf of the World Student Christian Federation (WSCF). Archival evidence suggests Stringfellow personally arranged this tour and its funding (Stringfellow, 1950c:1). It afforded him the opportunity to further encounter the Confessing Church, as well as to learn first hand about other Christian experiments in discipleship (e.g., Iona) and the character of the European churches in general. It was in these travels, and his previous time at LSE, that Stringfellow came to realize the importance of the Bible's authority in dealing with matters of church unity and Christian vocation. At the end of the tour Stringfellow returned to the United States whereupon he was called up to serve as a NATO soldier in Germany: a young protagonist's ticket to return to Europe. Stringfellow's courtship with controversy became very visible while serving in the army, and it was to continue to be so for the rest of his life. Despite serving in the army, Stringfellow's involvement with the SCM and WSCF, and the ecumenical movement they represented, continued unabated.[23]

As well as proving significant to the development of his thinking on faith and politics, this time overseas was also personally significant. It was a time of a dramatic renewal of his faith under the influence of new Christian groupings at work in Europe at that time, especially the Confessing Church and Bonhoeffer's theology. It was a period in Stringfellow's life described as one of "dying to career" (Stringfellow 1982b:125; McThenia 1995b), or put otherwise, dying to self; until this point the evidence suggests Stringfellow had predominantly been led by his ego. Exposure to the Word and the world, or context, of Europe in the aftermath of the war greatly influenced this transformation. This personal renewal led to an understanding of faith and politics that went beyond convention, central to which was the role and authority of the Bible.

While Stringfellow began college as an American loyal to the state, by this time his political and theological view had shifted somewhat, influenced by his experiences abroad. However, that he undertook military service rather than resist (as the Berrigan brothers were later to do, with Stringfellow's advocacy) can be interpreted in at least two ways, both essentially practical and contextual. The first is that resistance to National Service in America at that time was simply not an option: it did not occur to people. According to Alan Brinkley,[24] it was not that people were necessarily loyal to the state, nor that they were afraid of the state. Rather, the idea of resisting the draft simply did not occur to people as an

---

23. This is documented in a series of letters concerning an article he was asked to write for the YMCAs journal *Intercollegian* (Stringfellow, 1952). The article, regarding the role of the chaplaincy in the army, was censored by the army. Stringfellow, unwilling to make the changes and soften his criticisms, preferred it missed publication, which it did. The volume of *Intercollegian* it was due to appear in also carried other articles along similar themes—including one by Jack Lewis, who was soon to found the Christian Faith and Life Community (see chapter 5).

24. This was a conversation the author had with Alan Brinkley in 1999. Brinkley was Professor of History at Columbia University, New York.

option nor as a *form of protest*, predominantly because organized protest as we saw arising in the 1960s had not begun. The second is that the G.I. Bill was in place at that time, and this would have provided Stringfellow with a heavily subsidized route into post-graduate education. Coming from a poor background, he was aware of this option, and a handwritten ten-year plan found in the archives indicates he was at this time considering the idea of G.I. Bill-subsidized legal education, along with post-graduate and doctoral theological studies, which he envisaged undertaking upon his return (Stringfellow, 1953a). However, as mentioned above, whilst in the army Stringfellow was highly critical of it primarily concerning the abandonment he and all Christian servicemen felt and his article for the YMCSa Intercollegia magazine, on the role of the chaplain in army life, was subject to censure by the army and so never was published.[25] On leaving the army, Stringfellow went on a speaking trip to India, where it is likely that he contracted the hepatitis that was later to cause his health such problems.

The Politics of Ecumenism

As we are beginning to see, Stringfellow's commitment to ecumenism is the cornerstone to the development of his thinking on faith and politics, grounded in his participation in ecumenical student Christian movements. Looking at published histories of the ecumenical movement, this may appear an odd influence, for in such histories the theme of politics is afforded little attention.[26] However, Stringfellow's primary commitment is to context, the place where he stands accompanied by the recognition of the pedagogical and political significance of students despite their marginalized position in society, coupled with a desire for change. We need to look closer now at his involvement with student ecumenical movements.

25. His political involvement at this time was such that even prior to his national service, the FBI had a file on him. Unfortunately, the FBI are unwilling to make public this and later files, so the precise nature of their interest in him cannot be known. However, Stringfellow was committed at this stage to exploring leftist politics and was also already critical of some aspects of government activity. Such was the anticommunist climate that most American citizens who expressed an interest in socialism or leftist politics would have been monitored to some degree as a matter of "national security." It is therefore likely that these files are not of significant importance to our present discussions.

26. See Lossky et al. (1991).

The origins of his involvement in the ecumenical movement originates in the WSCF, and the Oslo meeting of the World Conference of
Christian Youth in 1947, at which time he also attended the inaugural
meeting of the WCC in Amsterdam. Deeply involved in the student
Christian movement, Stringfellow was described as the "one of the ablest
and most interesting products of our recent SCM work" (Johnson, 1953).
As a member of both the councils of the SCM and the United Student
Christian Council (USCC), by 1953 he had written two substantial papers: "Some Thoughts on the American SCM in Politics" (Stringfellow,
1950e)[27] and a proposal for an Ecumenical Institute of Theology and
Politics (Stringfellow, 1953d). Both papers acclaimed the central, amateur role of the student in the practice of faith and politics. He advocated "amateur" rather than "professional" theologians as the primary
inhabiters of theological practice. They also indicate a new direction in
his thought concerning the relationship of politics and evangelism. This
acclamation of the amateur is clearly dominant in his published work,
and here we see that this commitment is self-consciously predicated by
an early methodological premise.

Stringfellow felt that as a group, the student Christians were predis-
posed to "romantic and mellow liberalism" and failed to confront politics
realistically (Stringfellow, 1953e:1).[28] He sought to confront that situation
by exploring the way faith and politics relate. It reflects a realignment of
his thinking in the light of his European experiences and affirmed the
evangelical significance of politics and its ecumenical basis. Simply, the
integrity of Christian witness requires political involvement—a stark
contrast to the message of the churches.

> We do not retain our Christian integrity by refusing to enter
> politics because it is unpleasant or socially irresponsible. We may
> retain it if we search the problem of *how* to enter politics, rec-
> ognizing the peculiar conditions and resources which make up

27. Although this paper is dated 1950, it was not in fact released by Stringfellow
until 1953. His proposal was for an organized national study program to be undertaken
by USCC members, followed by local experiments, political apprenticeships, and local
national study [small] groups to reflect theologically and politically at a local level. This
harmony of study, the production of documents, hands-on political engagement, and
small-group theological reflection sought to build "a concerned fellowship of Christian
students vocationally interested in politics" and to serve them. It was a highly innovative
approach and a precursor to Stringfellow's later theological developments.

28. His view changed little over he years. See Stringfellow (1968e).

our situation; we may retain it if we seek some understanding of *how politics can be a positive instrument of evangelism,* as well as a weapon for social reform. (Stringfellow, 1953e:2)

This political-evangelical identity requires us to "develop the perception to see theological issues in politics, as well as political issues in theology" (Stringfellow, 1953e:3), and radicalizes the two dominant modes of Christian thinking in America at that time, namely the traditionally liberal and the conservative evangelical. It also requires us to develop a theological concern for politics that is relevant and accessible:

> Our concern for politics as Christians must have theological roots which we ourselves understand, and which have clear relevance to our own experience. This is perhaps not so much the job of the theologian as it is of the individual Christian student. It is a permanent task . . . surviving our student days. (Stringfellow, 1953e:2)[29]

In other words, theology related to our experience, arising perhaps out of our experience, is the basis of political action, and such theological politics is the content of the Christian life. This view is symptomatic of his lifelong disposition for developing a theology that is accessible, relevant, and faithful for the "long-haul"; his concern for fostering a theological predisposition amongst lay people, to which the de-specialization or de-professionalization of the theological task is crucial. The unity expressed in ecumenical identity is the basis of this Christian life.

> I contend that our response to the ecumenical fact opens us to completely untouched political frontiers, that our understanding of vocation *and* work (the two concepts are inseparable) has immense political importance for American democracy, that our problem of evangelization through politics is illuminated by the ecumenical character of the SCM. (Stringfellow, 1953e:4)

In sum: ecumenism, and moreover the unity of which it is an expression, is the basis for faith; all faith is necessarily political (but theologically so), and the primary context for faith is in the world (vocation and work). For Stringfellow, ecumenism has political implications precisely because its central theme is *reconciliation.*[30] His emphasis upon *politics* at this

29. Such a sentiment is, of course, expressive of his own future lifework.

30. This was the dominant theme of post-war theology in the ecumenical movement, and in fact became the core theme of Stringfellow's own thinking and has a strong emphasis upon incarnational Christology.

stage in his theological development radicalizes the theological understanding and implications of the ecumenical movement.

The theme of reconciliation leads to the discovery of Christian vocation, itself a political event unifying transformation, witness, and worship. Stringfellow saw that Christian vocation as ministry requires us to witness to the unity (reconciliation) we have with God in Christ through his incarnation, death, and resurrection, and that the ongoing witness of the church is a repetition of this reconciliation. His understanding of politics as essentially a missionary activity here is an exciting one, for it places faith at the center of his understanding of politics, and vocation at the center of faith. This existential bias (towards experience) and ecumenical commitment (towards reconciliation) is something that was to prove highly significant for Stringfellow in the years ahead.

Following his thoughts on the American SCM in politics, Stringfellow posed the following questions in his thinking about the nature of politics and faith in relation to vocation.

> Where can the young Christian who is to enter industrial work find guidance in the preparation for his ministry? Where can the young Christian who will spend his life in agriculture discover resources that are helpful in the fulfillment of his ministry? Where can the young Christian—armed with a law degree and a healthy zeal to make the world more tolerable—receive assistance in working out the intricacies of the Christian ministry in law and politics? (Stringfellow, 1950f.)

Stringfellow's own answer can be seen at this time in his initiative to establish the "Ecumenical Institute of Theology and Politics" (Stringfellow, 1953d).[31] The proposal was an attempt to redress an imbalance in a

---

31. All three papers (Stringfellow, 1950f, 1953d,e) were originally conceived and written in 1950, at the close of his time at LSE. He continued to develop them while in the army. However, his time in the army resulted in him being out of circulation. During those three years nothing whatsoever appears to have been done to address the problems identified: it fell to Stringfellow to envision and organize. Others, in those years, simply appear not to have seen the need, or if they saw the need, lacked the motivation or insight. However, from 1953 the need was quickly adopted as "a given." Stringfellow's vision, commitment, and passion directly preempted, inspired, and influenced this change.

The committee members at this time included Professor Julian Hartt, widely acknowledged to be the founded of the "New Yale" school. Also present on the committee was Professor Kenneth Underwood, professor of social ethics from Yale with whom Stringfellow was in good contact, and William Ellis, with whom Stringfellow was later to establish a legal practice in East Harlem.

church vigorously committed to preparing and sustaining people for church service—missionaries, ordained ministers, and the like—but consistently failing to apply itself to the secular work of Christians.

The two main objectives of the institute were to "develop a competent understanding of Christian theology especially in its vocational and political implications" and to help people to "grasp the relationship of their specific vocation to the total mission of the church and their personal responsibilities in evangelism" (Stringfellow, 1953d:2).[32] The vision for the institute was orientated around the radical life of the laity and sought to move away from both compartmentalization and privatization of roles and faith: "The religious discipline of public life is to come not from the occasional intervention of the clergy, but chiefly from the dedicated conscience of lay believers" (Stringfellow, 1953d:2).

The Institute sought to build and develop the theological discernment and engagement of Christians roused into action by the SCM and to prepare them for Christian leadership. Essentially, its purpose can be summed up in one word: discipleship.[33]

Echoing the Confessing Church, the intention was for the staff and students of the institute to exist as a worshipping community, and for the community to be sustained through this corporate ecumenical life of prayer, worship, and pastoral care. They studied the Bible and examined the political relevance "of such modern theologians as Barth, Niebuhr, Maritain, etc., problems in church history of the pertinence of the political order, the church and state relationship in America viewed theologically and politically" (Stringfellow, 1953d:5).

This proposal is an excellent example of the way in which Stringfellow identified and engaged the concrete implications of the debate on vocation in the life of the church at that time. Such a move was both political and theological and sought to recover the central role of the laity in the life of the church and the world.[34]

32. It is worth observing that Stringfellow's use of the term vocation here is in its more conventional sense. Despite his own personal thinking, at this stage he had clearly not consistently worked out his thought in this area.

33. The Institute was something of a forerunner to Stringfellow's later idea of the seminary underground, discussed further in chapter 5.

34. Stringfellow was constantly fearful that the institute would render its subject academic and as a result "professionalize" its students. It was set up in 1953 at Wesleyan College, and for a time Stringfellow remained on the board. However, quite quickly his fears were realized. In 1957 he resigned: professionalization and abstraction had replaced discipleship.

Stringfellow's proposal was an expression of the development and struggle with his own vocation and identity; he experienced a failure of the church in his own life, saw this pattern repeated in the lives of others, and sought to address it at a public level. As before, experience was giving rise to change, for as he put it:

> Christian faith is historical, not theoretical; it is objective, not subjective; it is knowledge, not conviction ... Christian faith is acknowledgement of what God has done for man. Confession of the faith is testimony about that event ... Christian life is evangelism ... Politics is the ordering of life by men in society ... The gospel is politics. (Stringfellow, 1954:2, 3, 6)

This perspective, being born out of his involvement with the ecumenical movement, constitutes the essence of Stringfellow's theological orientation and the politics of the gospel. The sentence is pointing towards a convergence between the politics of the gospel and his own thinking through the inspiration of the ecumenical movement[35] upon his position.

Politics and social action are the Christian imperative, and the form that should take is one of a concrete, obedient response of witness and evangelism. It is the cornerstone of the theology upon which he would build throughout his lifework, uniting politics and the practice of faith in the work-a-day world of the laity in the light of the gospel and the politics of reconciliation therein, and construing the church in the light of this.[36]

35. It was a context which afforded him access to a theological network which included Karl Barth, Jacques Ellul, Heindrick Kraemer, Reinhold Niebuhr, Gustav Wingrin, John Baillie, Emil Brunner, Joseph Hromadka, and Stephen Neill.

36. His work in the ecumenical movement was a significant part of his life up to the mid-1960s. In 1959 he was offered a job on the WCC in Geneva, but turned it down. Although chronologically much later than the material we are looking at here, his decision does shed some light on the emerging understanding of himself and his theology, which Stringfellow already possessed half a decade earlier. Vocationally aware in the letter he wrote declining their offer, he explained his decision in the following way:

> I withdraw because something else claims me, and I have understood that more lucidly by coming to Spittal. What claims me is just my work in the world in law practice and in politics in East Harlem and my life in a congregation. That claims me ... because I see more sharply how irrelevant the church is in my own neighborhood and how afraid the church there is of the neighborhood ... In a word, I am shocked by the reluctance of Christians in America to trust the gospel and I am persuaded by God's mercy that my vocation is just to trust the gospel. (Stringfellow, 1959i:1)

So far in this chapter we have been attentive to Stringfellow's engagement with faith and the law, and the place of politics therein. We have introduced some of the more important events and influences upon his life at this time, and focused upon the development of politics and faith (vocation), predominantly through his involvement with the ecumenical movement. We have uncovered the origins of his theological engagement with politics, in which the life of faith, or vocation, is the obedient and political response to God's reconciliatory love: the experiential embodiment of, and witness to, the truth of the gospel. That, in essence, was ecumenism's political force in Stringfellow's lifework. Keeping all this in mind, we now turn our attentions to Stringfellow's theological engagement with the law.

REBELLION: THE LAW AND THE CHURCH

The unfolding of both Stringfellow's vocation and his engagement with his context found sustained focus in his engagement with the law. This engagement with the law and the legal establishment on the one hand, and theology and its ecclesial establishment on the other, displays further his strong commitment to his context, and through it Stringfellow's attentions upon the debates on law and vocation came sharply into focus.

It was a busy period for Stringfellow, consequently our discussion makes selective use of the material in order to elucidate encounters which would provide further foundation for Stringfellow's theological outlook and orientation. Temporally, they take us to the end of the 1950s, and logically, to the beginning of his "mature" or published theology.

Back to School

Burning inside Stringfellow at the beginning of the 1950s was a passion and a confidence matched by few of his peers. Together, their focus changed as his thinking and experience developed and as he made himself vulnerable to the Word. Demobilized by the army, and prompted no doubt by his work on the Ecumenical Institute for Theology and Politics, in 1953 Stringfellow's emerging vocational understanding coupled with his exposure to circles of theological discourse (through SCM, WCC, WSCF, etc.) took him back to school, so marking the beginning of the uniting of law and theology that was to be so significant to his lifework.[37]

37. To put it in perspective, this is the same year the Civil Rights Movement got underway with the court case "Brown vs. The Board of Education."

Stringfellow's changing view of the nature and purpose of theology is perhaps reflected in his decision to abridge his once-desired year in theological school to a single semester. And so it was he spent the fall at the Episcopal Divinity School (EDS). This afforded him the opportunity to read, study, and receive formal tuition by many well regarded theologians, such as Joseph Fletcher. It was a time of theological intensification for him, allowing him the chance to consolidate his theological knowledge and experience thus far acquired through his student work. But while EDS provided Stringfellow with his first formal experience of theological education (especially of church history, ethics, doctrine, and biblical studies), it did not win him over to pursue academic study of theology; he survived intact, his mind enriched.

Immediately following EDS, Stringfellow entered Harvard Law School to train to become a lawyer. Along with his political ambition, it was clear to him that the law functioned as a kind of "secular theology"; it functioned as the arbiter of reality and the guarantor of truth, and most importantly to this end, *it informed people how to act.* Because the law was the way through which most people experienced the mechanics of the state at work, its relationship to ethics (politics) and in some sense its status as ethics was the focus of Stringfellow's attention. In other words, the relationship of law to theology, or indeed the legalization of theology (that is, the status of law as theology), was deeply significant to Stringfellow, for the joining of theology and law, Stringfellow wrote later, deals with the "more general interest in the laity in the world, and with the issues of moral theology or theological ethics" (Stringfellow, 1961b:3).

While attending law school[38] and after, he undertook to bring law and theology together in a number of practical ways. His aim was to get people thinking and talking about the law *theologically*, and hence vocationally. This included organizing and running a forum on law and theology (membership for which came from all levels of most of North America's leading universities and church organizations), along with a number of national conferences (Stringfellow, 1956g, 1957f,e). In different ways, these conferences addressed the relationship of theology and

---

38. Stringfellow's relationship with Harvard Law School was a strained one, and he made only occasional appearances there, spending much of his time at Tufts University, where he taught debate, and continuing to travel with the WSCF.

law in relation to ethics,[39] and those issues (vocation, work, worship) which occupied him during his ecumenical work with student Christians. Organizing these conferences in particular was something of a coup, derived from Stringfellow's own hard work and "larger than life" character.[40] It provided a networking opportunity that was unparalleled and a platform for engaging and encountering many well known and highly regarded thinkers in the areas of theology and law; included amongst these were Jacques Ellul and Markus Barth, with whom Stringfellow entered into fruitful correspondence and was to become good friends (Stringfellow, 1957d, 1958d).

Following the conference on Christian Faith and the Legal Profession[41] Stringfellow arranged for the publication in America of two books he became aware of through his time in London and his work with WCC: Barth's *Gospel and Law* and Ellul's *The Theological Foundations of Law*.[42] These law conferences also afforded him an extraordinary networking opportunity amongst legal and theological circles. In a press release Stringfellow acclaimed the conference as "the first attempt in more than a generation to bring together lawyers, law faculty, students, seminary faculty, and clergy to discuss the vocation of a Christian lawyer and the relationships of Christian faith to legal philosophy," and they formed part of a projected three year program of the National Council of Churches among law students and faculty (Stringfellow, 1957g).[43]

39. As McThenia (1998:7–8) points out, the law left little room for justice at that time, and issues of morality were sidelined in favor of notions of moral neutrality. Stringfellow was challenging that assumption theologically, as a lawyer.

40. And yet, despite this character, during these years Stringfellow spent much of his time alone and drank heavily (McThenia,1998:5–6); there was loneliness.

41. This conference was convened jointly by the Diocese of Western Massachusetts, the USCC, and the Faculty Christian Fellowship of the National Council of Churches. It was held at Harvard Law School April 12–14, 1957, and the program was essentially structured around four papers dealing with Christianity and law.

42. Barth and Ellul were also members of the WCC, and this is how Stringfellow came to be aware of their work. Gary Lee's account of the publication of Ellul's work seems to downplay Stringfellow's involvement and is therefore historically inaccurate (Lee, 1985).

43. In addition, Stringfellow was committed to running the law school discussion group at Columbia University, at which he was Associate to the Office of Protestant Counselor. He also worked at the Law School of New York University. Both were done under a grant from the Church Society for College Work (1956–57) (Stringfellow, 1957h). As well as conferences, Stringfellow wrote a proposal for a lectureship in the area of law and theology for the University of New York Law School, comprising three

Like many others, Stringfellow perceived the importance of the law in society: the law tells us how to act and so provides a framework for living our life. In view of the importance of the law, Stringfellow was particularly concerned to bring theology to bear upon it, but not in any way that his contemporaries may have anticipated. His faculty paper marks the beginning of this engagement.[44]

LAW AND CHURCH IN STUDY: LAWYERING AS WORSHIP

Stringfellow's faculty paper, "The Life of Worship and the Legal Profession," was produced while still at Harvard[45] and is significant to us both for the way it furthers our discussion as well as for the evidence it yields of the early development of his thinking. In it he engages the two areas of discussion that were uppermost in the realms of the legal profession and ecumenical Christianity at that time, namely the role of law and the nature of vocation. He elucidates what he perceives as their coincidence with each other and the fundamental problem to which this gives rise, as the discussions impinge upon the life of the lawyer who is a Christian.[46] Throughout this paper Stringfellow engages the issue in terms of the relationship and nature of reconciliation of church and World—or *justification* and *justice*—and how each is related to creation (Stringfellow, 1955b:4).

---

formal lectures (Stringfellow, 1956e). There is documentation to suggest that Paul Tillich or James Pike was being lined up for the first lectureship, and it took place in Spring or Fall of 1957.

44. Despite Stringfellow's evident academic ability and mixing in academic circles, he chose not to pursue an academic career as a lawyer or a theologian. He declined many academic job offers throughout his life, preferring to remain in practice. Rather than out of an academic environment, it was out of the "screwy dialogue which ... takes place between my daily work and common life and the Word of God" (Stringfellow, 1960e:3) that he decided his writing would emerge. His commitment to the non-academic lay Christian life led him to refrain from undertaking formal theological education in the university, despite initial plans to the contrary (Stringfellow, 1953a). It was not an easy decision for him to make, but one driven by his commitment to social context and the unity of faith and politics.

45. The paper totals just twenty-two pages, which in later years he was to regard a "tentative" position. Such a view further supports its significance at this time, representing a new direction in his thinking, even if the loose ends had not been tied.

46. This paper is also less polemical than his later writings and seeks to be a rigorous theological engagement with the issues.

In essence the conflict at hand was this: if a lawyer who believed on the one hand in the gospel of grace, and on the other finds him or herself responsible for upholding the law, how should he or she act? Which commitment must take priority, and could these conflicts in any way be resolved? How must a Christian act in the work-a-day-world? Stringfellow saw that this problem brought together not only the debate on law, but also the debate within the church on vocation.

Prevailing discussions concerning equipping Christians for the workplace were driven by ethics: determining ethical norms as the basis for Christian practice. This, thought Stringfellow, was "an entirely wrong—and unbiblical—approach. The problem of work is not primarily or originally a problem of ethics, but a problem of worship, a problem of how in our daily work in the world there may be manifested the relationship which God has given to us concretely in Jesus Christ" (Stringfellow, 1956c:4). Therefore, his description of Christian work as worship emphasizes "being" over "doing" as determinate of vocational authenticity: in worship we are most fully authentic (Stringfellow, 1959k:4,7).[47]

Meanwhile, prevailing discussions on the relationship of law and faith rendered solutions which variously attempted to vindicate the law or transform it and conform it to what was perceived as God's will. Stringfellow believes all approaches are reductionist, for they abstracted and objectivized the subject of faith (Jesus Christ) and used the resulting set of Christian "concepts" or "principles" as a means of relating secular law and Christian faith (Stringfellow, 1955b:3). These discussions fail to deal with

> the question of individual Christian vocation in terms of the corporate Christian life in history as the Church; for, in the end, the Church would be at best a fellowship in common principles, not a community in common worship... Moreover, the very intentions, to vindicate or to transform secular law, which inform this effort beg the question of the meaning of sin in secular law. They really assume that sin is mastered, or at least profoundly mitigated, by secular law in so far as the latter is vindicated or transformed. (Stringfellow, 1955b:3)

47. This paper is in many ways a re-presentation of his previous *Life of Worship and the Legal Profession*, but represented around the axis of *mission*. In support of work as mission, Stringfellow cites a number of biblical references, including 1 Cor 3:9–13, which begins "We are fellow workmen for God; you are God's field."

Stringfellow's alternative proposition emerges from this critique. The issues at stake are those of grace and law, justification and justice, and the solution, according to Stringfellow, is derived from conceiving of the problem evangelistically. What is at stake, in essence, is nothing other than the gospel (Stringfellow, 1958a:2). As he later summarized: "to contort the word of grace into the law of nature is to make the gospel unintelligible, however neatly it resolves the query about the relations of law and theology" (Stringfellow, 1957a:81). For Stringfellow, the gospel is the very content of the Christian vocation.

We turn now to examine his proposal. First, we must examine the role of church and worship in his proposal, second, the role of law and vocation.

Church and Worship

The theme of Stringfellow's paper is that of reconciliation and response, and as such lays before us the foundation of his future lifework. The origin of his argument lay in an explication of the doctrines of creation and the fall.

For Stringfellow, creation is no mere sign of God's love for us, but is the medium of that love, through which we may love God. Creation is good, it manifests who God is, and it glorifies God. In short, creation is grace, and the theater of God's glory. Humanity lives amidst the fall, the ruination of creation. Stringfellow suggests that we inhabit the fall most fully, and creation is ruined primarily, when humanity seeks to worship its own achievements and ends. The saga of creation and the fall is the saga of life and death, being and non-being. In the moral reality of the fall, he says, the church is shattered and we literally "work to death" (Stringfellow, 1955b:6). In the fall

> the futility of men's struggles to restore life groans for restoration by Him. The emptiness of men's search for reconciliation cries out for reconciliation through Him. . . . Sin involves perception of the need to be saved. Upon this very perception men chiefly are motivated in history to try and save themselves. But in history Christians, having the same perception, attest that men are saved, that creation itself is restored by Jesus Christ alone . . . Men who are Christians are still men. Christians are fully implicated in fallen creation. They participate in its ruination. (Stringfellow, 1955b:7–8)

Note here the hermeneutic being used, whereby history is interpreted in terms of the saga of the fall. For Stringfellow the world of the Bible is understood as the means by which the world is understood; it is not so much "our history" as "God's history," whereby reality is interpreted biblically. This commitment is further supported by the many meetings in university law faculties which he organized or spoke at, when he worked with "law students and lawyers devoted to considering the gospel and law through Bible study" (Stringfellow, 1958g:1). He was convinced that "the whole point of having such a meeting is to listen to the Bible and not so much to listen to ourselves" (Stringfellow, 1958g:2). Here, then, we see the theme of *listening* emerging—a theme which was later to prove to have such fundamental importance, especially in Harlem.

Furthermore, the universal condition of our humanity is our implication in fallen creation; in faith, our humanity is not lost, but redeemed. The only difference between Christians and others is simply that Christians know they are saved by Jesus Christ; they recognize Christ as implicated in (the restoration of) their humanity and the whole of creation. Reconciliation does not mean forgoing our humanity, but is contiguous with it; it is the process of it being restored along with all of creation in which we act. Christ's gift is reconciliation of humanity and restoration of community, and the name of that community is the church (Stringfellow, 1955b:8).

> The identity of the Church with Creation, the Church as Creation being restored, emphasises the visible Church, the Church living in history, not to the exclusion of other affirmations about the Church, but only to emphasise the Church as the new life actually taking place in the midst of ruined life. (Stringfellow, 1955b:9)

The unity of the church, which is at the heart of his ecclesiology, is not derived through its invisibility in history but by its concrete physical manifestation in the life of the congregation.[48] Through the congregation the life of Christ is lived, the new age is begun, and the event of reconciliation of God and humanity takes place. The congregation is the key to humanity's partaking in reconciliation, for "no adherence to Christ exists outside the congregation; there is no membership in the Church

---

48. Here, he quotes Barth: "a *civitas platonica* or some sort of Cloud-cuckooland, in which Christians are united inwardly and invisibly, in which the visible church is devalued" (Barth, 1949:142).

except in the congregation" (Stringfellow, 1955b:9–10). For Stringfellow, the church is both incarnational and re-creational.

Despite this emphasis upon the concrete, it also has a deeply *mysterious* quality, and that mystery is Christ. The congregation arises in obedience and response to Christ's summons, not humanity's creative or organizational efforts, and that response is worship. The church of which he speaks while visible and concrete is not in itself a human institution.

> Men tamper and fiddle and perhaps call "church" what is not the Church, but the Church comes into being only because Christ summons His people. He sets them apart. He names them as a holy nation.... to live the new life in Him, to manifest that life to the world and in the world, so that the world may believe in Him and come to Him. (Stringfellow, 1955b:10)

The church is constituted by its response in obedience, and the "characteristic fact about life in the Church is worship." In the midst of ruined creation, the church is the place "where God is glorified: where his glory is manifested, where his glory is witnessed, where his glory is seen" (Stringfellow, 1955b:11). God justifies us, and our response in community is one of obedient worship, and it is in worship that we most readily encounter the subject of our faith.[49]

Worship describes and enacts restoration and declares the reconciliation or reunion between God and creation, and creation to God. Worship is our sacrificial response-in-love rendering to God all which he has given to us—in other words, his gift of creation. While the "appropriation in worship is focused upon the sacramental elements" (Stringfellow, 1955b:13) it extends beyond the bread, wine, and water to

> the building, the garments and (most essentially) the people gathered. Everything is given to Him: everything which He first has given men. The appropriation in worship is the offering of ourselves: the offering of that which He gives is making us. *Now the very event is taking place: God reconciling men to himself. Now prophecy is fulfilled. God is with His people. Now Creation is restored: His people glorify God.* (original emphasis Stringfellow, 1955b:13)

---

49. Stringfellow recognized the divergence between the reality of worship he described, and the practice of worship in the nation's churches which by and large scandalized the worship of God (Stringfellow, 1955b:12).

For Stringfellow, worship takes place in the church when it is gathered and dispersed in the world (Stringfellow, 1955b:13). The Christian life is the life lived in worship of God, *in the world*. In dispersion worship is not individualized, and nor is this some notion of the invisible church at work uniting the otherwise visibly separate in their lives at work. Rather, "wherever there is a Christian, *there* is the Church in representation" (Stringfellow, 1955b:15). Simply, what goes on amidst the gathered community is the same as what goes on in the world.

> It may be said that in each Christian, in work in the world, the Church and the world confront each other. In each Christian, restored Creation and fallen creation meet, collide, come, really, into concrete and awful struggle. This is the same struggle that happens when a congregation celebrates Holy Communion in the midst of, before the eyes of, secular community. It is the struggle of Church and World. (Stringfellow, 1955b:15)

Worship leads onto work. Amidst the reconciliation of creation, the fall lingers and humanity's relationship with creation is characterized by toil, pain, and death. Amidst the fall our relationship with creation is work, for work is the burden of death. It is grace, not work, which restores our relationship with God, and so grace, not work, which justifies us in the sight of God's justice. Worship, not work, is therefore the task of authentic humanity.

The struggle between the church and the world is, for Stringfellow, never more evident than in the discussion over vocation and law. Here the world seeks to reconcile the church to itself, and when conformed ceases to be the church. When the church is the church, it confronts the world and reveals the reality of the fall in its midst: "the World really cannot tolerate the Church . . . it bears the truth about reconciliation; it calls the World into the Church; it evangelizes the World, which is, of course, to say, it calls really for the death of the World . . . for the World to cease to be itself—so that it may be restored, so that it may live" (Stringfellow, 1955b:15). The vocation of the church is worship, and the issue at hand is one of justification and justice: grace and law, church and world, faith and politics as they confront one another.

This theological framework is the basis of Stringfellow's understanding of the relationship between the Christian faith, the church, and the world. It is the basis for his discussion of vocation and law, and it is to that discussion we now turn.

Law and Vocation

In bringing this theological framework to bear upon the concrete discussion of work, he contrasts dominant notions of work as vocation (i.e. undertaking a particular job) with the work of mission as the only true vocation. Our vocational decision is not a concern of this job over that, but is in fact a decision made in conversion, embodied as the "single, common vocation of worship" (Stringfellow, 1955b:17).[50] Our vocation is our unity, and is "the life-work of Christians" (Stringfellow, 1955b:17). In unity, God can be worshipped anywhere, because any work in the world can be sacramentalized. The choice of secular work is therefore (ultimately) of little consequence, in so far as it (does not) determine our identity; it does not justify us. Essentially, the scandal of the gospel is that our only true work is witness to the work of God—witness to God's life and activity in the world.

In order to emphasize the importance of the ordinary, Stringfellow asserts that secular work can be missionary activity originating in Jesus Christ and in "the work accomplished by God in him for the world" (Stringfellow,1955b:17).[51] Gone here is any notion of "applying faith to daily work" or "making the gospel relevant to secular work" (prevalent views at the time). For him the gospel is the work of God in the world and on behalf of the world, and the work of God cannot be overlooked or ignored when we speak of our own work in the world.

In bringing this view to bear upon the lawyer, we must first acknowledge his view of the law. "Human law originates in sin ... Men try to save themselves; men try to justify themselves. Law is thus an instrument" (Stringfellow, 1955b:19). However, while law is a sin, it also has the unusual power to name sin—e.g., murder. But while it names specific acts as sin, it does not, and cannot, "disclose the dimension, the reality of the *state* of sin into which men fall" (Stringfellow, 1955b:19). While the law can limit sin (specific acts), it cannot overcome it. The law, in short, is paradoxical; it identifies sin, yet at the same time is bound up in the power of sin. It is a paradox shared with the church.

Despite his criticisms of the law, elsewhere Stringfellow recognized there was also a place for it. "Christ demands of his followers a passion-

---

50. Stringfellow identifies vocation as lifework; see Stringfellow (1955b:7).

51. Here we see the way Stringfellow takes seriously and absolutely the notion that God became Man in Christ—God himself became subject to the Fall—subject to work.

ate love for justice, a belief that law should be an instrument of justice, and a desire to convert law and justice into instruments of Christian love" (Stringfellow, 1956d:1). The issue, naturally, is one of justification and justice. He was eager to make clear the limitations of the law, in that it functions instrumentally not foundationally, and that in so doing its inherent value lay in its ability to facilitate or deliver justice (Stringfellow, 1956d). At the heart of the practice of the law was justice, not, as had become the norm in legal education, *technique*.[52]

> The law can not be vindicated in Christian faith ... The law guar-
> antees the order of secular society, and Christians are subject to
> the secular power. Law is an aspect of historical existence, of hu-
> man life in the world. Now Christians, though they live in expec-
> tation of the fulfillment which God promises to men in Christ,
> live in the world, and in that sense under human law, as the *locus*
> of their proclamation of the gospel in which law and all of his-
> torical life is transcended. (Stringfellow, 1956a:49, 50, 51)

For Stringfellow, there can be no joinder between the law and theology. The justice of the law, while important in the secular order, is limited to that order, and is not the basis for the ordering of restored (authentic) humanity (our justification/the ordering of the church).

Given Stringfellow's theological redescription of vocation, work, and law, we are left with the one final practical question: how does the Christian worship God when he or she is engaged in work in the legal profession? "[S]urely it does not consist of ... mumbling the *Te Deum* before crossing the courthouse threshold or while waiting for a jury's

---

52. Furthermore, any critical self-reflection on behalf of the legal profession upon its role was generally absent. When it was raised, the issues of gospel and law ensued:

> The gulf between legal philosophy and the practice of law in the United States
> marks both legal education and the legal profession. The sense of law as a schol-
> arly profession is lost in an emphasis upon training students to become skilled
> technicians. The law student does not become learned in the law, but skillful in
> analysis and advocacy. Legal history and jurisprudence have little stature in legal
> curriculum ... since the Korean War especially law faculty and law students, and
> some lawyers have indicated dissatisfaction with the narrowness of legal educa-
> tion and legal work and there are some signs of new interest in legal history and
> jurisprudence ... But the quandary in these discussions extends further: to the
> significance of law in the social order and the relevance of a consideration of the
> gospel and law to the wider problems of social ethics. (Stringfellow, 1957c)

verdict. Nor would inscribing 'In God We Trust' upon a legal letterhead be worship of much reality" (Stringfellow, 1955b:21).[53]

The life of worship is one of appropriation of vocation (Stringfellow, 1955b:21), and our work becomes sacramentalized in worship so that work itself becomes worship. This evangelical theology of the sacramental Christian life resists the message of Christian autonomy which was the mainstay of evangelical revival.

> Being a Christian, belonging to Christ's people, really precludes the possibility of autonomous decision in any circumstance. Perhaps Christians nowadays have little sense of their peoplehood, little sense of being the Church; but in any case, notions of individual, autonomous decision by Christians are incomprehensible in Christian faith. Where mere autonomous decision is called for from Christians . . . the erroneous attempt is made to centre Christian faith upon God and the individual rather than upon God and His whole people, into which each individual is called. (Stringfellow, 1955b:18)

The life of the gathered church sustains us in this life, as well as providing understanding and knowledge. Vocation is derived by both its proximity to the gathered church (Christ's body), and the representation and inhabitation of that body within the particular context in the world in which one finds oneself. Consequently, the meaning this life takes on is witness (Stringfellow, 1955b:22). Vocational understanding and decision therefore is something which takes place within the context of Christ's church, in the world.

By encompassing the life of work within the activity and identity of the life of the church, Stringfellow provides a means of understanding the church engaged with, rather than removed from, our sociopolitical and cultural setting; he internalizes the discourse on work within the discourse on faith theologically, while establishing the fundamental place of the church in the world of work, rather than removing all in that world from their work in order to fulfill their vocation, as was otherwise so commonly the practice (e.g., the only work truly faithful to vocation was to give up work in the world and take up full time work in the church). In short, he redescribes reality from a biblical faith perspective, and does so in a literal and concrete manner. This sacramentalization of daily life

---

53. Mention of *In God We Trust* is clearly a passing critical reference to the introduction of this banner upon the U.S. currency at this time.

and the rethinking of mission have been at the center of his attentions in this paper.

In light of this later discussion, we can perhaps better understand why Stringfellow's paper seeks to reconceptualize the problem of vocation from the ground up. The place of ethics is secondary in Stringfellow's theology, a consequence of our response-in-love. His later writing on ethics needs to be understood in light of this. There are no Christian ethics which can be formulated as norms for the whole community of believers—they are truly dynamic and existential, not static or legalistic. Worship, not ethics, is therefore the means of unity. Ethics, presumably, is the expression of diversity.

Conclusion

To summarize, in this faculty paper Stringfellow brings the debates on law and vocation to bear upon each other from a theological perspective. From a legal perspective, his treatment of the issue of the law is brief. Yet from a theological perspective the issues of law (and grace) were the subjects throughout. His work met with a mixed reception.[54]

Through this paper and subsequent work, he had a growing realization that being at odds with the organized church meant being at odds with America itself (McThenia, 1995b:69); the church had become theologically and epistemologically subservient to the secular culture of threat and prosperity in which it was immersed. One of the central and guiding motif's of Stringfellow lifework is clear in this paper: the *church* is the society and social order that Christians should uphold, not the world.

He was not negative about the law as such, but about incorrect attempts to place the law above Christianity, or to "legalize" the law—

54. Perhaps the clearest example of the positive reception is the correspondence and relationship the paper initiated between Stringfellow and Wilbur Katz, Head of Law at Chicago Law School. Katz writes to Stringfellow, being impressed by his faculty paper, and wanting to know more about the Committee on Christian faith and the Legal Profession (Katz, 1955), and Stringfellow replies (Stringfellow, 1955a). Criticism, for example, came from Dr. Hanft (Hanft, 1956). Hanft, a professor of law who was particularly concerned with the relationship of faith and law, argued that Christians motivated by love act in the world to make it a more tolerable place, and that was their work. Stringfellow's responds by saying that "this is just the social gospel, and I invoke all the neo-orthodox arguments against it ... on its merits as social gospel theology it is heretical because it is a doctrine of justification by works ... it speaks in terms of sociology and psychology rather than theology" (Stringfellow, 1956b:2–3).

attempts in other words to externalize into jurisprudence the internal discourse of faith, rather than to understand jurisprudence in the light of the internal discourse of faith (whose language is theological).[55] The law was the first principality Stringfellow engaged, before he could name it as such. As we can see, the fall occupies center stage of his writing and thinking even at this stage, as a consequence perhaps of it being the "moral reality" which the law engages. However, it would not be until he left law school and moved to East Harlem to engage the issue empirically that he would understand with greater clarity the moral and spiritual reality he had here identified in a more academic context.

With this in mind it is time to examine the second of his engagements with law and theology: the practice of law in East Harlem.

LAW AND CHURCH IN PRACTICE: SOJOURN TO THE MARGINS

In a decade preoccupied with wealth creation, the creation of personal and national security, and urbanization, it is perhaps surprising to see that upon leaving law school Stringfellow went out of his way to turn his back on these values. And so on Labor Day, 1956, at the age of twenty-eight, Stringfellow relocated from the delights of Massachusetts where he had grown up and was schooled in law, to the poverty of New York City. It was to be this encounter with poverty, and the poor, that taught him concretely, empirically, about the relationship of faith and law and the reality of the biblical world which he had thus far glimpsed. It was a reality that was to take him far beyond the imagination of his faculty paper. So, it was to East Harlem he went, taking with him the now practical issues of law and vocation. Little could have prepared him for what he was to find; it was literally and figuratively a different world.

55. See for example Stringfellow (1956d), in which he speaks quite positively about the role that law can play to "correct our culture's exaltation of economic over other value" and to "hold together peoples of different national, racial and ideological loyalties." Given Christianity's demand for justice, he also stresses the need for the church to once again teach civil disobedience to laws which infringe Christian faith, and to reform oppressive laws. The law, however, remains for Stringfellow subordinate to Christian faith, acutely aware that the secular morality of Western law is derived from Christianity, and without Christianity it remains partial and ineffectual. Once again, then, we see the beginnings of his theological outlook. This early perspective upon what he would later understand as the principalities and powers, and the church's response of resistance, is one which was to undergo some further revision.

Stringfellow's encounter with this world is the subject of our examination in this section.

Entering A Marginalized World

On entering Harlem, Stringfellow was an alien in a strange land. For Stringfellow, East Harlem provided a context in which the gospel came to life, and that theological reality which he had glimpsed, he now focused upon with clarity.[56]

Located just to the northeast of New York's Central Park, East Harlem is a place of squalor, depression, overcrowding, unemployment, neglect—a place of poverty. A place, at least in the late 1950s, surrounded on all sides by the splendor, luxury, and wealth of the city; a place abandoned, as people either ignored it, fled to the suburbs, or were relocated through the development of housing projects which, as we have heard, ultimately left them displaced. It was a place of contrast.

> Outside are air purifiers, private toilets, hi-fi, gourmet food, imported cars, and the extra dry martini; inside Harlem are the smells of sweat and waste, bathtubs in the kitchens, antiquated direct current, predatory vermin, second-hand clothes, and a million empty beer cans in the gutters. Outside the ghetto are secure jobs, some chance for education, and even space to play; inside there is chronic unemployment, much illiteracy, and the numbers game. (Stringfellow, 1964d:4)[57]

East Harlem was home to about 200,000 people.[58] The tiny apartment where he lived (25' x 12') previously housed eight people, and it continued to be a home for a multitude of cockroaches and rodents.[59] In fact,

---

56. While himself from a working-class background, Stringfellow was by this time a well-educated white Anglo-Saxon Protestant lawyer—a sharp contrast to the poverty of Harlem's native, mostly African-American, inhabitants.

57. The language Stringfellow uses is reflective of his theology in the early 1960s, when this book was written, rather than his theology while in Harlem, and this will need to be borne in mind. What is also significant is the title of the book, *My People is the Enemy*, which seems to echo Myrdal's perception of the racial crisis as a white problem, and Cory's adoption of that thesis.

58. In order to get some idea of this level of overcrowding, it was estimated that if the entire population of the United States (then 190 million people) lived in the same proximity to each other as they do in East Harlem, the entire population would fit within the five boroughs of New York City (Stringfellow, 1964d:7).

59. It was so small that the bath was in the kitchen, raised at sink-level.

overcrowding was so great in Harlem that people spent their lives on the street; the street was the place he would practice law. Predictably, education, health care, and representation before the law went predominantly unknown in Harlem. It was a place forgotten by the rest of New York, unless and until a scapegoat was needed.

Stringfellow, a man at odds with himself, the church, and the world, had arrived. This was to be his reality, more or less. For of course, while living here he continued his work with the SCM arranging law conferences and seminars, speaking at law schools and theological seminaries, and meeting and socializing with professors, bishops, politicians. Yet far from distancing him from Harlem, this routine seemed to ground him all the more; it was of Harlem and his life there which he spoke to these others most often.

Stringfellow's account is, by his own description, a witness, testifying to what he saw and experienced while in East Harlem. Giving its residents a voice, through advocacy and representation in life and law, was Stringfellow's ambition. To outsiders it was hell on earth, to residents it was reality, but to Stringfellow it was a sacrament of the Kingdom. He was home (Stringfellow, 1964d:2).[60]

BEING A CHURCH IN HARLEM? THE EAST HARLEM PROTESTANT PARISH

Harlem had a significance to many people. Stringfellow was not alone in recognizing the need for Christians not to abandon Harlem amidst the prosperity of the age, nor to recognize the extent to which that prosperity was the root of what Harlem was. The East Harlem Protestant Parish (EHPP) also recognized its significance and was a highly regarded pioneer of urban ministry, founded in 1948.[61]

60. In fact East Harlem was brought further to life for America through a CBS film of Stringfellow's life and work there, which Stringfellow wrote and narrated (Stringfellow, 1965d, 1968b).

61. It was founded by Don Benedict, George Webber, and Archie Hargraves. A full account of the EHPP can be found in Kenrick (1963). Kenrick's book came out before Stringfellow's own, and his correspondence with Stringfellow can be found in the archive (Kenrick, 1960a; Stringfellow, 1960f; Kenrick, 1960b). Of course, there were many that did ignore Harlem and other places of poverty, especially the more conservative evangelical revival which had taken hold throughout the United States at this time. Christian concern traditionally came from the more theologically liberal wing of the church, and this was generally true of the concern expressed in Harlem. This, essentially, is one of the key features of Stringfellow's conflict with the EHPP.

According to one of its members, while the rest of the church in America was essentially dead, EHPP was the "New Jerusalem" of American Protestantism: a flag-ship for the future church.[62] Its work consisted of a number of store-front congregations, considerable practical help, and something called the Group Ministry (GM). An early document in the life of the parish described it as "a group ministry of twelve men and women working at the neighborhood level to help people face and work on their problems" (Stringfellow, 1964d:86).

Members of the group ministry necessitated commitment to four disciplines: political (they debated and attained shared positions on issues), economic (they paid according to need, and they paid speaking fees received into a common fund), vocational (there was joint decision making over each members work, plans and problems), and devotional (there were communion and retreats). Furthermore, membership to the Group Ministry normally necessitated membership of one of the store-front churches in East Harlem. The work of EHPP was essentially political and social with evangelistic consequences; it engaged the social context of East Harlem, and the social problems and issues facing its residents (e.g., housing, drugs, arrest, employment, health), by, for example, helping residents to obtain housing benefits.

Stringfellow joined the EHPP upon the invitation of George Todd,[63] a friend whom he had initially met in 1949 at the World Student's Christian Federation Central Committee in Ontario, and with whom he had kept up correspondence (Stringfellow 1964d:35, Stringfellow 1956b:2). The EHPP were looking to get a lawyer amongst their ministry in Harlem in order to provide legal representation and utilize it in support of the various social problems facing East Harlem residents. Todd knew Stringfellow and his theology and urged him to consider joining to undertake this new role.[64]

62. Quoted by Stringfellow (1964d:89).

63. Todd visited Stringfellow in Cambridge, and there said: "You should come to the Parish, join the group ministry, and work as a layman and as a lawyer" (Stringfellow, 1956b:2).

64. Although in *My People is the Enemy* (Stringfellow, 1964d), he suggests a set of events that introduce the EHPP to him for the first time, the presence in the archives of a thesis by Hostetler (1950) from Princeton examining aspects of the EHPP may serve to indicate that his knowledge of the East Harlem Protestant Parish extends back much further than previously thought; this may or may not be significant in relation to his motives and his decision to join, whether Stringfellow obtained it retrospectively is not known.

At the time, Stringfellow appears to have been considering a number of other attractive options, which included joining large law firms in either Northampton or Boston, which he felt would not provide sufficient client-contact, and an invitation from the Church Society for College Work in a ministry developing Christian vocation for lawyers, for which he felt he lacked sufficient experience of legal practice. Stringfellow was already involved in the newly emergent Civil Rights Movement, and he was acutely aware in his deliberations of the issues of race and poverty in relation to faith and the legal profession.

Therefore, according to Stringfellow, there were two main reasons for his move to Harlem. Firstly, to test the health and maturity of the legal system (Stringfellow, 1962j:3),[65] and secondly, to take seriously the demand for Christians to be found at work and witness in the world among those for whom no one cares (Stringfellow, 1964d:38). However, the archives reveal a third reason for his move to Harlem, and that was politics—specifically, elective politics. Election to political office was high ambition to Stringfellow,[66] and while he had learnt much about vocation, at the time of going to Harlem his own political ambition for office remained. Weighing things up, Stringfellow recognized that his chances of obtaining political office in Massachusetts as a Democrat for statewide office were at best very slim: "I am a Protestant, have a Yankee name, too much education, and am not Irish" (Stringfellow, 1956b:1), and in Massachusetts Irish Roman Catholics dominated the political scene. Taking up George Todd's invitation afforded him an opportunity for statewide elective politics,[67] and there was no doubt that Stringfellow's own political ambition drew him to this opportunity; a centripetal force was at work, with Harlem at its center.

This decision also marks an attempt to connect these parts of his life empirically. Stringfellow expressed a desire and preference for consolidation and engagement and recognized the unrivalled freedom that this opportunity afforded him—a freedom which was to become

---

65. A kind of "contextual experiment." See also Stringfellow (1964d:37–38).

66. While he acknowledges being "concerned about the politics in such a community" (Stringfellow, 1964d:65), he does not mention his desire for political office, nor in fact does this mention of politics in this quotation allude to it—this refers instead to the political nature of everyday life.

67. According to Stringfellow, George Todd indicated that "elective politics would not be at all precluded from this picture; quite the contrary" (Stringfellow, 1956b:2).

increasingly significant, and a source of contention between him and the EHPP.

> What appeals to me about this is that it involves a joinder of law and theology in the place where I would be working; whereas, were I to enter an orthodox law firm, the locus of whatever theological study and discussion I continued would be in another place. This has been the recent situation, and I do not like it. One foot has been in the law school, another in work at Tufts, another (figuratively) in the seminary community and among friends hereabouts who are Christians and who share some of the theological concerns that I do have. Most of my life is spent commuting between these segments, and so it appeals to me that East Harlem would bring them together in a single situation in which I lived and worked. (Stringfellow, 1956b:2)

From the beginning of his time there, Stringfellow's desire to "be himself" placed him to some degree at odds with the group ministry. For example, unlike the other members he did not join a storefront church but instead attended an Episcopalian church located just outside the EHPP. By many on the GM this was seen as dissent, resented, and over time became the cause for considerable friction. Todd believed he had recruited a valuable member to EHPP who could provide services they needed; Stringfellow found himself increasingly at odds with this, as his commitment to Harlem and disquiet with the EHPP grew.

BEING HIMSELF IN HARLEM: ARRIVAL

The reality of loneliness was ever present upon the horizons of Stringfellow's lifework, and his search for self-acceptance prominent. Upon entering Harlem he was actively in search of self-acceptance and self-understanding. This can be seen, for example, in his reflections upon the power of grace, which he understood to mean "the real knowledge of self, the freedom of self-acceptance and the freedom to accept others" (Stringfellow, 1957b:1). What is most interesting, however, is the way in which Stringfellow identifies that grace, or self-understanding and self-acceptance, is a matter of *community* not *autonomy*; it is a matter of the church—the community of grace, the community of freedom and forgiveness, in history—"in relation to which the vocation of any Christian has integrity and responsibility and is sustained and empowered" (Stringfellow, 1957b:1). Self-acceptance takes place within Christ's reconciliatory unity embodied in communion, not in isolation. Hence his thinking that even when in the world, the Christian is not alone, but a part of the church.

Accordingly, for whatever other reasons Stringfellow came to Harlem, he came to be himself: he came seeking acceptance; he came seeking self-understanding. He found it amidst the marginalized and dispossessed, he found it amidst poverty. It was a vocational journey; a sojourn of discipleship. It was a journey that was intense—at once intensely personal, and intensely political; for this reason, its wide-ranging effects upon his life and theology were to make Harlem forever personally significant to Stringfellow. After the death of his partner Anthony Towne, he described it as "his beloved old neighborhood," "the place in the city where I had first felt accepted and at home" (Stringfellow, 1982b:141).

Against a background of crisis, the late 1950s were days dominated by existentialism, and with his concern towards incarnational theology and vocation Stringfellow had become attracted to this school of thought, especially the work of Kierkegaard and Berdyaev. A number of characteristics of the existentialism seem to have had an impact upon Stringfellow's lifework, including its emphasis upon avoiding systematization and rational categories, the freedom of rejoicing in the spirit (whether human or divine), being authentic, and the emphasis upon experience over observation.

Accordingly, there should be little wonder at his apparent preoccupation at this time with "being himself"; it was a concern arising out of his commitment to live authentically and his desire to be accepted. This desire for authenticity and acceptance appears to be augmented by a feeling of "ugliness" (of non-acceptance) which he struggled with for many years; a struggle which is not readily apparent in his published work, and is at least in part associated with his sexuality. Theologically, this feeling might also be viewed in terms of fallenness.[68] However, we can see evidence of this lurking feeling of ugliness, and his desire for acceptance and "being himself," in the archives. For example, an undated

---

68. It is, moreover, a more universal existential situation in which we all find ourselves before God: ugly but accepted. Our attempts at beauty are therefore nothing other than worldly (fallen) attempts to justify ourselves before each other and before God. Stringfellow's personal experience put him onto the empirical and theological reality of this.

handwritten note shows his own personal dealings with the themes of ugliness and acceptance in theological terms through his understanding of the vocation of the church, and thus the transforming (shattering) work of grace. As we shall come to see later in this section, the role of the church in being oneself (being authentic) he considered both crucial and central—a view which was to produce both conflict and creativity.

Harlem was the empirical catalyst through which his theological understanding of ugliness and acceptance began to take concrete expression. Acceptance was for him a matter of grace, and the community of the church (as the gift of Christ) was a sacrament of that graceful action, free of the limitations and restrictions of the world.

> This community shatters all barriers—not in the sense that *everything* is disclosed or shattered at once—but in the sense that in this community there is nothing which cannot be disclosed— there is no barrier to disclosure—nothing is too mean or nasty or ugly or true or distorted. (Stringfellow, undated)

Stringfellow's desire for acceptance is a significant theme in the formation of his lifework and was a need constituted by his humanity, but also the specific existential circumstances of his sexuality.[69]

Any attempt at "being himself" would inevitably involve his consideration of his sexual being. Stringfellow's homosexuality was at this time a closely guarded, personal secret, as it remained throughout his life.[70] While Stringfellow was clearly aware of his sexuality by this time,

69. The need for acceptance in relation to sexuality is suggested in an address he gave many years later on the subject of Christians who are homosexuals, just as they were emerging into the public arena. Stringfellow himself never quite came out. "I commend you to consider sexuality in the context of conversion—in the context of the event in which one becomes a new person in Christ ... not ... the denial or suppression or repression of anything that we are as persons. It involves instead the renewal of our persons in the integrity of our own creation in the Word of God ... to welcome and affirm our sexuality as a gift ... Love yourself, in that way you will be enabled to love others and honor the Word of God that loves you" (Stringfellow, 1979a).

70. This was no doubt due to the culture of secrecy which surrounded homosexuality. Despite this, Stringfellow did address homosexuality publicly through his written work and lectures and talks. In these, he ranges from being highly critical of the way in which homosexuality is perceived and judged in America (Stringfellow, 1976c:51–52), to more positive support for homosexuals (Stringfellow, 1979a).

Instead of Death (Stringfellow, 1976c) was initially published in 1963, with some parts having been previously published in 1959 (Stringfellow, 1963g). Here and elsewhere we cite from the second edition. The only significant difference between the two editions is the inclusion of a preface in the later edition.

archival evidence seems to suggest that his relationships were quite few (Andy, 1947; Denham, 1962),[71] and in his view "sexual appetite is biologically given and morally neutral. Motivation is key in sex behavior" (Stringfellow, 1953a). This thought was later developed in *Instead of Death*.

> In sex, whatever the species or practice, the issue is not pleasure or lust, but personal identity. Sex is by no means the only way in which the quest for personal identity is pursued ... [But] the search for self is the most characteristic aspect of sex. The discovery of self, or, more precisely, the recovery of self—the gift of personal identity—is, at the same time, the very theme of the gospel. Christ is, pre-eminently, the one who knows what it is to be a human being ... It is impossible to consider sex seriously in terms of the search for self without eventually confronting the promise of the gospel that the secret of personal identity for *every* person is found in Christ. (Stringfellow, 1976c:37–38)

For Stringfellow, sexuality and authentic personal identity (authentic vocation) are intrinsically and christologically connected and revealed in the gospel. The sojourn to Harlem was about discovering the reality proclaimed in the gospel—personally, publicly, and most importantly empirically. This was the meaning of his "vocational sojourn."[72]

So, in his sojourn to Harlem, Stringfellow's acceptance-seeking gaze becomes (in part) more introspective, partly shifting attention from the world of America to questions of his own identity. In a concrete way, he begins to learn the reality of reconciliation and acceptance of himself (humanity) by God. It is an acceptance which stood in opposition to the world of America going on around him.

The poor are the marginalized and poverty is their suffering; their role in Stringfellow's lifework a catalyst. And so it is to poverty he owed his most fundamental insight: that in Harlem, *his work was to live his life as authentically as he was able.*

Stringfellow tells a simple story which illustrates this point. Generally, for the first two or three months after his arrival Stringfellow

71. According to Bill Wylie-Kellermann, the Mount Morris Baths, located on upper Madison, were nearby to Harlem and were an interracial cruising spot at that time. Stringfellow frequented baths which may well have been these.

72. It is quite likely that his move to Harlem as an advocate for the marginalized may have arisen from sublimation of his homosexuality and from a shared inner knowledge of his similarity with those for whom he was an advocate.

had not spoken to anyone, nor they to him; but he had been watched very carefully. Then, late one November night, Stringfellow was out walking when he noticed two figures down the block, and they noticed him. It was Archie.

> Archie was a pusher . . . He is part Negro, part Puerto Rican. He is married to a woman with whom he seldom stays. Archie is always hustling one thing or another. "I want you to meet Bill," he said to the girl friend. She was a young Negro woman, dressed somewhat shabbily. "He's my friend" Archie continued, "Take care of him whenever he wants it." I shook Archie's hand and went home. I knew I had been accepted . . . thereafter I felt welcome on the street. People sought legal counsel of me there. The street was as much of an office as I ever had in Harlem. (Stringfellow, 1965d:14)

An offering of welcome had been extended to Stringfellow, and he realized that while it may seem culturally and ethically foreign, Archie's offering was one of friendship and embrace, despite their obvious differences. In a world of absolute poverty, gifts and tokens of friendship take on a new yet equally symbolic form. Archie's was a sign of acceptance, a sacrament of grace. To be accepted, just as he was, was an event of vocational freedom.[73]

As we saw in his paper on worship, for Stringfellow the question of vocation is not determined by work, but by grace; the work of the Christian life is *solely a consequence* of faithful obedience to the Risen Lord (our response to grace). This is the life of worship and mission, in which we can "go anywhere and do any sort of work" (Stringfellow, 1964d:25) in absolute freedom, unrestrained and unencumbered by conformity to the world, and guided by conformity to grace.[74] In Harlem, this was brought practically to bear upon his lifework, and he was free to be himself, and therefore free to honor the gift of his vocation, experience acceptance in his own life, and think through the theological significance of this for him and all Christians. In Harlem he *experienced*

73. Stringfellow attributes the origins of his knowledge of vocational freedom to his time in the army, where he learnt that he could be fulfilled as a person no matter where he was nor what he did (Stringfellow, 1964d:25).

74. It was this same self-knowledge which was to lead to his falling out with the EHPP, for as his self-knowledge grew, so, as we shall see, he grew at odds with EHPP. As we shall see this self-knowledge was essentially obedience-in-faith, or put in terms of the theme of the introduction to this book, orientational knowledge of the Risen Lord.

the response of life to the power of death. It was a very personal yet very political experience, as he was later able to appreciate; East Harlem was the place in which he became "sufficiently enlightened about institutionalized death so that death was no longer an abstraction confined to the usual funeral connotations. I began then and there to comprehend death theologically as a militant, moral reality. The grandiose terms in which the Bible describes the power of death had begun to have a concrete significance for me" (Stringfellow, 1976c:5).

In summary, moving to East Harlem was in the deepest sense a vocational journey for Stringfellow, for it was a journey governed by his desire to "be himself" and to be accepted for it; it was a personal and a political journey. His discovery of the power of death, and ultimately the principalities and powers, which marked a significant moment of intensification in the development of his lifework, was *not* a theoretical or academic discovery; it was a practical, empirical, and existential one that arose out of the coincidence of the Bible and his context. While he conceived of the power of death predominantly in public and political terms, at work in him personally was the transforming work of grace. Theoretical understandings and influences followed this experience and helped him to understand the reality he was experiencing.[75] Stringfellow realized with some immediacy the concrete reality of the world which the Bible narrates; he saw the "spiritual reality" of the world and the struggle between the power of life and the power of death which is its work, embodied in people, institutions, images, ideologies, etc. Simply, in Stringfellow's lifework, Harlem functions apocalyptically: it makes reality known. This revelation literally transformed Stringfellow's faith and his way of seeing reality. As such, it needs to be understood as a fundamentally significant moment in his theological biography.

THE CHURCH BEING ITSELF: RESIGNATION AND REDRESS

Stringfellow's unfolding vocation was the force which shaped his lifework in East Harlem. Empirically, we can see this most noticeably in his controversial resignation from the GM of the East Harlem Protestant Parish. His resignation was a theological matter.

---

75. Markus Barth and Jacques Ellul were especially influential here. Stringfellow also undertook another study period in 1959 at the Episcopal Theological Seminary summer school: an opportunity for retreat and reflection.

It was the church which initially attracted Stringfellow to Harlem, and the EHPP embodied a hopeful possibility of its concrete manifestation. Yet Stringfellow resigned from the Group Ministry just fifteen months after joining, on April 30, 1958, and he did so in the most public fashion.[76] It was not, however, resignation from ministry in Harlem, but separation from the EHPP; it was an issue of authenticity—he believed he had to resign from EHPP to be more committed to Harlem. His resignation was over the matter of grace, although Stringfellow's somewhat antagonistic manner may have done much to disguise this fact. In this section, as well as identifying some of the salient facts surrounding his resignation, we will explore the implications and insights this action, and accounts of it, reveal to us about his lifework at this time.

Characteristically, Stringfellow's resignation letter runs to seven pages and takes a form somewhere between polemic and critique. It largely represented the substance of his discussions and criticisms that had taken place between him and the GM over the fifteen months he had been a member. Its direct and critical manner meant that it was not especially well received, and his duplication and public circulation to many of his friends and colleagues around the country[77] did little to diffuse the situation. He was aware that others in the ministry perceived him as outspoken and impertinent, and on the surface this letter seemed to confirm this perception: his was an uncompromising voice (Stringfellow, 1958h:1–2). The incredible influence that EHPP had, and the high regard with which it was viewed, meant that in resigning it was equally important to Stringfellow that the EHPP's failings enter into the public arena, and this he ultimately ensured when he published the letter and expanded upon it in *My People is the Enemy*. At the time of the resignation and after, the letter upset many people in the EHPP in general, and the GM in particular.

The letter is a theological polemic, which is perhaps most appropriate given the way in which his resignation was, strictly speaking, over theology. This theological expression itself was a point of dissent from most others in the GM and placed him once again on the margins; due to the ecumenical and non-denominational nature of the GM, its

76. Along with the other citations, I wish to acknowledge the unpublished written reflections of Bill Wylie-Kellermann upon Stringfellow's resignation, from which I have benefitted (Wylie-Kellermann, undated).

77. The letter is also reproduced, with modifications, in Stringfellow (1964d).

members had agreed to refrain from theological debate and discussion. Stringfellow would not hear of such a thing. We can see this polemic most evident in its conclusion:

> I resign for your sake, both for the sake of those within the group ministry whom I can confirm and for the sake of those within it whom I cannot do so. I resign to enhance my availability to East Harlem and to the Christians of East Harlem. I resign to be more disposable for the Church in East Harlem. That is, I resign to point to the disunity in the group ministry, which is a disunity also manifest among the parish congregations, and thereby to attest a unity given in Jesus Christ which transcends even the group ministry . . . I resign, thus, not in malice, but in zeal . . . not harshly, but hopefully; not with guile, but with realism; not to make gossip, but to be persuasive; not to be stilled, but to be heard more . . . not in self-reliance, but in reliance upon the presence and power of God; not to conserve myself, but to be more fully expended. (Stringfellow, 1958h:7)

Stringfellow resigned because he felt his "loyalty to Christ" conflicted "with participation in the group ministry as it is conceived and constituted" and functions on a day-to-day basis (Stringfellow, 1958h:1). Essentially, his critique amounts to the fact that the GM and the EHPP were a fallen principality and would not recognize this fact and respond in faithfulness and obedience.[78]

Four main points are raised by the resignation. The first point is *politics*. Stringfellow felt his activities in East Harlem were constrained by the GM through the apportionment of "abstract limits" to his freedom "as a Christian in involvement in the world" (Stringfellow, 1958h:3). He wanted to be free to be engaged wholeheartedly in the politics of East Harlem, and the internal politics, or "attrition of membership in the group ministry greatly inhibit[ed] this" (Stringfellow, 1958h:3). He thought the GM met too often, and required constant attention upon relationships with its individual members. His concern was to "be free to engage in neighborhood politics rather than continue to be engaged in group ministry politics" (Stringfellow, 1958h:3).

The second point of departure concerns the "contrived arrangement" of the GM's *economic discipline*. Stringfellow found himself in-

---

78. Stringfellow himself did not describe them in terms of fallen principalities, for he had not yet made that connection. In essence, his resignation did much to prompt that discovery.

creasingly uneasy with the way in which the work he did as a lawyer was not at all related to whether or not he ate (Stringfellow, 1958h:3). This might sound an odd complaint, for clearly there was a communitarian ethic of equality at work in the GM's mind, not dissimilar to monastic communities. So what was the problem? In short: context and engagement. Stringfellow felt that the GM had lost sight of the demands of both: "In a community so much afflicted by poverty, I think that to continue in this arrangement amounts to my abstention from the world—amounts to a reluctance to share the most primitive risks of life in the world. So I resign for that, so that my work is related to my livelihood, as it is for most human beings" (Stringfellow, 1958h:3). This decision seemed to coincide with his passing the Bar exam, so *enabling* him to work for a living—in other words, he no longer needed their money.

The next point concerns the place of the *Bible* in the GM's work, and the way in which some of the GM are "appallingly diffident toward the Bible. Where there should be expectancy and vigilance, there is slothfulness and slumber. Those who are most selfserious in, say, the analysis of culture, are more often the dilettantes in Bible study" (Stringfellow, 1958h:3). It is, he felt, this lack of attention to the Bible, or moreover, the lack of authority of the Bible over the life of the GM, which accounted for its disunity. He felt the GM were far too preoccupied with social outreach based upon worldly knowledge rather than (existential) knowledge of the Word. Now we must remember that Stringfellow's comments are delivered here amidst the emergence of Protestant Revivalism, and his criticisms on the face of it are not dissimilar to many which proponents of the Revival had of liberal Protestantism. While this may well have colored the EHPP's reception of his comments, Stringfellow was not part of this revivalism nor its fundamentalism and was in fact equally critical of them, and particularly their emphasis upon individualism and their abuse of the Bible.

This brings us to our final and connected point, which is one of *theology*. "I count," wrote Stringfellow "the diffidence apparent in Bible study as the reason for the misapprehension among some in the group ministry about theology" (Stringfellow, 1958h:4). Speaking out against the view of theology as the theory of Christian faith, which is brought into action by the Christian in the world (theory-practice model), he articulates a different model:

> Theology is not out of this world; it is rather the knowledge of
> God given to men in this world, it is the integration of faith and
> existence in history, it is the appropriation of the whole experience
> of men to faith; it is confession, not speculation; it is existential,
> not ethereal; it is personal, not propositional, at the same time it is
> corporate—the knowledge of the whole church, not private—cut
> off from the Church's knowledge; it is, in short, Scriptural, not
> non-Scriptural. There is no such thing as being a Christian with-
> out having theology. Christians will vary in their articulation, but
> there is no Christian faith where there is no knowledge of God.
> (Stringfellow, 1958h:4)

Naturally, he goes on to distinguish confessional theology of all Christians from theology as a "discipline of scholarship in the church"
(Stringfellow, 1958h:4), but views this second-order reflection as intrinsic but essentially of secondary importance; while Christians can
be a congregation without second-order theology, they cannot come
to life as a congregation without a confession of faith.[79] Thus, primary
importance is given to what we might refer to as performative personal
practical theology of the whole people of God, for forming, sustaining and nurturing the congregation: it is a corporate and confessional
act. This, then, is Stringfellow's understanding of theology in general,
and his own theology in particular. In Stringfellow's case, the center of
theology was spirituality, i.e., the Christian life in the world lived in the
power of the graceful spirit.

Clearly, the four points identified here speak of a more substantial
underlying issue—namely, the nature of the church—for the same issue is at stake here as we saw in his faculty paper: grace and law, faith
and work, the Word and the world. It was in terms of the church that
Stringfellow comprehended his work in East Harlem, rather than in
terms of the district's problems in themselves: "My concern for an addict
is not simply informed by his addiction, but is far more informed by the
estrangement in East Harlem between Protestants and Roman Catholics
... This is ... the difference between the Church in the world and the
police department; it should be the difference between the Parish and
Union Settlement;[80] it is the difference between the work of faith and

79. The use of the term "congregation" here is Stringfellow's, and by it he means the
church of Christ, the authentic church, described in Stringfellow (1955b).

80. The reference here is to Union Theological Seminary, who sent many of their
ordination students to work in the Parish on placement. George Webber, one of the
EHPP's founders, worked at Union, eventually as Dean of Students.

good works" (Stringfellow, 1958h:6). There was little being done and said in the EHPP which could not have been said, for example, by a social worker, psychologist, or anthropologist; it lacked the distinctive voice of a church rooted in the radical reality of the Word in the world.

Furthermore, Stringfellow was concerned that the EHPP was dependent upon the culture of East Harlem or the rejection of "middle class culture" outside Harlem, for its unity, rather than Christ. If it were Christ, he maintains, unity would be located not in the GM but in the congregations themselves: decentralized. The ordering of the GM and the distribution of power therein are central characteristics of his concern for the nature of the church; he felt the description of the EHPP as "twelve men and women working at the neighborhood level to help people face and work on their own problems" not only betrayed an inappropriate imperialistic notion of mission, but furthermore made the presumption that the GM was a congregation (Stringfellow, 1958h:5). This, Stringfellow thought, was paradoxical, because he considered the way in which the EHPP actually operated to be

> the chief and constant threat to the emergence of living congregations among the people of the neighbourhood while at the same time the emergence of some congregations here is the most substantial threat to the group ministry. (Stringfellow, 1958h:5)

It seems the GM, in Stringfellow's view, understood itself to be operating as a congregation, relegating the store-front congregations to "good works" rather than congregations in any real sense, and so derived its unity from its allegiance to the principals and theories of ecumenism, non-denominationalism, and theological silence. It was a view which he felt promoted the "pompous superstitions" that the GM was the "new Jerusalem" betrayed; it was a "cultus unity" (Stringfellow, 1958h:6).

Essentially, this vainglory had come about by the EHPP's withdrawal from the wider church and their lack of dependence upon the "sufficiency of God's grace in all things" (Stringfellow, 1958h:6) and their "ignorance of the reality of the Church elsewhere" (Stringfellow, 1958h:2). It was not until the GM "understand and bear the burden of anxiety for all churches" (Stringfellow, 1958h:6) throughout history that the unity and freedom which Christ gives would begin to be seen. It was, simply, only when the EHPP realized it was part of, not apart from, the wider Church, and therefore not quite as unique as it may believe itself to be, that it could in any way be thought of as a congregation; the "manifestation in the world of God's accomplishment of reconciliation" (Stringfellow, 1958h:6). The sign of this freedom in the EHPP would be "when all of its members are willing even to give up the group ministry" (Stringfellow, 1958h:7). It was in such freedom that Stringfellow resigned. Ultimately, Stringfellow's biggest and unspoken criticism appears to have been of their failure to comprehend and dwell in the work of the Holy Spirit.

Stringfellow's own commitment to the wider church grew out of his Episcopalianism and a "sense of belonging to the Church, wherever I happen to be in the world" (Stringfellow, 1958h:2); it spoke of continuity and unity. He saw with clarity the importance of the church honoring its vocational calling in East Harlem, and it was his strongest desire that this might come about and was convinced of its importance in Harlem for the wider church:

> The emergence of the Church in East Harlem with integrity and a lively conscience about the unity of the whole Church, which is also the real concern for the world, could be by the grace of God a real instrument of reformation of the whole Church . . . I am all for changing the face of Harlem, but the mission of the Church depends not on social reformation in the neighbourhood, as desperately as that is needed, but upon the presence of the Word of God in the society of the poor as it is right now. (Stringfellow 1958h:6, Stringfellow 1964d:99)

Resignation was, according to Stringfellow, primarily a matter of grace and a means of obtaining freedom. He resigned the more to be committed to Harlem and its people, and it is through the practice of law that he worked out this vocational commitment:[81] "The decision [to resign]

81. This commitment is further consolidated by correspondence regarding a job offer with the WCC, which followed shortly after his resignation. See Stringfellow (1959f, g, h, 1958c, f, 1959j) for a discussion of the job, in which he reflects "it would mean leaving my present work, whatever it is, in a way just as it begins" (Stringfellow, 1958f). He also sought Markus Barth's counsel, who seemed to confirm Stringfellow's suspicions about the post. See also Stringfellow (1959i) in which Stringfellow withdraws his name from consideration for the job following a trip to WCC headquarters in Spittal, Austria. Part of the letter reads: "I withdraw because something else claims me, and I have understood that more lucidly coming to Spittal. What claims me is just my work in the world in law practice and in politics in East Harlem and my life in a congregation. That claims me—I am bold enough to confess it—because I see more sharply how irrelevant the church is in my own neighborhood and how afraid the church there is of

permitted both the group ministry and myself to persevere in the work which each felt called to do in East Harlem, in society at large, and in the ministry of the Church" (Stringfellow, 1964d:96).[82]

Lawyering provided Stringfellow with a way of engaging the world as witness to the Word; it was, in other words, work as worship and brought together both the personal and the political. It is upon this that we now focus our attentions.

MINISTRY AT WORK: THE LAW AND POVERTY

Poverty permeated every part of the lives of East Harlem's inhabitants. A place to sit, play, find privacy, or simply be alone in Harlem was a luxury craved. Not that the streets were safe: they were not; they were a violent place, in which shootings were a reasonably regular occurrence, and bookies, pimps, and drug dealers variously fought over their turf. As Stringfellow observed: "the street [was] a jungle" (Stringfellow, 1959d). Yet still the street provided some measure of escape, if not from poverty, at least from some of its insufferable accompaniments, and Stringfellow was quick to see this (Stringfellow, 1959d). In East Harlem, Stringfellow took to the streets, and there amidst poverty he practiced law.[83]

> Poverty was my very first client in East Harlem—a father whose child died from being bitten by a rat. Poverty is a dope pusher who wanted to learn from me his rights if arrested because he knew that would sooner or later happen. Poverty is a widow on welfare whose landlord cuts the heat knowing that winter will end before the complaint is processed. Poverty is an addict who pawns the jacket off his back to get another "fix." Poverty is a young couple who married only to obtain public housing but now have no grounds for divorce in New York and are tempted to collusion. Poverty is a boy who wants to be adopted because

---

the neighborhood. And that is just, of the complacency of the churches in the United States, one scene" (Stringfellow, 1959i).

82. Following his resignation, changes did begin to take place. There appears to be some debate about whether these changes were already begun at the time of Stringfellow's departure or whether his departure caused change to take place. Stringfellow notes the changes that took place since his departure (Stringfellow, 1964d:96), but Kenrick (1963:136–44) seems to locate Stringfellow not as a decisive catalyst, but rather as a voice amidst change already taking place. Stringfellow's correspondence with Kenrick over this book shed no further light on this (Kenrick,1960b,a; Stringfellow, 1960f). There is, I suspect, truth in both views.

83. His flat fee was one dollar.

his mother is alcoholic. Poverty is the payoff to a building inspector not to report violations of the building code. Poverty is the attempted eviction—finally defeated—from a project of a family whose son was thought to be "undesirable" by the project manager. Poverty is the wife of an addict with whom I worked out a budget to manage her while her husband was in prison. Poverty is a Puerto Rican shopkeeper whose store was stoned when he tried to relocate to 96th Street. Poverty is a kid in trouble who comes to my place in the middle of the night because his foster parents have thrown him out. Poverty is the relentless daily attrition of contending with the most primitive issues of human existence: food and cleanliness and clothes and heat and housing and rest. Poverty is an awful vulnerability. (Stringfellow, 1959d)[84]

Here in Harlem's jungle he practiced street law, with incarnational ministry in the form of advocacy being his *leitmotif*. Stringfellow knew the poor had no significant voice in the making or implementation of the law; they were usually just its victims. Indeed, he found that the only impact the law had upon the poor was a hostile and negative one, and that troubled Stringfellow, for he realized the failure of the law to uphold the rights of the poor within the American legal establishment jeopardized all of society.[85] Despite the overcrowding that surrounded him, life on the streets as a lawyer was a lonely and isolating experience. It left him exposed as much before the legal establishment as before the poor he represented.[86]

Yet his commitment to the poor and their suffering was as much a theological commitment as a legal one. His experiences there exposed him to the ubiquity of death's reality, and "first comprehended the veracity of the resurrection" (Stringfellow, 1970d:1346); this was a radical awakening.[87] In their poverty, the poor saw the presence of death vividly

84. This paper is also published in French in *Foi et Vie* (Stringfellow, 1960a). This was most likely arranged by Ellul.

85. See for example Stringfellow (1965g, 1961c).

86. Loneliness, he came to realize, was a characteristic of poverty. In due course, he reflected upon this experience. Understanding law as the state of sin, and echoing Rom 3:22–24, he wrote: "Loneliness is the most caustic, drastic and fundamental repudiation of God, the most elementary expression of original sin. There is no man who does not know loneliness. Yet there is no man who is alone" (Stringfellow, 1962f). See also Stringfellow (1976c), and Wink (1995:19).

87. His exposure to poverty was not limited to Harlem, however, but took in the gas chambers of Auschwitz, the slums of Glasgow, lepers begging in Bombay, and later was also to include Vietnam (Stringfellow, 1964b:66).

and actively at work in their lives, and at work everywhere in the world. Quite simply, they saw reality: as people on the margins of society, they saw the counterside to the gloss, acquisition, and appeal which passed for life. The marginalized of Harlem saw death. There is, in short, an apocalyptic character to such marginalization.

> What is special about the suffering of the poor is not innocence nor extremity, nor loneliness, nor the fact that it is unknown or ignored by others; but, rather, the lucidity and the straight-forwardness with which it bespeaks the power and presence of death among men in this world ... (Stringfellow, 1965d:11)

Thus in Harlem he saw for himself empirically how "death is a living power in this world, greater, apart from God himself, than any other reality in existence. Death is no mere abstraction or mere destination, but the pervasive power which apparently overrules everyone and everything else in the whole of creation ... A man's death begins at his birth, but before then death has been at work in this world ... In this world, men and all the principalities and all other things exist within the realm of death" (Stringfellow, 1964b:69,66). Amidst death, the secret of the Word was proclaimed. Stringfellow's ministry in law was to expose this secret and testify to it: it was the life of worship.

> There is a boy in the neighbourhood ... whom I have defended in some of his troubles with the law. He used to stop in often on Saturday mornings to shave and wash up, after having spent the week on the streets. He has been addicted for a long time. His father threw him out three years ago ... He has contrived so many stories to induce clergy and social workers to give him money to support his habit that he is no longer believed when he asks for help ... He is dirty, ignorant, arrogant, dishonest, unemploy-able, broken, unreliable, ugly, rejected, alone. And he knows it. He knows that at last he has nothing to commend himself to another human being. He has nothing to offer. There is nothing about him that permits the love of another person for him. He is unlovable. Yet it is exactly in his own confession that he does not deserve the love of another that he represents all the rest of us. For none of us is different from him in this regard. We are *all* unlovable. More than that, the action of this boy's life points beyond itself, it points to the gospel, to God who loves us though we hate Him, who loves us though we do not please Him, who loves us not for our sake but for His own sake, who loves us freely, who accepts us through we have nothing acceptable to offer Him. Hidden in

the obnoxious existence of this boy is the scandalous secret of the
Word of God. (Stringfellow, 1964d:97–98)[88]

Lawyering in East Harlem was murky, precarious, and risky. Stringfellow
represented the alienated, was the advocate for those who had no voice,
touched the untouchable, and called those who did not to account. What
marks his work out is his ability to *see* the poor and poverty through
the gracious eyes of the Word of God and be a witness to the reality of
the resurrection: there are no ethical imperatives, just a life lived in faith
(McThenia, 1995b:178). His life as a lawyer was characterized by the acts
of listening, compassion, and surrender; implicated him immediately
and existentially; and resulted in his marginalization. His life as a lawyer was the life of worship, and led to the most dramatic and empirical
discovery of his lifework to date: the principalities and powers. We shall
now examine how this came about.

His understanding of lawyering was vocationally formed and biblically determined, incarnational in character, and christological and soteriological in outlook. As an advocate and a lawyer, he believed his job
was nothing other than to intercede on another's behalf, and "to become
vulnerable (even unto death) in the place of another" (Stringfellow,
1982a:19). Indeed, for him the law was a pastoral gift rather than a
profession. For Stringfellow lawyering took on the costliness, character,
and intimacy of pastoral care, rather than the costliness, character, and
abstraction which characterized law in general. Stringfellow's lawyering was grace-full action, adopting the role of advocate and mediator.
As a lawyer, like so much else in his life, he didn't fit, for "he refused to
let modernity colonise his mind" (McThenia, 1995b:172). Stringfellow
undertook legal practice on his terms; it was a mixture of obstinacy and
obedience. Lawyering was his ministry.[89]

The origin of this ministry was the act of listening, an act he
considered

---

88. He also tells this story in Stringfellow (1961c:585–86).

89. Note his previously discussed realization that politics was ministry: Harlem is the
empirical verification of that decision. In correspondence, Bishop Appleton Lawrence,
the Bishop of Western Massachusetts, with whom Bill had long been associated, said: "I
reiterate that I think you were quite right in not going into the ministry, as such, but in
having a ministry which is really far more effective than that of nine out of ten clergy-
men" (Lawrence, 1963).

> a rare happening among human beings. You cannot listen to the
> word another is speaking if you are preoccupied with your ap-
> pearance or impressing the other, or if you are trying to decide
> what you are going to say when the other stops talking, or if you
> are debating about whether the word being spoken is true or rel-
> evant or agreeable. Such matters have their place, but only after
> listening to the word as the word is being uttered. Listening, in
> other words, is a primitive act of love, in which a person gives
> himself to another's word, making himself accessible and vulner-
> able to that word. (Stringfellow, 1967a:16)

Listening amidst the clamor of voices, each waiting and wanting to be
heard, was perhaps Stringfellow's most profound witness. This act of love
was at the heart of his lawyering, for he thought practicing law required
more than professional identification or sympathy, more than knowledge
of the human issues, needs, and complaints of deprivation. It required
something very different from the social project Stringfellow saw at work
in the EHPP and pervasive in the hopeful liberal social constructions
that were present in politics, the church, and the nation at that time and
since. Rather, it was necessary "to experience the vulnerability of daily
life here. It is necessary to live within the ambiguity and risk the attrition
of human existence. In a way, it is even more simple that that: it is just
essential to become and to be poor" (Stringfellow, 1959d). Lawyering in
Harlem was an act which implicated him in the lives of those to whom
he ministered. Therefore, amidst poverty the issue which Stringfellow
felt was crucial for the law and its authenticity was "whether it stands at
the intersection of life, aware of the self-interest of adverse contentions,
free to be the advocate of each. For that, the law and the lawyer must be
radically exposed to the existential situations of each party and person
. . . [and] law itself must be genuinely implicated in and wrought from
the realities of human existence" (Stringfellow, 1959d). This was a stark
contrast to the mechanics and technique which dominated the legal
academy at that time.

> Cases in East Harlem invariably require face to face encounter
> with a client. For that communication it is important to have
> known a client as a person before the case arose . . . to have ac-
> cepted him and to have been accepted by him, to have lived in the
> same place and similar circumstances as his own, and to expect
> a continued relationship after the case is closed. (Stringfellow,
> 1959d)

Thus, there is a priest-like quality to Stringfellow's ministry, in that his life is implicated in the lives of those to whom he ministers. For him, these were the uncompromising demands that vocational authenticity required. From his own experience of the Word and the world, he realized the need to move beyond theories *about* humanity, and the need to engage *in* humanity in the "here and now" of Harlem. In so doing he brings together in his own practice and the practice he advocates both law and vocation. Living authentically as a lawyer required him to live under grace and make himself vulnerable to that reality; the practice of the law was for him about engaging people as subjects, not objects, and necessitated acceptance of the client and by the client—embracing and welcoming the stranger or the outcast just because they are the outcast, for their own sake, and for the sake of the gospel. This is the essence of his legal practice.

Stringfellow's practice of the law is an incarnational witness in obedience to the Word and a loving commitment to those the rest of society had turned its back upon. His practice conveys deep personal commitment to the gospel. In his commitment to creatureliness, we see the incarnation; in his commitment to grace, we see the resurrection; and in his confrontation with the power of death, we see Christ's work on the cross.

Stringfellow's ministry was immersed in the subjective, but was focused upon the objectivity of God's self-revelation which that subjective encounter presented. Advocacy of this sort is existentially costly for the lawyer, rather than financially costly for the client. Stringfellow realized that the Christian life in the Spirit is this life of advocacy and calls us to be radically different. As a lawyer he turned his back upon the values of the legal establishment and turned instead to face his clients, and there *served* them as their advocate and himself became marginalized.

However, while *My People is the Enemy* does not indicate it, Stringfellow was no stranger to marginalization. Amongst his peers at Harvard he was a social and economic outsider (coming from a working-class background through hard work and scholarship); he treated the law with a healthy dose of criticism, rather than the reverence the establishment felt such a guarantor of truth deserved; while politically a democrat, he was more politically radical than the norm (something we see in his college paper); he made a decision in his youth not to get ordained, which meant turning his back on a profession in the priesthood (so snubbing the church); amidst a culture moving out to the suburbs and enjoying their growth and expansion, Stringfellow moved to the inner city; he was evangelical, but politically so; he was high church, but evangelically so; amidst a culture which legally and socially prohibited it, he was (a closeted) homosexual; and when it came to legal practice, Stringfellow shunned the power and personal financial gain afforded him through the law, so bemusing both his peers and his parents. We need to dwell a moment on this, for this was an act of self-marginalization.

Stringfellow marginalized himself through his ministry. He did this by insisting that the origin of law is grace, and the nature of vocation is worship. We saw this in his faculty paper: here we see it in practice.[90] Stringfellow engaged the law as a critic, not because he wished to dismiss it, but because he thought passionately that the law could only be most fully the law—most fully the advocate—when it recognized its anthropological limitations.[91] In his practice, Stringfellow is affirming the true

---

90. In his lawyering amongst the marginalized Stringfellow was acutely aware of the coincidence of poverty and race, and his concern in some ways foreshadowed the rise of the Civil Rights Movement and black consciousness: his concern dated back to his time at college. He provides the following account: "I myself was involved in what must have been one of the original sit-ins—back in 1943—when I was in college in Maine. Some of us had observed that Negros were not served at a certain hotel and that discrimination existed and was practiced in some other public accommodations . . . A bill was introduced into the legislature that condemned racial or ethnic discrimination, and that sought to establish a commission against discrimination. Several of us were working for the Bill's enactment. One day the legislator who had sponsored the measure . . . came to see us to report that the legislation had almost no chance to pass, since there was so little public interest in the issue. After long discussion, it was decided that three of us would go with a Negro to the hotel which barred Negros and ask to be served." Now the senator would be there with a newspaper man, and the expectation was that Stringfellow and his friends would be refused service and then the publicity which arose would help the passage of the ailing bill. "The senator and the newspaperman were halfway through their entrées. After we had been sitting at the table for several minutes, we noticed that the waiter had gone to speak to the manager . . . soon the waiter came to take our order. We had to order something of course. Ironically, we had already eaten at the college, so sure we were that the hotel would not serve us. Among the four of us we had only about five dollars, so the unfortunate senator ended up paying the check . . . That was the result achieved in this pioneer sit-in" (Stringfellow, 1964d:104). We shall look at Stringfellow's engagement with the issue of race in theological terms in much greater detail in the next part of this book, when we examine his lifework during the early 1960s.

91. Indeed, much later Stringfellow came to wonder if in fact the two were mutually exclusive: "I continue to be haunted by the ironic impression that I may have to renounce being a lawyer, the better to be an advocate" (Stringfellow, 1982a). Note here that his priority was for advocacy—a character he associated most strongly with the Christian life.

identity of the law as it exists under grace: the law defined theologically, rather than the law as secular theology.[92]

It is out of his life of advocacy, predicated upon his commitment to the Word and the world, that he gradually learned what those indigenous to Harlem knew already:

> namely, that the power and purpose of death are incarnated in institutions and structures, procedures and regimes—Consolidated Edison or the Department of Welfare, the Mafia or the police, the Housing Authority or the social work bureaucracy, the hospital system or the banks, liberal philanthropy or corporate real estate speculation. In the wisdom of the people of the East Harlem neighbourhood, such principalities are identified as demonic powers because of the relentless and ruthless dehumanisation which they cause. (Stringfellow, 1976c:5)[93]

While he had probably first come across the principalities and powers in Oslo,[94] the influence of Jacques Ellul and Markus Barth was also seminal. He met both through his work on faith and the legal profession (especially the conference he was arranging during 1957) and had since established friendships and correspondence.[95] Stringfellow discovered

92. He mapped this relationship between law and theology initially in Stringfellow (1956a,1956f).

93. Stringfellow leaves his definition of the principalities and powers for another book: *Free in Obedience* (Stringfellow, 1964b). Where *My People* is autobiographical, *Free in Obedience* seeks to reflect specifically upon the book of Hebrews in relation to what he saw as the juxtaposition of the church and the world. Where one explicitly and preferentially utilizes the Word in his life-experience (his biography), the other utilizes the Word in the Bible (biblical witness).

94. This is originally argued by Wylie-Kellermann (1999). According to Kellermann, Stringfellow was also influenced by Caird (1956).

95. Ellul in particular appears to have impressed Stringfellow, and they corresponded for many years. In correspondence to a friend at Yale Divinity School, Stringfellow expresses a desire to indefinitely keep hold of a paper by Ellul which had been lent to him, and in fact to try and obtain copies of everything he had ever written, something it appears he did not in the end do (Stringfellow, 1958b). Stringfellow wrote the jacket blurb to the American edition of Ellul's *The Meaning of the City* (Ellul, 1970), which appeared on the cover, along with the Foreword to the 1967 edition of Ellul's *The Presence of the Kingdom (Ellul, 1967)*, which in themselves highlight the harmony between the two theologians' thought and which commend Ellul to the American audience. On commending Ellul, see also Stringfellow (1970b). Markus Barth later described their relationship as "yoke fellows" in relation to their work on the principalities and powers, when he was seeking Stringfellow's advice about leaving Chicago and returning home to Basel (Barth, 1972).

the reality of the biblical understanding of the principalities and powers in the specific, particular encounter with the people of East Harlem. It was a discovery with huge significance for the future direction and shape of his theology.

These principalities or angelic powers are living realities, the creation of God, created for God's pleasure. In creation they are a gift of God to humanity, placed under our dominion, and are the "means through which men rejoice in the gift of life to all men and to the whole of creation ... All men, all angels, and all things in creation have origination, integrity, and wholeness of life in the worship of God" (Stringfellow, 1964b:52). But in the fall, the principalities and powers are captive to the power of death; in the fall, they literally work to and for death. Thus, as we encounter them, the fallen principalities challenge and reject the sovereignty of God, claiming "sovereignty over human life and history" (Stringfellow, 1964b:64) for themselves.

Stringfellow understood them in the following way. The principalities and powers are what we might also refer to, although not by any means exclusively, as ideologies, institutions and images, "ism's," corporations, and idols.

Ideologies include the various "ism's" to which we pledge our political, economic, or ethical allegiance: for example, capitalism, communism, democracy, racism, fascism, nationalism, rationalism, free markets, and globalization. None of these, least of all the nation which embodies them, is the benevolent entity it is so often perceived as, and amidst the era of threat and prosperity, Stringfellow therefore warned that "Americans are now constantly, incessantly, and somewhat vehemently assailed with the word that the ultimate moral significance of their individual lives is embodied in and depends upon the mere survival of the American nation and its 'way of life'" (Stringfellow, 1964b:58).

Institutions make moral claims upon individuals for their commitment, whether "a great corporation, a government agency, an ecclesiastical organization, a union, utility, or university" (Stringfellow, 1964b:56) in order to ensure its own survival; the survival of the institution is the primary concern of the institution and that to which all its work is focused, and is therefore dehumanizing. While often portrayed as benign, or even somehow to the benefit of the employee, "in the end, the claim for service which an institution makes upon a man is an invitation to surrender his life in order that the institution be preserved and prosper. It is an invitation to bondage" (Stringfellow, 1964b:56–57).

Images are broad in their scope and most common. While often displaying less influence than other principalities, we are each of us accompanied by one throughout our life. Most obviously these images can be associated with celebrity (whether an entertainer, actor, politician etc.), but each one of us conveys an image and leaves an image—a public image—in the minds of those we meet both during our life and after it. Of course, celebrity makes some such images more widely known than others: Barack Obama, Bill Clinton, Michael Jackson, Drew Barrymore, Patrick Swayze. Furthermore, image today is also portrayed in advertising and branding. Therefore, in our culture the principality of image can be seen at work when we give up our own identity to the pursuit of an image, for example through fashion and brand acquisition, as much as in the idolization of the image of particular people. It is an idolatry which costs us our lives. "The demand . . . made in the conflict between the principality and the personality is one in which the whole life of the person is surrendered to the principality and is given over to the worship of the image" (Stringfellow, 1964b:55).[96]

CONCLUSION

That the principalities themselves are subject to death means, of course, that they are void of saving power; while their power for creating bondage is very real, their power for giving freedom is not. "The principalities are themselves acolytes of death in this world, and man's idolatry of them is really the concrete form of his bondage to death" (Stringfellow, 1964b:65). While worship (vocational allegiance) of the principalities and powers brings death, worship of God (through vocational authenticity) brings life.

Stringfellow's encounter with the principalities and powers was and remained primarily and most importantly an empirical one. Harlem helped him literally to see the world differently, and in writing about it Stringfellow is attempting to re-orientate us as we seek to live the life of worship as well. In East Harlem he experienced the growing realization that being at odds with the church and the law meant being at odds with America itself. It was a position about to radicalize and be realized, as the next decade dawned.

96. Further, angelic powers include money, folk heroes, sex, fashion, sport, the Crown, patriotism, religion, and idealized notions of various ways of life—Stringfellow cites the example of Motherhood (momism), implicitly pre-empting what was to become the feminist movement.

PART TWO

Movement—Faith and Politics

4

Social Context II

INTRODUCTION

THE 1960S HAVE BEEN characterized as an end to the Dark Ages and "the beginning of a more hopeful and democratic period that lasted until the early 1970s": a modern Great Awakening, heralding a new American identity (Patterson, 1996:442). This is the period of focus in this chapter. Significantly for us, along with the 1950s, this period in America's history reshaped the landscape of its morality. Naturally, to say the changes were unwelcome in some culturally and politically conservative quarters would be to understate the obvious, but as Patterson points out, both sides "were correct in recognizing that unusually tumultuous events shook American life in the 1960s. Cultural and social changes seemed to accelerate rapidly in the early 1960s, to reshape public policies in the mid-1960s, and to polarize the nation in the last few years of the decade" (Patterson, 1996:443).

It was a period characterized by faith and politics, and faith *in* politics. But if one word were to sum it up, it would be *movement*: it was the period characterized by, on the one hand, the political mobilization of the search for authenticity, freedom, and equality, which a generation had inwardly pursued in the 1950s, and by, on the other hand, the continuation of economic growth, despite the recession of 1958. The 1950s had been the decade of a people and a nation seeking to understand and identify itself in relation to a new personal, political, and economic environment, characterized by identification and understanding, and seen for example in the rise to prominence of existentialism (and in America, especially Christian existentialism), centrist politics, and Christian social projects (like EHPP) which were attempts to assimilate the secular thinking of the time into Christianity.

The 1960s, however, were a decade of action. This is an environment in which Stringfellow flourished, if providing a somewhat belated socio-political framework with which to characterize him.

It was a time of political change, transformation, and hope: embodied most in the presidency of John F. Kennedy. It was also a time in which marginalization gave rise to popular movement, strongly led by baby-boomer students eager for change—it was a period in which marginalization almost became mainstream. For Stringfellow, the 1960s marked a period of radical and controversial public encounter, prompted most notably by his published work, and episodes where the significance and impact were far more personal.

In this chapter we shall introduce some of the key elements of this social context that were especially relevant or prominent in the story of Stringfellow's lifework, and in chapter 5, we shall explore his engagement with many aspects of the context we describe here.

HISTORICAL BACKGROUND: ROADS TO FREEDOM?

The history of the United States is a complex web of interconnected hopes, dreams, and actions. It is a story which encompassed change or movement working actively from two directions: from the top down and from the bottom up. Here, and in the chapter which follows, we shall see it from both sides.

There was a certain expectancy in the air as the decade commenced. For some it was driven by the legacies of economic promise lingering from the 1950s and the freedom it entailed, while for others it was the search for authenticity and a different kind of freedom. This expectancy was an energy which embraced the nation; America was literally buzzing with optimism and hope, but at the same time it was also burdened by fear and despair, and this tension remained throughout the 1960s and beyond. And at the outset of the decade, nothing appeared to capture this mood and tension better than John F. Kennedy's presidency and Civil Rights, and in these (and others) "threat" and "prosperity" continued but took a somewhat different turn.

America's Icon: John F. Kennedy

The dawning of a new decade brought with it a battle for the Presidency, which was won by John F. Kennedy. Despite the extremely narrow margin by which he won, his victory spawned a mood of hope and optimism for many. He was a political phenomenon, and the most charismatic politician of the post-war period. But despite the image now idolized since his death of embodied hope and tragic loss, according to Patterson and Brinkley he was a leader of little political substance: in Kennedy, the age of the "processed politician" had arrived.

The main issues upon his political horizon, and those of his challenge for the 1960 presidential election, Nixon, remained the issues of the 1950s: the Cold War and the economy (threat and prosperity). He continued to embody and maintain the centrist politics of the 1950s, albeit from a more youthful perspective. "He symbolized in the 1960s a sort of generational imperative: the need for youth to carry forward the battles that the older generation seemed no longer capable of fighting" (Brinkley, 1998:215). At forty-three years old, he was the youngest president to ever be elected to office, and, succeeding the oldest, he symbolized a coming of age for a new generation, and through that he embodied hope. He had been considered by many critics before his presidency as little more than a rich playboy—a reputation he did little to resist.

Kennedy had presence and charm also in his favor, and his command of media skills made him well suited to the newly emerging television generation.[1] His image was carefully crafted and controlled, his manner graceful, his life appearing blessed (Brinkley, 1998:217).[2] However, all was not as it appeared, and America was served a carefully crafted and orchestrated illusion. He was not athletic, but quite ill, suffering from Addison's Disease (Patterson, 1996:523). Nor was he the doting father and contented husband, and his squalid sexual exploits, both before and after marriage, are now well known. Neither was he much interested in high culture, having a closer affinity with more culturally popular figures like Ian Flemming and Frank Sinatra. Finally, while being intelligent and literate, he was neither an intellectual nor a writer.[3]

---

1. Television came into its own during the 1960s, a major force in providing and shaping a national culture, and bringing into people's homes quite graphic (and hitherto unseen) images of the quite violent and profound divisions within America (Patterson, 1996:446–47).

2. See also Patterson (1996:437).

3. "There is strong reason to believe (although Kennedy always denied it) that his connection with the writing of *Profiles in Courage,* the book that won him the Pulitzer Prize, was at best casual. His aid ... and others wrote most of it, and family retainers ... maneuvered it through the jury to secure it the Pulitzer Prize (for which it had not been recommended by the historians on the advisory committee)" (Brinkley, 1998:218).

Yet his appeal can be understood in relation to the public need for a national purpose or goal, for which support had been steadily growing since the Second World War. Kennedy seems to have captured that mood and provided a mission around which people could muster themselves. He provided a sense of confidence, and purpose, and a reason for hope. His assassination in 1963 was a specter of disillusionment and mystery that hovered over 1960s America, and brought about a resulting change in American self-understanding. For many, America was no longer a place of infinite progress and ever-expanding promise, and suspicions of conspiracies loomed. In the wake of these events, and Kennedy's assassination itself, conspiracy and fear rode high on the wave of the public mood.[4]

During his presidency, Kennedy's gaze of concern was predominantly international (foreign affairs), yet around on the domestic scene there was unrest, and his commitment to civil rights, for example, was somewhat lame according to Patterson. His interest in generating the Civil Rights Bill, which Johnson's administration eventually turned into law, was driven by political expediency, not commitment to justice (Patterson, 1996:440).

PERSISTENT THREAT

During Kennedy's short Presidency, the Cold War escalated to new heights. Kennedy declared that for Americans "the enemy is the Communist system itself—implacable, insatiable, increasing in its drive for world domination ... This is not a struggle for arms alone. It is also a struggle for supremacy between two conflicting ideologies: freedom under God versus ruthless, godless tyranny" (cited in Beschloss, 1991:25). It was a view far removed from Stringfellow's own, yet its polarization of good and evil reflected well the Cold War mood. It would be fair to say that the Kennedy administration was primarily concerned with containing communism rather than advancing social reform (Patterson, 1996:496).[5]

4. Many conspiracy theories have been put forward for this; most include the involvement of the Mafia, Cuba, and the CIA in some measure. See Brinkley (1998:210–21) and Patterson (1996:521).

5. Despite acknowledging there was no missile gap between the United States and the Soviet Union, his administration undertook massive spending in increasing conventional and nuclear weapons and showed few of the fiscal concerns that had occupied

Cold War threat can be seen at the heart of one of the most expensive political and technological icons of the Kennedy administration: the Apollo project, which began in 1961. The effort to get Armstrong to the moon cost $25 to $35 billion, and it failed to produce much in the way of scientific knowledge. However, it captured the imagination of a huge number of Americans throughout the 1960s and was therefore a triumph of pride and patriotism for Kennedy. It was an icon of the progress and supremacy which Kennedy's America craved.

With Soviet–American relations deteriorating in the days immediately leading up to Kennedy taking office, and he and Khrushchev battling head to head in a desire to both look tough and save face, the shooting down of a U-2 spy plane over the Soviet Union did much to harden relationships between the two nations.[6] These were days in which Billy Graham preached about the end of the world. The fear of nuclear annihilation was widespread amongst the American people, and anti-communist sentiment was at an all-time high—sentiment which spilled over directly into restrictive immigration practices and fear of foreigners or aliens. Amidst this, Cuba became the central and defining issue.[7]

With his attention firmly focused upon foreign affairs, Kennedy had a less masterful appeal to the newly emerging restlessness, especially prominent among young people. A new and undefined zeitgeist was emerging, and its "restless spirit pushed with special insistence against the political centre" (Patterson, 1996:447) which Kennedy occupied.

---

the mind of his predecessors. Over the course of the next three years spending on defense rose 13 percent, from $47.4 billion in 1961 to $53.6 billion in 1964. Much of this spending went on America's already vast nuclear arsenal.

6. On May 1, 1960, a U-2 spy plane was shot down by the Soviets inside their borders. The timing, just sixteen days before a summit between the leaders of Britain, France, the Soviet Union, and America, couldn't have been worse. Khrushchev used the opportunity to show the world that he was a force to be reckoned with. He began by announcing it was a weather balloon, lured America into a tissue of lies, and then sprung the surprise of pilot Powers' capture and the spy plane upon the world. Anger and embarrassment ensued. Tension and mistrust grew.

7. Emphasizing once more his disdain for domestic politics and his preoccupation with foreign affairs, Kennedy once remarked to Nixon: "Foreign affairs is the only important issue for a president to handle, isn't it? . . . I mean, who gives a shit if the minimum wage is $1.15 or $1.25, compared to something like Cuba?" (Beschloss, 1991:48). However, as others observed, Cuba was more a thorn in the flesh than a dagger in the heart, and Kennedy's almost self-destructive fixation upon it was damaging. The Bay of Pigs and the Cuban missile Crisis, in which the imminent and real danger of nuclear war loomed, are told by Patterson (1996:492–509).

While there are similarities between Kennedy and Stringfellow,[8] there are clear and significant points of contrast. Kennedy was an icon of American hope and under his administration the feeling of *threat* and its associated fears rose to an all-time high. It is in this wider context that Stringfellow's East Harlem discovery of the principalities and powers was made.

THE GREAT SOCIETY

Owing to Kennedy's assassination, Lyndon Johnson literally continued where Kennedy left off, but his gaze and vision were distinctly different. If Kennedy's was a centrist presidency of foreign affairs and containment, Johnson's was one characterized by liberal, predominantly domestic, reform. In his presidency he would have to deal with a number of complex problems, and the growing popular expectations which Kennedy's promises had fuelled.

But the presidencies of Johnson and Kennedy were offices of contrast: Kennedy came from a wealthy background, Johnson came out of poverty; Kennedy had a gift for self-presentation, Johnson's vanity and cold personal style and desire to dominate and humiliate were legendary;[9] Kennedy's ability to create fragmentation, rather than heal its wounds, are witnessed to by his dealings with Cuba and the Soviet Union, but Johnson's gift for coalition building was to prove invaluable for healing the domestic wounds.

> Johnson entered the fray amidst a national mood desiring strong presidential leadership, and the mood was optimistic. Kennedy's expansive rhetoric about a New Frontier . . . had kept the liberal agenda alive. Surging growth of the economy since 1962 helped enormously: the nation, it seemed, could afford expensive federal programs. And highly optimistic liberal bureaucrats . . . were certain that social science expertise and computerization gave government the tools to change the world. (Patterson, 1996:530–31)

8. For example, their oratory abilities, their illnesses which were kept private, and their high achieving status despite their relatively young age.

9. See Patterson (1996:527–28) for more information about his style. One story tells of a visit he made to the Pope. The Pope presented him with a fourteenth century painting as a gift, and in return Johnson gave the Pope a bust of himself. It was quite common for Johnson to be parodied in jokes as Abraham Lincoln, Jesus, or God.

Johnson seemed to embody the grand expectations which had captured liberals in the 1960s. He believed unflinchingly in the power of government to develop public programs and policies that could benefit society "and secure the progress of the Free World" (Patterson, 1996:531). And, moreover, he believed with equal certainty that America had the resources to achieve this. "I'm sick of all the people who talk about the things we can't do," he told an aide in 1964. "Hell, we're the richest country in the world, the most powerful. We can do it all" (Patterson, 1996:531). This was the mood which characterized Johnson's presidency, whose agenda was liberal (equality of opportunity), not radical (equality of social condition), and strongly backed the New Deal programs which had preceded him in the 1930s. Johnson was on his way to building his Great Society.

The Great Society was the vision which embraced his social policies of reform and dated to May 1964. It was a vision which encompassed not only a society growing in wealth and power, but also one growing "upward." The Great Society was where "the city of man serves not only the needs of the body and the demands of commerce but the desire for beauty and the hunger for community . . . It is a place where men are more concerned with the quality of their goals than the quantity of their goods" (Patterson, 1996:562). Central to this rather idealistic and utopian vision was the guarantee of rights. Single-mindedly, Johnson forged ahead with his vision, putting into place a vast number of bills in rapid succession. Driven by ambition and determination, his desire, in terms of his presidency, sadly focused upon the *quantity* of bills and laws, rather than their *quality*.

The Great Society consisted of a number of measures, including immigration reform and the controversial introduction of Medicare.[10] However, for the purposes of our study, and in order to gain some insight into the contextual, political, and cultural forces which were shaping and influencing America and Stringfellow, we shall look here briefly at the three which are most pertinent to our discussions.

10. According to Patterson, in all his policies, such was Johnson's concern for implementation and change that haste took precedence over thinking through the mid or long-term consequences of his actions. Many of his policies and decisions can be traced as the cause of later recession and fiscal and political difficulties, especially during the 1970s and 1980s.

WAR ON POVERTY

In his State of the Union address in January 1964, Johnson declared
war: "This administration, today, here and now, declares unconditional
war on poverty in America" (Patterson, 1996:533). It was an idea he had
taken from Kennedy, but which fit nicely into his vision for the Great
Society nevertheless. At the heart of the initiative were programs like
Mobilization for Youth in New York City. The idea behind the initiative
was, simply, to provide government help and guidance in order to promote *opportunity* amongst the poor.

Poverty, as Stringfellow discovered, was a widespread and oppressive problem throughout America. Government statistics put the poverty
line at an annual income of $3,130 for a family of four, and $1,500 for an
individual. Accordingly, some 40.3 million people were poor, accounting
for 21 percent of the population at that time. However, it is not surprising that certain groups were represented more than others: over half of
black Americans, about a half of those living in female headed house-
holds, and a third of people over sixty-five, were to be found catego-
rized as poor (Patterson, 1996:534). While not exclusively so, racism and
poverty were nevertheless intimate bedfellows. Moreover, by this time
in the 1960s, poverty in America was headline news. In his usual style,
Johnson was eager to tackle it, and quickly; with all America's wealth and
resource, he reasoned he must be able to do something.

> Johnson also believed unquestioningly in another liberal faith:
> that government had the skills to improve the lot of its citizens.
> What motivated Johnson to fight poverty . . . was not the worsen-
> ing of a social problem—higher percentages of Americans had
> been poor in the 1950s—but the belief that government could,
> and should, enter the battle. These optimistic expectations, not
> despair, lay at the heart of American liberalism in the sixties.
> (Patterson, 1996:534–35)

Of course, Johnson was not talking about welfare—that remained a dirty
word. In fact, he intended that anything he did to fight poverty would
not increase government spending on public expenditure, nor would he
raises taxes; Johnson's was a "hand-up, not a hand-out," opening doors
of opportunity rather than financing floors under income (Patterson,

1996:535). The backbone to Johnson's war was therefore education and training programs, and it predominantly targeted young people.[11]

It is worth noting two unforeseen consequences of the Poverty Bill arose from the haste with which it was passed through Congress, which together were to have a profound significance. First was the idea of "community action." The hope was that community development would arise as a consequence of local poverty programs in such a way that local community leaders would somehow be intrinsically involved in fighting the war at a local level. The inclusion in the bill of the provision for poor people to have "maximum feasible participation" was also highly significant. Both became adopted by radical activists and resulted in clashes with local authorities. Together, these two notions "became fighting words that divided the Democratic party" (Patterson, 1996:536): liberals on the one hand, radicals on the other.

The war on poverty failed to tackle the structural roots of poverty. In their haste, Johnson and his team failed to wait for studies which would have shown that most poor people in America at that time needed more than education and training; we can see as much in Stringfellow's account of Harlem, and his account of the "other America" which existed there. Widespread racism, discrimination over housing and jobs, age and illness, low wages, and the problems associated with single parenthood, were issues which stood firmly in the way and needed addressing. Critics were of two kinds: radicals—who claimed Johnson failed to comprehend the problem with sufficient gravity—failed to see the separate nation which the poor inhabited, and conservatives, who said the "poor" of the 1960s were in fact rather well off compared to the poor of the 1930s, and that Johnson's plans would have little effect other than create a generation of un-deserving drunks and deadbeats.

While in absolute terms the poor were better off, in relative terms they were not. In fact, many poor were relatively worse off in the 1960s: the gap between poverty and wealth was growing, fostered by the growing expectations of both groups of people. Advertising on the television, for example, conveyed for the first time to the poor what it was they were missing and so created an even more profound sense of relative depriva-

---

11. This notion of enhancing opportunity, although no embedded in British government, is a "profoundly American idea, rooted in a tradition dating to Thomas Jefferson and the Declaration of Independence" (Patterson, 1996:535).

tion. Feelings of anger and apathy amongst low-income families at this time did much to expose racial and class divisions.

In his war on poverty, Johnson was not much concerned with inequality and remained unaware of these rising feelings of relative deprivation. Nevertheless, poverty, his administration hailed, could be wiped out within a decade with sufficient funding.

Politics of Success

While Johnson's war on poverty was being fought, so were his attempts to ensure continued prosperity and economic growth. The economy had been surging ahead since 1962 and provided everyone in government, and many people in the nation, with an optimistic outlook.

Pushing forward on another of Kennedy's proposals, in early 1964 Johnson implemented a tax cut. This cut was set to shed $10 billion over two years, but because of its structure it was of help mainly to corporations and those who were relatively wealthy. Loopholes, readily exploited by these two groups, also persisted. Many economists at that time hoped that the tax cut would further stimulate the economy.

Compared to the $800 million the government spent on its war on poverty (which totaled less than $200 per poor person), this tax cut was of staggering generosity, representing more than a six-fold reduction of income through taxes over expenditure on the poor.

The politics of Johnson's government, seen in his dealings with taxes and with poverty, were the politics of success: emphasizing opportunity over equality. They were liberal policies.

War on Racism

The Civil Rights Bill, again begun by Kennedy, was implemented finally by Johnson as part of his project for The Great Society. Unlike Kennedy, for whom it was motivated by a mood of political expediency, Johnson was committed to this bill because he believed in it. He had grown up in the South, witnessed discrimination, and had empathy for its victims. It was his most important and long-lasting piece of legislation and did much to raise rights consciousness and guarantee in law, even if not in practice, the rights of millions of black Americans. The process of getting the bill passed absorbed practically all of Johnson's "time and effort for the first six months of 1964" (Patterson, 1996:542).

On July 2, 1964, the bill became law. Racial discrimination was banned in "privately run accommodations for the public," like hotels, petrol stations, theaters, cinemas, and restaurants, and the Attorney General was authorized to eliminate segregation in public places. Institutions like schools faced withdrawal of federal funding if they persisted with discriminatory practices, and the Attorney General would take up cases on behalf of parents and the government would pay their legal costs. These, just some of the highlights of the bill, were far-reaching and profound changes brought to bear upon a nation literally at war with itself over the issue of racism.

Another important section of the bill, Title VII, was added by the chairman of the House Rules Committee, Howard Smith, of Virginia. It stated that discrimination in employment was also forbidden, and that discrimination on the grounds of sex should be added to those of race, color, religion, or national origin. It was to prove a highly significant change. Smith, ardently against the Civil Rights Bill, had made the amendment in the hope of destroying the bill. "He figured [that] liberals committed to protective legislation for women might feel obliged to oppose the bill, which would then fail. But Smith miscalculated" (Patterson, 1996:545). So it was that federal enforcement of gender equality, a movement which was later to rise to prominence, became American law.

> No other President cared so much as Johnson did about domestic policies or about civil rights, and none since FDR in the 1930s had come close to securing so many laws ... It was a high tide of American liberalism in the postwar era. (Patterson, 1996:587)

But miracles were not worked overnight, and overt discrimination remained in many Southern states for some years, and still does in places. Nor did it do a great deal to positively improve the lot of black people. "The law did not pretend to do anything to better the mostly abysmal economic condition of black people in the United States. Like the war on poverty, it was a liberal, not a radical, measure. It aimed to promote legal, not social equality" (Patterson, 1996:546).

Furthermore, the civil rights legislation did not cater to all discriminated groups. Muslims in America were "deeply alienated from whites [and] had no use for the interracial civil rights movement or for 'corrupt' and 'evil' white society" (Patterson, 1996:550). The Muslim radical movement received growing support, and Malcolm X, who broke away from the Nation of Islam to head his own group, the Organization of Afro-

American Unity, became one of the most prominent in this movement. Nevertheless, the significance of the Civil Rights Act was so great a piece of legislation that Patterson describes it as "far and away the most important in the history of American race relations" (Patterson, 1996:546); without doubt, it has transformed contemporary America.

Johnson's efforts to get the bill passed were legendary[12] and not without opposition. One of these who stood most squarely opposed and publicly vocal was the conservative senator Barry Goldwater of Arizona (Stringfellow, 1964c). Goldwater was well liked in Washington. He opposed almost all the efforts of Johnson's government to intervene in domestic affairs, especially the new civil rights legislation. Furthermore, a strident anti-communist, he was keen to deploy American military force in order to settle foreign disputes. Despite his popularity amongst conservatives, he did not want to be president, and ran for the nomination (which he won) with some diffidence. Goldwater's politics and views contributed significantly to anti-civil rights violence, and won much support in the South. It is important to note, however, that he ran his presidential campaign not on the issue of race, but on that of ideological opposition to Big Government: what he considered the greatest threat to America's freedom. The presidential campaign of 1964 was especially dirty, with more negative campaigning (over 40 percent of advertising) than ever before.

In the end, Johnson's vision for the Great Society appears to have won him favor and support amongst the American people. It was a generally popular policy, and he swept home with a strong and convincing victory.[13] Johnson was the champion of liberal politics, and they dominated the decade: as much the fruit of increasing expectations, hopes, and dreams, as that which sought to produce them.

Legislative changes dominated the history of the 1960s, but the story has two sides. And while the government ventured into liberal policies as solutions to national problems, the movement from below was more radical. While Johnson's efforts were seen in a generally positive light, his policies were nevertheless reactionary, and they were reacting to grow-

---

12. See Patterson (1996:542–44) for details.

13. Johnson polled 43.1 million votes over Goldwater's 27.2 million—61.2 percent of the total vote. Johnson also swept the electoral college, 486 to 52. Democrats also ruled the House and the Senate. On Goldwater, see also Stringfellow (1964c), in which Stringfellow is highly critical of his politics.

ing movement at the grassroots.[14] It is to these movements that we now turn our attention.

CIVIL RIGHTS

Martin and Malcolm

The campaign for civil rights, which dated back to 1954 and *Brown vs. The Board of Education*, had predominantly been a series of well-orchestrated protests, boycotts, and speeches, organized in the main by the National Association for the Advancement of Colored People (NAACP) and Martin Luther King Jr.

King, well respected and well regarded in the black community, was the leader of the SCLC[15]—a leading organization in the Civil Rights Movement. Theologically, he was aligned with Reinhold Niebuhr and ideologically committed to the pacifism of Gandhi: "Niebuhr's great contribution to contemporary theology is that he has refuted the false optimism characteristic of a great segment of Protestant liberalism, without falling into the anti-rationalism of the continental theologian Karl Barth, or the semi-fundamentalism of other dialectical theologians" (Branch, 1988:87).[16] King was no academic, and what roused him to action and impassioned eloquence was the injustice he saw and experienced in America's South. His combined commitment to Niebuhr and "Gandhism" (as he referred to it) fostered a commitment to nonviolent social action, and this is what he conveyed so eloquently. He called followers to social action, but to stand up for what's right while staying within the law, which would show the power of Christian love and forgiveness.[17]

14. Johnson's emphasis upon creating a rights culture also contributed in some measure to ongoing grassroots movement throughout the 1960s

15. SCLC stands for the Southern Christian Leadership Council. By far the most thorough and well researched account of King and the Civil Rights Movement can be found in Taylor Branch's three-volume work on the subject (Branch, 1988, 1998, 2006).

16. While Branch is right to point out Niebuhr's influence, it is worthwhile noting also that by the time of the Vietnam War, King had moved beyond Niebuhr.

17. Montgomery, a city of about 70,000 whites and 50,000 blacks, was the location of the most dramatic action of the 1950s. The blacks in Montgomery were poor, and they used buses for transportation. They were subject to victimization and ridicule on a daily basis (and victims of Klan brutality at night), forced to pay at the front of the bus but then enter the bus at the rear and sit there. One day in 1954 a woman named Rosa Parks refused to move down the bus: an action which sparked a huge organized protest, which

But despite the charismatic leadership, the heroes of the Civil Rights Movement were predominantly unsung and anonymous: those local people who were willing to put themselves on the line and say "no" to the injustice they suffered. One woman protestor—and most were women—remarked on her action "The Reverend [Martin Luther King] he didn't stir us up. We've been stirred up a mighty long time." King's role was predominantly to help people focus, organize, and strategize, and his desire for reform of the system, rather than its overthrowing, was not entirely out of step with Johnson's liberal agenda. It did however place him at odds with the more radical wing of civil rights, like the Black Panthers, or other campaigners like Malcolm X.

Malcolm X's rhetoric was quite distinct from that of King, and unlike the Nation of Islam from whom he separated, was preferred by Stringfellow. His belief was in the brotherhood of all people, not just black people.[18] He also believed that black people should take up arms to protect themselves. He believed the most important thing black people could do, indeed the burden facing them, was to think for themselves. But his position is probably best summed up in his lively and radical rhetoric. King had just organized an action in Birmingham, Alabama, in which dogs had been set upon peacefully protesting demonstrators, including women and children. The events had been widely broadcast on television and shocked the nation. Malcolm X made the following remarks in later broadcasts:

> Any man who puts his women and children on the front lines is a chump, not a champ . . . You can't call it results when someone has bitten your babies and your women and children, and you are to sit down and compromise with them . . . and drink some coffee with some crackers in a cracker restaurant, desegregated lunch counters. Now what kind of advancement is that? (Branch, 1998:86)[19]

---

drew heavily for its participants upon the black churches. Income of bus companies plummeted, and after almost a year the Supreme Court ruled the discriminatory practices must stop. Note that it was the Court, not the local bus companies, which relented. It was a huge triumph for civil rights.

18. Following his separation, his relationship with the Nation of Islam was, at best, a hostile one. It is they who assassinated him in 1965.

19. I use this quote to highlight the radical nature of Malcolm X's thought, rather than to enter into a debate about relations between him and King.

The Quickening[20]

In 1960, through a spontaneous action, civil rights changed from a campaign to a movement, and it resonated with Stringfellow's own actions some years earlier. In Greensboro, North Carolina, late in the afternoon on February 1, 1960, four black freshmen spontaneously decided to go downtown to the local Woolworth's store and sit at the whites only lunch counter, waiting to be served. People in the store didn't know how to respond, the management floundered: they had never experienced such direct action before. A policeman nervously slapped his club in his hand, the waitress fearing reprisal refused to serve them, and in the end, the store shut early in order to bring the situation to an end. The boys returned to college only to discover they had become heroes—others, even white students, wanted to join them; the atmosphere was electrifying. The next day, Tuesday, it was more organized, and nineteen students took part; by Wednesday the numbers had swelled to eighty-five. And with this single spontaneous spark, the fire of direct action in the Civil Rights Movement, throughout the nation, was well and truly lit: it helped "define a new decade" (Branch, 1988:272).

> A week later fifty-four sit-ins were under way in fifteen cities in nine states in the South. It was obvious from the way that the spark of protest jumped from place to place that black resentments, which had somehow failed to ignite other sit-ins between 1957 and 1959, had exploded. (Patterson, 1996:431)

The impact of this single action is highly significant. According to Branch there had been a number of other similar demonstrations in around sixteen other cities, and none had the slightest catalytic effect anywhere else. Greensboro was different, and their spontaneity holds the key.

Because the four students at Woolworth's had no plan, they began with no self-imposed limitations. They defined no tactical goals. They did not train or drill in preparation. They did not dwell on the many forces that might be used against them. Above all, they did not anticipate that Woolworth's white managers would—instead of threatening to have them arrested—flounder in confusion and embarrassment. The surprise discovery of defensiveness within the segregated white world turned their fear into elation (Branch, 1988:272).

---

20. This title is taken from chapter 7 of Branch (1988).

In the first half of the 1960s, America's civil rights relations progressed decades. This period of dynamic change was largely due to two things: politics from the bottom up, and politics from the top down.

But the Watts riot of 1965 was a stark counterpoint to this hopeful optimism; it was an ominous omen of the future. As black people began to take direct action, fear eventually gripped white America, and violence ensued. As a consequence, the decade was peppered with the use of extreme violence and brutality by law-enforcement agencies and white people against blacks. Savage beatings and murders of men, women, and children, as exemplified in the events in Selma, Alabama, were all to take place.

In 1965, tensions were running high in the South. The FBI maintained a high profile ensuring the Civil Rights legislation was enforced, and this met with quick tempers of whites. Protest in Selma, organized by King and others, began as a demonstration against the denial of voting rights[21] and represented a significant post-legislation shift in the focus of civil rights, from protest to attain equality in law, to protest to attain what the law now prescribed: equality in action. The build up had been going on for some time. To add to the tension of protest leaders, in February Malcolm X arrived on the scene. Malcolm, who did not support the non-violent ideology, preached to an eager crowd—one of the last addresses he was to give before his assassination later that month.[22] Selma was to prove to be one of the most violent and bloody protests in the entire duration of the movement.

Protest in Selma had been taking place for some time, and King had chosen Selma as the location for this series of protests because he "anticipated that whites would resist fiercely and violently, thereby dramatizing his cause on television and forcing the government to act" (Patterson, 1996:579). The Sheriff, Jim Clark, was well known as an unreconstructed segregationist, and his department had a history of manhandling protestors. King was correct. In January and February many people were arrested, including King.

21. Out of a population of 29,000, some 15,000 were black. However only 355 of these were registered to vote. Blacks were subjected to discriminatory tests in order to evaluate their eligibility.

22. When Malcolm X's biography was finally published, in October 1965, a critic from the New York Times wrote that Malcolm "understood, perhaps more profoundly than any other Negro leader, the full, shocking extent of America's psychological destruction of its Negros" (Branch, 1998:601).

Many protestors were kicked or clubbed before being taken away, including one occasion when a woman was knocked to the ground, held down by deputies, and beaten indiscriminately by Clark.[23] Then again, on February 10, he arrested 165 protesters and forced them to march out of town, he and his men using cattle prods on the demonstrators. Clark punched members of the clergy, state troopers ambushed marchers and shot one young black man who was trying to save his mother and grand-father from a beating; he died eight days later.

But the events on Sunday March 7, 1965, have gone down in history as America's own Bloody Sunday. In order to raise the profile of the cause, King organized a march from Selma to Montgomery, the state capital. When they arrived they would petition Governor Wallace to protect black people who wished to vote. The march started on Sunday, March 7; what followed was one of the most violent and frightening encounters in the history of the movement (Patterson, 1996:581). State troopers shouted through a bullhorn, giving the marchers two minutes to turn back. One of the leaders of the march asked for "a word," but was told there was "no word to be had." A minute later, the troopers advanced.

> They tore forward in a flying wedge, swinging clubs at people in their way. Lewis [the SCLC leader] stood his ground, only to be cracked on the head. He suffered a fractured skull. With white onlookers cheering, the troopers rushed ahead, hitting the dem-onstrators and exploding canisters of tear gas. Five women were beaten so badly that they fell down near the bridge and lost con-sciousness. Sheriff Clark's horsemen then joined in the assault. Charging with rebel yells, they swung bullwhips and rubber tub-ing wrapped in barbed wire. More demonstrators fell, seventy of whom were later hospitalized. (Patterson, 1996:581)

The events were brutal, savage, and indiscriminate. Repeatedly shown on television news programs, it outraged Americans.[24] Malcolm X, while he abhorred the violence of Clark and his men, would also have abhorred the fact that the protesters did not defend themselves. A flood of white helpers from the North arrived in Selma, among them clergy, rabbi, and

23. It was an action widely circulated in photographs, and appalled Americans throughout the country.

24. Television served as an astonishingly effective tool in bringing to light the struggles present within a country which had until now been largely unaware of events in other states. The use of visual moving image was uniquely effective in capturing the horror of this event, and others like it.

nuns. Inevitably, Congress took action, but a fury had been unleashed which the president had to address. King spoke out. In a speech which moved him to tears, he spoke on television with emotion and sincerity:

> Their cause must be our cause, too. Because it is not just Negros, but really all of us who must overcome the crippling legacy of bigotry and injustice. And we shall . . . overcome. (King, cited in Patterson 1996:582)[25]

This was not the end of the violence, but it was the beginning of the end of the government's failing to enforce the law they and the movement had struggled so hard to create.

VIETNAM

While "wars" on poverty and racism were fought on domestic soil, another more perilous, devastating, and unpopular war was being fought by America on foreign soil, and by 1966, as interest in the domestic wars subsided, Vietnam took the political center stage. For Johnson, it had become something of an obsession, and he threw himself behind it as enthusiastically as he had previously the domestic policies of the Great Society. His liberal politics meant that he held on to a view of the might, ability, and invincibility of America: it can do anything it wants, and it can win.

America's interest in Vietnam was political: it feared both the loss of the democracy in South Vietnam to the powers of communism in the North, and the associated ideological images that this might portray to the world. It also feared the perceived subsequent dominance of communism in the Far East should Southern Vietnam fall to the North. The Soviet Union and China both provided the North with financial aid, totaling about $2 billion between 1965 and 1968.

At the end of 1963 about 17,000 American military "advisors" were posted in Vietnam, and in 1964 there were 23,000. There was then a significant escalation following North Vietnam's attack on an American airbase in February 1965, and American bombers began a campaign of bombing North Vietnam. By the end of 1965 there were 184,000 American military personnel stationed in Vietnam, a year later, 450,000, and by early 1968 the number had risen to more than half a million.

25. King's words, remarkably, resonate with those of Stringfellow's *My People is the Enemy.*

A similar escalation can be measured in terms of casualties (killed, wounded, hospitalized, and missing):[26] in 1965, there were 2,500, by the end of 1966 the figure had risen to 33,000, then to 80,000 by the end of 1967, and up to 130,000 at the peak of American involvement at the end of 1968.[27] But perhaps most alarming of all, about 415,000 civilians were killed while America was involved in the war, and about a third of South Vietnamese became refugees. "American planes unleashed more bombs, many of them napalm, on Vietnam between 1965 and the end of 1967 than they had in all the theatres of World War II," and by 1970, the total tonnage of bombs dropped in Vietnam was more than that of all previous wars in human history (Patterson, 1996:595). America dominated the air, and they had more firepower than the North. However, the North had two great assets: it outnumbered them, with a seemingly endless supply of conscripts, and their commitment was driven by a dictator with unyielding determination, which ultimately wore down American resolve. Amidst American's onslaught, North Vietnam remained undeterred and became more resolute.

However, the cost of American involvement was not only in terms of human life and suffering. Vast resources were directed to the military-industrial complex, the arms race escalated, and attention was diverted from various foreign problems in other quarters. The culture of South Vietnam became subject to American corruption, and at times America unnerved many of its allies. Finally, the financial cost was vast, and the war created huge budgetary deficits which were a major contribution to the inflation and economic instability that plagued the early 1970s (Patterson, 1996:597).

America's involvement in Vietnam was a defining force that shaped and determined the lives and identities of a generation of Americans, and it was a force itself determined not by valiant victory, but by futility, despair, and failure. It symbolizes faded hope, or perhaps an awakening of a new awareness: a loss of confidence in America's moral righteousness, military invincibility, and readily apparent ideological and economic destiny. It marks, in short, an awakening, a maturity, a recognition of self-limitations. "With the young men who died in Vietnam died the

26. These are measured cumulatively.

27. The Vietnam memorial in Washington DC contains the names of 57,939 Americans who either died or who are missing in action in the Vietnam.

dream of an American century" (Karnow,1983:9) and with it, the great expectations that had dominated American politics since World War II.

While it was an outcome which was by no means inevitable, it was also an outcome which grew out of an involvement "planted and nurtured in . . . America's concept of its own 'exceptionalism'" (Karnow, 1983:11). As Martin Luther King put it, in characteristic tone: "The Great Society has been shot down on the battlefield of Vietnam" (King, cited in Patterson 1996:614).[28]

Vietnam and civil rights violence like that seen at Selma did much to shake liberal optimism in America. The ebbing of liberal hopes in the 1960s has caused many to blame Johnson, and according to Patterson they have a point. Driven by his ego, he was preoccupied with trying to outdo Roosevelt (and every other President), and he measured his success in relation to the number of programs passed. His focus was upon getting things done quickly, with little research into their long-term sustainability or politically divisive consequences. In getting things done quickly, he often sacrificed getting them done well (Patterson, 1996:589). The backlash which ensued polarized the nation, and protest was at its heart.

LIBERATION: POLARIZATION, PROTEST, AND POWER

The latter half of the 1960s was dominated by the rise of protest. These protestors were in dissent and sought to recover power: they were radical movements seeking to recover power from liberal movements (including the government). Their expression was diverse and polarized: "This is the twenty-seventh time I have been arrested. I ain't going to jail no more. We want black power!" (Patterson, 1996:656). Stokley Carmichael spoke these impassioned words to the waiting crowd as he emerged from jail after being arrested for taking part in one of King's non-violent protests. This was more than a slogan. His words changed the course of the Civil Right Movement, giving rise to a backlash which organized itself into the Black Panthers and Black Power. It was a politics which moved away from assimilation into the great American melting pot. In

28. According to Patterson, Johnson realized escalation would have a negative impact upon his Great Society programs, and this is one reason he put it off until 1965 and tried for the first few months to hide that escalation from the American people and Congress (Patterson, 1996:600).

the radical movements which arose at this time the political (public) and the personal were bound tightly together.

Carmichael was just one example of the transformation to a more radical politics of protest which took place in the years following 1965, that polarized America, and was orientated, in all its expressive diversity, around people reclaiming power: the power to say "yes," and the power to say "no."[29] From the mid 1960s, the era of protest changed direction in a more radical and violent direction. Activists were now engaged in explicitly violent and angry protest, and towards the end of the decade there were bloody riots in many major cities (especially in their ghettos) and on many university campuses. Indeed, the campus was the hotbed of rebellion.

Polarization was rooted in wealth and class. So, at a time in which inequality and poverty were significant, the ongoing advance of prosperity at this time[30] did much to contribute to this polarization. Furthermore, from 1965 onwards, activism was fostered by the rights culture which Johnson's administration had fostered, although much of it radicalized Johnson's liberal implementation. Ironically, this commitment to rights can be seen in the legal implementation of Miranda rights.[31] Rights consciousness became embedded in American culture by the time the 1970s dawned. While there was a general allegiance to the language of rights, the mainstream considered the demands for the right to social equality for certain groups to be taking it too far.

And such demands were prolific and high in expectation. Organized movements arose out of marginalized groups. The rest of the decade saw activism concerned with women's rights, black power, gay rights, sexual liberation, anti-war protest, anti-nuclear protest, environmentalists, and free love, to name but a few. Finding one's "*real* authenticity" from the many on offer was becoming increasingly difficult. On what grounds was a person to decide—on the grounds of politics, age, economics,

29. The latter half of the decade saw Johnson commit to many more liberal goals, including rent supplements for the poor, urban mass transit, low-cost housing. One of his major concerns was to improve the quality of life for people in the cities: a stark contrast to the late 1950s (Patterson, 1996:648).

30. The economy finally peaked around 1967–1968.

31. According to Patterson, *Miranda vs. Arizona* was the landmark case in 1966 which prompted the introduction of explicit rights for criminal suspects. Chief Justice Warren, from the Supreme Court, gave liberals much to celebrate until his retirement in 1969.

color, race, religion, sex, and sexual orientation? All were represented,
and many were combined in some organizations. In fact, the interrelat-
edness between the groups was widespread and profound. There was not
inconsequential rivalry between the groups, and one thing was certain:
the movement(s) you joined sent a clear message about your personal
identity.

On that note, it is important to recognize that the culture of movement for equality and power that was forged in civil rights gave rise to
a significant shift in the way in which homosexuality was understood
and interpreted by some parts of American society. Ultimately, this climate also gave rise to the Gay Rights Movement. It was a movement
that was perceived as being at the more radical end of the spectrum of
protest. However, in a decade dominated by sit-ins, freedom rides, assassination, Southeast Asia, and violent and bloody protest, the issue of
gay rights "created hardly a stir in the nation's consciousness" (D'Emilio,
1983:147).

Despite this, developments during this time were of great significance: barriers to discussion about homosexuality began to fall, and
there was a noticeable shift in the self-perception and life style of many
gay men and women. It was a highly significant time, and 1965 saw
the stirrings and growth amidst the Mattachine Society's membership.
However, while membership had increased, it was still tiny compared
to the number of homosexuals in America at that time, and few of its
members had come out of the closet: whether or not this organization
can be understood to represent American homosexuals, as compared
to the Civil Rights Movement representing American black people, is
therefore debatable. Within the movement at this time there was a decisive break by militants away from the "accommodationist spirit of the
1950s" (D'Emilio, 1983:174).[32] This move towards radicalism marked a
significant change in the homophile movement in America. "Young gay
radicals exhibited as little respect toward the homophile movement as
they did towards institutions of American society. They scorned its mod-
eration and reformist politics" (D'Emilio, 1983:240), and they had little
regard or knowledge of the work of the previous two decades. However,

32. The militants broke away from the medical model, asserted their equality, sought
recognition of their place as a persecuted minority, and proclaimed homosexuality as
a viable way of living. In short, they proposed a radical, positive gay identity (D'Emilio,
1983:174).

the changes around this time had little immediate impact upon the consciousness of New York's gay or straight population.

While there were a number of rights-orientated undercurrents, and a number of supportive institutions like The George Henry Foundation, with whom Stringfellow was closely associated,[33] liberation didn't begin to come until the end of the decade, when homosexuals and lesbians began to realize the way in which the ideology and tactics of radical movements might transform their struggle for freedom and the condition of their life. Consequently, they began to appropriate it. Like Black Power and other radical movements, they sought to move beyond the integrationist politics of civil rights.

There were many actions which this movement took across the country, but the most significant took place in New York. On June 27, 1969, police from Manhattan's Sixth Precinct set about what they no doubt thought would be a routine raid of Stonewall Inn, a gay bar in Greenwich Village. It was a normal practice in New York at that time. After many arrests, the mood changed:

> The scene became explosive. Limp wrists were forgotten. Beer cans and bottles were heaved at the windows and a rain of coins descended on the cops . . . Almost by signal the crowd erupted into cobblestone and bottle heaving . . . I heard several cries of "let's get some gas," but the blaze of flame which soon appeared in the window of the Stonewall was still a shock. (Village Voice, 1969)

The rioting persisted for some time. By the second night, the slogan "Gay Power" had appeared on walls (D'Emilio,1983:232). History's first gay riot was underway, and its effects far reaching. The liberating effect of the Stonewall riot owes much to the radical movements which dominated American sub-culture in the 1960s, and especially since 1965:

> Gay liberation used the demonstrations of the new left as recruiting grounds and appropriated the tactics of confrontational politics for its own ends . . . The apocalyptic rhetoric and the sense of impending revolution that surrounded the Movement by the end of the decade gave to its newest participants an audacious daring

33. The George Henry Foundation was established in 1948 in New York City. George Henry and Alfred Gross worked to counsel homosexuals on parole who had been arrested for offences relating to their sexuality, and sought to find ways of helping them integrate into society. Stringfellow was on their staff as their General Counsel.

that made the dangers of a public avowal of their sexuality seem insignificant. (D'Emilio,1983:233)

A radicalized movement, gay liberationists became involved as groups in other protest movements, especially that against the war in Vietnam. Marches and public demonstrations often resulting in violence, did much to raise the public profile of gay people in America's consciousness. While other movements of the 1960s faded as the decade drew to a close, the same cannot be said for gay liberation. According to D'Emilio there are two reasons for this. Firstly, there was the way in which "coming out" had shifted from the private to the political—from signifying one's private decision to accept one's homosexuality and acknowledge it to other gay men and women, to a public declaration, a political act, a witness, which "symbolized the shedding of the self-hatred that gay men and women internalized, and consequently it promised an immediate improvement of one's life" (D'Emilio,1983:235). Coming out functioned as a strategy for building the movement and encapsulated the personal and the political of 1960s radicalism. Secondly, it gave rise to a strong lesbian liberation movement: a distinct entity which coincided with the emergence of women's liberation, thus collectively launching a large number of women into radical politics.

In the history of homosexual politics, Stonewall marks the transformation of thinly spread reform to a large grassroots liberation movement. It gave rise to the beginnings of gay sub-culture: gay churches, hospitals, publishing houses, travel agencies, etc. "The quality of gay life in America was permanently altered as a furtive subculture moved aggressively into the open" (D'Emilio,1983:239). Being gay, publicly, politically, and personally, became a way of life. So far as gay people were concerned, the fruits of liberation were authenticity.

In conclusion, rights language fostered increased expectation, and this in turn led to burgeoning disillusionment by many sectors of society—disillusionment in the promises of government to deliver the freedoms it promoted, and its control of the power to do this. Faced with this reality, there appear to have been two reactions. In the activism, the baby boomers who had been seeking authenticity, now come of age, had spoken out.[34] And while the mainstream considered many activist claims

34. Many of these boomers also had their roots in 1950s Beat culture. However, it is also important to make clear that while this culture was predominantly populated by this generation, there were significant numbers of older people involved in the move-

to be excessive and outrageous, they also desired autonomy in respect to power. As a result, the culture grew increasingly conservative and made ever greater demands upon the economy, the government, technology, and a burgeoning consumer-culture. In some ways, this period was a domestic battle for personal and political power, between two cultures: the consumer-culture and the counterculture.

While there are many radical examples, it is important to realize that rights affected everybody in everyday life as well. By the end of the 1960s, notions of rights literally redefined America's moral self-understanding. Rights became the currency of authenticity; they became a moral and legal entitlement that allowed wholeness. As people's thirst for their rights grew, they turned increasingly to litigation. Lawyers flocked to join a new class of "highly trained, well paid 'experts'—technocrats, consultants, medical specialists, scientists—that flourished in these dynamic years" (Patterson, 1996:641).

Amidst this, Stringfellow's lifework was distinctive—a radical and dissenting voice which still remained distinct from the dissenting counter-culture. Many of the movements of the 1960s, and in particular the issues and movements discussed in this chapter, were of particular explicit concern to him, but what made him unique was his commitment to biblical politics and the ongoing emergence of his moral theology.

CONCLUSION

The history of the 1960s is vast and complex, and libraries have been written upon its various themes, issues, influences, and moods. In our discussions we have laid out some of the salient themes, issues, influences, and moods which bear upon our forthcoming discussions: for example, the idolic status of JFK and his privatized religion; the role of Johnson's Great Society and its programs for reform; the Civil Rights Movement and the war in Vietnam; along with the rising desire for liberation and freedom which characterized this decade's ending and another's beginning.

It is, perhaps, hard for us now to imagine the fear and the "clear and present danger" of the Cold War which the world, and especially America, felt at this time. These were not distant days of academic scru-

---

ments. One case in point is the Women's Movement, which emerged in response to Betty Friedan's book *The Feminine Mystique* (Friedan,1963).

tiny but days heady with more primal emotion: fear, threat, risk, mortality, outrage, and an imminent sense of impending destruction. Threat ignited fear as nuclear holocaust, which had loomed ominously in the background (and was to continue to do so), now entered the foreground of the horizon of people's lives as a real possibility. Death was imminent; its scale seemingly apocalyptic. Amidst this turmoil America pitted itself publicly and privately as the victim, claiming for itself God's blessing. And from the church, there thundered the collective voice of silence.

Stringfellow addressed America amidst both its feelings of fear and threat and its bullish attitude of invincibility. He was critical of America's position, proclaiming its lack of innocence and identifying it as much a part of the fall, and as much under the power of death, as any other nation. America was not subject to God's special blessing. Therefore, amidst what became seen as his prophetic utterances, it was especially poignant that the politics of the Bible concern living in freedom from the power of death, and this indeed was the dominant theme of Stringfellow's public and private encounters throughout the 1960s and beyond. For this reason he was often described as a critic: indeed *Time* magazine described him as "one of Christianity's most persuasive critics from within."[35] However, instead of understanding his theological focus to be that of *offering criticism*, we should understand it as that of *restoring hope*.[36] For while his words were often harsh and uncompromising, it is the restoration of hope, not the condemnation of judgment, which was its ultimate focus. His hope was for people, the nation, and the church to embody the authentic vocation of salvation.[37]

In sum: in the 1960s and beyond, Stringfellow's understanding of the state of death in America and American Protestantism radicalized further. As his lifework changed, his biblical politics developed. During this time he understood, gradually, the full and pervasive extent of the death which he first identified in Harlem. The next three chapters are an examination of this radicalization, and the way in which his moral theology, and the place of faith and politics therein, developed in its wake.

35. Quoted on the dust jacket to Stringfellow (1966c).

36. It is a matter of emphasis here, for hope and criticism are two sides of the same reality: God's reconciliation of creation. In emphasizing hope I am not omitting criticism, but seeking to ensure that Stringfellow's voice is heard in its fullness: the hopefulness of his theology is often missed amidst the seemingly more prevalent criticism.

37. Stringfellow is a universalist, and the place of judgment is understood in eschatological and soteriological terms: it is a price Christ bore, and it is a judgment which will come. He is keen to remove the notion of human judgment—interpersonal condemnation—as in anyway part of Christian ethics.

5

Resisting Religion

The Vocation of the Church

A S WE PICK UP the story of Stringfellow's life-work, we find him still
located in his beloved East Harlem. Along with the cultural and
political movement which characterized the decade, the 1960s was also
a time of movement for Stringfellow. Initially, this can be seen in the way
he became a national figure—something which appealed to his sense of
the absurd[1]—as he began to write books.

THE VOCATION OF THE CHURCH OF CHRIST

Halfway through 1960, Stringfellow attended a WSCF conference in
Strasbourg. It was not a happy time, and his passion for it was on the
wane, disillusioned, "restless and bored" (Stringfellow, 1960b:1), for they
were too much concerned with systems, bureaucracy, procedure, and abstract attempts at church unity; a "certain absence of the wonder and the
surprise of the gospel" (Stringfellow, 1960b:1) prevailed. He described
the conference in the following way: "Each day we hear recitations of the
historic doctrine of the faith, but what is missing is the authentication
of that in the personal confession of the faith that is characteristic of
Christians" (Stringfellow, 1960b:1).

There were two notable exceptions, Karl Barth and Joseph
Hromadka,[2] both of whom were speaking at the conference; they made
a lasting impression upon him. In particular at this time, Barth conveyed
an "enchanting humanity" (Stringfellow, 1960b:1), while Hromadka

1. See Berrigan (1995:101) for Berrigan's reflections on Stringfellow becoming "infamous."

2. It was also an opportunity to meet with Jacques Ellul, which it seems he did
(Stringfellow, 1960d; Ellul,1960a).

spoke about the way in which Jesus was not respectable and was always found in the midst of those who were not respectable: "He is found in the world—the real, ordinary, broken, perishing world" (Stringfellow, 1960b:1). The conference made Stringfellow restless to return to East Harlem and to his work there. It helped him

> see how much I have learned there and have to learn there, and
> it recalls my affection and affirmance of the world. In that way it
> has helped me much to come here, because I had become, I guess,
> fatigued in East Harlem in the last few months. But now I feel
> refreshed and glad to return. (Stringfellow, 1960b:1)

But in recognizing this, he also recognized that it was time to relinquish involvement in "ecclesiastical and churchly affairs" (Stringfellow, 1960b:1) in order to avoid becoming "as hackneyed as [he] observed some [had]" (Stringfellow, 1960b:1), or worse, a professionalized layman. He was able to give up this involvement because of that which he prized more: his legal practice[3] and his beloved East Harlem. Ensconced in his commitment to Harlem, having turned down high-level appointments to the WCC and various attempts of embrace by the academy,[4] the 1960s commenced in earnest, the themes of Stringfellow's thinking were affirmed by these experiences.

The summer months of the new decade were spent in France, where Stringfellow met up with Karl Barth and Jacques Ellul. In particular, he recalls a most passionate discussion with Ellul over Algeria and the atrocities which the French committed there. It was an event which had considerable impact upon Stringfellow.

Speaking about the state of the churches in western Europe, Ellul explained how many Christians were trapped: on the one hand they do not wish to stay in the church because it was so apostate and decrepit, and yet on the other they cannot leave it and its precincts for to do so would be to turn their back on their responsibility for the "debilitation and unfaithfulness of the church" (Stringfellow, 1962a:4). Initially, Stringfellow protested that things were not yet so acute in the United States. Later he came to think differently, realizing that Ellul described the problem of

3. With two friends, Stringfellow set up a law firm, Ellis, Stringfellow and Patton, in 1961.

4. These included four offers of academic posts, and participation in a colloquy on the church and the University, at which he first met Hans Frei. Stringfellow's views at this colloquy were unpopular. See Church Society for College Work (1958a,b).

American Protestantism most succinctly. And while many in America could complain about the failure of the church, Stringfellow became convinced by Ellul that it was only the Christian who truly knows "the burden of the disunity and apostasy of the churches" (Stringfellow, 1962a:5). What he thought the churches needed was a voice of criticism from within.

Two years later, in 1962, Stringfellow had assimilated Ellul's words and responded in print.[5] What Stringfellow had to say on this subject (the state of the church and religion in America, and the nature of the Christian life) is the focus of this section, for it provides the foundation of the rest of his lifework throughout the 1960s and beyond. His thinking emerged out of his exposure to the power of death and life as they confronted one another, experienced especially, though not exclusively, in East Harlem. Much of his thinking was published in the remarkably dense and slim volume *A Private and Public Faith* (Stringfellow, 1962k).[6]

In *A Private and Public Faith* Stringfellow explores the relationship of the church to religion. His criticisms of religion are similar to those of the law, which we read about earlier. However, what is significant is both their focused and specific nature, and the radicalizing effect the discovery of the principalities and powers appears to have had upon his thinking. While he does not use the language of principalities and powers explicitly at this time, he is clearly working them out,[7] and consequently the way in which his polemic conveys the feeling of distance is much stronger here than previously. Stringfellow was finding his prophetic and proclamatory voice; he was learning his vocation.

5. This was also the year in which he began to write his account of his time in Harlem, *My People is the Enemy* (Stringfellow, 1964d).

6. In this chapter we shall draw mainly upon material from this book and its background sources. One of these, *The Campus Conference on Religion* at the University of Rochester (Stringfellow, 1962o,a), stands out as particularly lucid and relevant to our discussions, and much of it became included in *A Private and Public Faith*. Preparation for this book extends well back into 1961 and can be seen for example in the minutes from the Princeton Study Group, February 3–4, of that year (Princeton Study Group, 1961a,b).

7. It is the central focus of his questions to Karl Barth during the conference which took place in the year of this books publication. See the section "The Advocacy of Karl Barth" in chapter 6.

WRITING

Stringfellow's life as an author began with a direct engagement of the captivity of Christianity: an impassioned polemic—a tract on the state of religion and the churches in America (Stringfellow, 1962k:7). It is at once both personal and political, and bespeaks of his deep and passionate concern for the significance of religion's subject upon America and its people in their relationships with one another.[8]

A recurring theme in Stringfellow's lifework is the desire to avoid being pigeon-holed. In fact, he was strongly antagonistic towards such attempts. He was also concerned that religion avoid the same fate. Such efforts, he thought, were simply ways of avoiding taking him, or life in Christ, seriously. The temptation in American Protestantism was to systematize religion and permanently locate it—and so obscure its fluid and dynamic form—and such attempts were simply expressions of an inability or an unwillingness to take their subject seriously, "obviating the necessity of a real conversation or exchange" (Stringfellow, 1962a:1). Real exchange, he thought, necessitated openness to the dynamic and fluid form of faith: a participation in, or mimicry of, the activity of the Holy Spirit. The polemical style of Stringfellow's writing itself seemed expressive of this form.

Stringfellow's approach to writing was to begin with speeches or sermons, revise them into papers for publication in journals and periodicals, and then refine them further often in publication in his books. Often the process of delivery and revision in periodical form was a lengthy and repetitive one, and clearly this was the process by which he crystallized his thought. However, it is also reflective of the immediacy and fluidity of the message—his was an eternal response to an immediate context. In some ways then, reading his books was the worst way of engaging Stringfellow—far better to go and hear him and experience his words as they come to life. In adopting this style, his desire was to bring to the reader some sense of the Word in his words, and address the reader as he would an audience. His choice of style also speaks to his concern to avoid being pigeonholed. As we have seen, his academic abilities were not lacking, and it would have been quite feasible to write

---

8. The similarities with Barth (1939) are apparent, and further driven home by Stringfellow's use of such headings as "The service of the priesthood to the laity" and "The service of the laity to the world."

in more academic prose, but his style told something about his under-standing of the nature of theology.

> The work of theology is the work of the whole people of God
> . . . Some aspects of theology—that is, specifically the work of
> apologetics and moral theology—are peculiarly the office of the
> laity in the encounter in their practical lives between the Word of
> God and the ordinary life of the world. (Stringfellow, 1962k:47)

For Stringfellow, theology needed to be accessible and down to earth, and it needed to be contextual: listening to the world amidst the Word. Stringfellow's chosen style goes further; it witnesses to the presence of the Word in the world by mirroring our encounter with that same Word in the world. His writing is generally biographical—empirical reality aris-ing in anecdote and parable, witnessing to and reflecting upon the life of the Spirit in the world. The narrative becomes self-involving, drawing the reader in, moving the reader from observation to participation; his style and his writing are orientational. Therefore, at its most fundamen-tal level, he chose this polemical form because he wanted us to listen to the Word of God. What better way than proclamation (Stringfellow, 1962k:48)?

One final thing worth noting about his books is their format. Continuing the polemical theme, all of them are effectively commentar-ies and expositions, and each book tends to focus upon a specific book of the Bible for its theological discourse with the world or situation Stringfellow engages. In the case of *A Private and Public Faith,* the book is Colossians.

Religion

As the new decade got underway, Stringfellow spoke passionately about the state of American Protestantism, eager to rescue it from its decline and demise. This was a period of "moral revolution" in America, and the mainline churches went out of their way to try and accommodate the modern world.[9] At the heart of his criticisms was the function and survival of American Protestantism amidst the eschewing tendencies of what were considered the very means of maintaining American freedom

---

9. The emphasis in moral revolution was private and personal: personal morality as the key to living the public life.

of religion and democracy: the constitutional provision of individualism (privatization), and the separation of church and state.

For Stringfellow, the problem with religion is that it represents the human quest for God (or some God-like substitute) rather than a faithful response to God's quest for us in Christ. Religion, in short, is an idol, and what is at stake is the question of how we know ourselves and our authentic existence—simultaneously the questions of knowledge of God and vocation.

> The gospel tells when and how and why and where God has sought us and found us and offered to take us into His life. Religion is the attempt to satisfy the curiosity of men in this world about God; Jesus Christ is the answer to the curiosity of men in this world about what it means to be truly a man in this world which God created . . . religion supposes that God is yet to be discovered; Christianity knows that God has already come among us. (Stringfellow, 1962k:15–16)

For American Protestantism the answer had, especially at this time, been mined from the provinces of privately held faith.[10] The problem of the privatization of religion goes deep into the American psyche, and it confronted Stringfellow head-on as a lawyer through the constitutional separation of church and state. And yet, working within this framework Stringfellow came to see its paradoxical nature and became aware of its distorted and distorting character.

> The American law of separation of church and state and of freedom of religion represents, somewhat paradoxically, the insinuation of a particular confessional theology into public policy, and, at the same time, that public policy assumes that polity and theology are severable. Superficially, of course, the supposed dichotomy between polity and theology, reflected in court decisions and in statutes dealing with religious societies, sounds as though it upholds the separation of state and church. Yet responsible ecumenical discussion in this country among the churches denies any dichotomy between polity and theology. Such a denial challenges anew the notion that the law is neutral toward religion; it exposes the law as still serving the requirements of the polity of Protestant dissent. (Stringfellow, 1961a:17)

10. In that way, the existentialism of the Christian Faith and Life Community fitted quite well into the established patterns of American Protestantism and religion. See "The Adventure of Biblical Politics" below.

He saw, as we shall come to appreciate when we examine one of his most public encounters during 1963, that the influence of White Anglo-Saxon Protestantism (WASP) was at the heart of American identity. Moreover, he thought that WASP was part of the problem and was so in a very public and central way.

Constitutional provision of the separation of church and state resulted in the *overt* removal of religion from the political and public life—the everyday life—of Americans. Combined with the emphasis upon the individual and individualism, through which each person becomes "the author of their own religion" (Stringfellow, 1962k:19), "a personal faith in God" is manifest in the private life of individuals, and together as they seek God in the sanctity and safety of the church. But the church exists generally to foster and encourage this personal faith: it provides a public space for individuals to manifest their God. Faith in God is therefore publicly manifest in the form of personal ethical decision making and morality, detached from God's activity in the world. Stringfellow sees the consequences of such introspective, individualized thinking in terms of three interrelated manifestations, that beguiled American Protestantism, in which knowledge of God is replaced with the practice of religion.

The first is the cult of "positive thinking," which religion uses for "the aggrandizement of whatever interest or objective the practitioner of religion wishes to attain or acquire" (Stringfellow, 1962k:26). This kind of religion makes an association of God with the goals of personal success, wealth, personal security, and good fortune, with little, if any, regard for the victims of their good fortune. Stringfellow thinks it was seen most clearly in the doctrines of free enterprise, which American Protestantism had done much to support. Religion does little other than promote and confirm one's own ambitions and desires. God will help those who help themselves, and those that get ahead, deserve it.

Second is the "vaguely spiritual values to which the nation is just as vaguely committed" (Stringfellow, 1962k:30)—in other words, the dominant American belief that one should have some sort of religion, in that religion provides a foundation for moral behavior. The notion that religion was only concerned with conduct and behavior—a private belief which gave rise to particular moral conduct, was embodied most prominently at the time by John F. Kennedy's wife, who "allowed that religion was very important and very good for children but ought not to enter something important and adult like politics" (Stringfellow, 1962o:2).

It is alleged that the constitutional treatment of religion as a private and personal thing provides for religious freedom in America. Yet from his experiences overseas and with the ecumenical movement, Stringfellow indicates how other nations allow for religious freedom without this constitutional conception. Rather than harmony, he contends, it brings little more than the public profession of atheism. Protestantism, in short, has been accommodated into American culture and its religious notions: an accommodation which Stringfellow's moral theology would eventually reverse.

Perhaps the clearest example of this is the third manifestation, which in fact grows out of the first two. This took the form of the extremely popular religious revival which had swept across America in the post-war period, and had embraced a nation's craving for "religiosity" or morality as a basis for identity and personal success/wealth creation. Amongst its protagonists were evangelists like Billy Graham.[11] American Protestantism had identified very strongly with this revival, and Stringfellow injected his criticism as it reeled to the news that the revival which it sponsored was now in steep decline. Church attendance plummeted, and religious affiliations were no longer canvassed, especially upon the nation's campuses. Yet while concern was abroad amidst American Protestantism about recession and decline, Stringfellow takes solace, describing the decline as the happiest and healthiest thing "to happen in America for a long time" (Stringfellow, 1962k:11). It was a so-called revival, which did little more than reflect the "fat of post-war America" (Stringfellow, 1962k:11), sanctify its way of life, and lend credence to its indulgence and wealth, amidst a world of poverty and need. Out of the wilderness of East Harlem, Stringfellow's was an isolated voice of dissent, proclaiming the covert and troubling way in which the church and state in America embraced and upheld one another. The revival and its protagonists merely exposed, in a popular way, that which was already latent in American Protestantism.

> The post-war religious revival represented an outburst of allegiance to and acclaim for what are deeply embedded notions about religion in the American mentality. And more specifically,

---

11. Stringfellow had planned a book on Billy Graham, the working title for which appears to have been "The Apostasy of Billy Graham." Although never finished, the project was planned to the point of including photographs, including one of Graham holding Nixon's coat (Langkjaer, 1969).

one suspects that the religious revival was a response to and exploitation of the self-confidence, sense of destiny, and realization
of power that marked post-war America, a response nourished
by an idea of religion which American Protestantism, at least,
had harbored for generations . . . How far have the strange shib-
boleths spawned in the American pluralistic experience infected
Protestantism? Or do American Protestants much care anyway
what they believe, or what the Church is, or how the gospel relates
to contemporary life, so long as the institutional existence of the
churches is protected and the churches retain an amiable reputation in the community? If the public idols of the recent religious
revival are repudiated, or what is more likely, just increasingly
neglected and ignored by society, does American Protestantism
have anything, or, more precisely, any One to offer or commend
as replacement, or will Protestantism retract and conserve and
wait until attracted by some idol in the offing? (Stringfellow,
1962k:12–13)

In his impassioned plea, Stringfellow believes American Protestantism
had arrived at a crossroads: could it extricate itself from the mistaken
thoughts and practices of the revival in which religion functioned as
the "religious disguise and aura of American society" (Stringfellow,
1962k:13), and thus return to the gospel, or had it, in its association
with the revival, irrecoverably abandoned and disassociated from the
gospel?

However, those of the revival held the Bible in high regard, and
Stringfellow acknowledges that for this at least, they should be com-
mended. Yet their focus upon individualistic religion, detached from,
and occasionally in disdain towards, the church as Christ's body in the
world and serving the world, is problematic. For revivalists extolled personal sin as the cause of our own fallenness and the fallenness of all
creation, and took the view that if we suffer at the hands of principalities
and powers then it is a direct consequence of our own sin. The ills and
disorders of society were therefore seen as a direct result of the sinful
desires of humanity: individual sin is to blame, and only repentance will
lead to positive change and the eradication of the ills which afflict the
nation and its people.

The emphasis upon human sin of course extols the place of humanity in the world; it makes us central. The focus of this religion is "not the
initiative of God in history but the practice of religion by the individual
in some singular, stereotyped act of personal volition and emotion" in or-

der to bring about some desired result (Stringfellow, 1962k:28). It places us at the heart of our own religion, a kind of "positive thinking," and one suspects, this is "positive thinking for the lower classes" (Stringfellow, 1962k:28).

Against these three manifestations, movement was afoot to redress the problem amongst those who saw the dilemma and decline of religion in the modern age. Predominantly, those concerned with lay Christianity and the Christian faith in the modern world were asking a similar set of questions to Stringfellow's, and were increasingly drawn towards the "Death of God" movement for an answer.[12]

However, again taking a stance of opposition and resistance, Stringfellow believed this movement was part of the problem, not part of the solution. He was surrounded by American Protestantism on the one side, and radical movements on the other—each mistakenly pigeon-holing him in one or other "camp."

Stringfellow thought the popularity of the Death of God move-ment obscured many of the real issues of church life at that time, and especially the fundamental and important difference between religion and the gospel. To his mind, there was little to separate the movement from the establishment it rallied against, for it did nothing other than re-invent and repackage that which the biblical adventure already dis-closed. Illustrating both his criticism and the authenticity of the Bible in his thinking, Stringfellow later wrote:

> If these voices are asserting that acculturated conceptions of God are inappropriate and impotent, they are categorically right. They are also very tardy with the news, since Saint Paul made that the theme of a sermon to the Athenians twenty centuries ago. If these self-styled radicals are arguing that institutional religion is no longer worthy of the allegiance of men, they are also quite correct, though that's hardly a revelation. The ministry of Christ himself in this world made mere religion trivial and obsolete. If they are, on the other hand, propounding as *Time* magazine reports that they are, some "new" idea of God fitted to twentieth-century secular life, then they are pathetically confused. They are imitating the very thing they repudiate . . . What the "death of God" movement authentically could expose, I suggest, is the radi-cal, original, biblical distinction between religion and the gospel.

12. The Death of God movement was represented most succinctly, for example, by John Robinson (Robinson, 1963).

... [For] the theme of the gospel is not man seeking God, but just the opposite, God in quest of man. (Stringfellow, 1966b)[13]

While they were in agreement that for the church to be the church religion must end, Stringfellow thought this movement wanted to merely substitute one idolatrous edifice with another. What is at stake here is the gospel, and the division between gospel and religion is biblically determined. The Bible, in other words, is the primary witness to the truth of God's presence in the world; the primary witness of God seeking us. The Bible reveals the politics of the Kingdom, the way in which creation is ordered and the way in which its parts relate to its creator. Biblical politics, therefore, is the response of faith to the call of God; the response of obedience to hearing the Word. It is the antithesis of the religion which so swamped America at that time. The gospel reveals the truth of God's presence primarily in the world, not the sanctuary, and so any faith which takes the God who reveals Himself to us on the cross seriously must be engaged in the world, the common life. It is to this God to which the gospel bears witness, and in the gospel, knowledge of God is a matter of God's revelation, not our imagination. Faith originates from our response to God encountering us in the world (our response to God seeking us) and not from our private thoughts or abstract notions.

> God's presence and action in common life means that it is possible that man may know something of God—something beyond speculation and surmise—something quite concrete and certain—something, also, immediately, intimately and truly personal. God's witness to himself in history encompasses His specific grace and action in your own life and mine ... The possibility that I may know anything of God originates in His first coming to me, in His first knowing me ... The possibility of my faith belongs to His existence. The opportunity for faith is given in His initiative toward me, or any other man. Faith in God begins and is sustained in and consummated in the fidelity of God to his own creation. (Stringfellow, 1962k:17–18)

For Stringfellow this is the journey of obedience which we take into the world. The issue Stringfellow is dealing with here is the place of faith in politics, addressing the way in which religion is preoccupied with "the sanctuary, not the marketplace" (Stringfellow, 1962k:20), and the way the

---

13. This article was also reprinted as Stringfellow (1967c).

presence of God—alive, active and living in the world—had become so obscured.

Stringfellow thought religion was essentially the consecration of a power or an ideology or a person, or a projection of God outside of history or inside the self, the unknowable, the absolute, the subjective, the archetypal deity. But the God of the Christian faith is found not in philosophy, not in ideology, idols, imagination, speculation, nor *any* attempt by us to construct a means, no matter how well meaning, to attain knowledge of who God is or how God acts, including for example, law, justice, democracy, Marxism, or indeed, free-market capitalism. American Protestantism stood on the brink, and he sought to call it back. His message was clear: remember, repent, return, recount. The gospel, not religion, is the key to vocation; the key to who we are and how we act, the key to identity and ethics.

Throughout this confrontation, Stringfellow focuses his gaze internally: on the life of the church, theology, and discipleship. However, his writing is located in the world, which at first sight would appear to suggest his attentions were actually externally motivated (that is, motivated by a perspective external to faith). This apparent juxtaposition of perspective is of significance to Stringfellow's task, for his argument is essentially that the life of the church and the life of faith have been removed from the presence of God have and become defined and understood predominantly by the external perspective upon faith, either in terms of privatized religion, pietism, and personal morality, or in terms of philosophical or ideological positing of notions of God. In all, God has become a matter for private speculation rather than public obedience, and God has come to be understood as being located in the church, a sub-culture or sub-location of wider society. In what might appear little more than a confusing paradox, he insists that the internal perspective of faith is located not in the church nor in private prayer life but in the world, for the world is the location of God's being and God's action through the Holy Spirit. Rescuing the identity of the church therefore necessitates the recovery of biblical politics, for at its heart is our encounter with God in the mundane everyday world.

Religion is the (fallen) work of human hands, sustained by our own efforts; faith in God is "a work of the holy spirit" (Stringfellow, 1962k:18), sustained in God and his creation, and in this faith our lives are returned to us as a gift, by God (our vocation).

> Religious speculation suspects there is God, somewhere, some-
> time; the gospel reports His presence and action in this world
> even in those circumstances within which we are unaware of
> Him. Religion suppresses the truth, because the truth obviates
> Religion . . . The news of God embodied in Jesus Christ is that
> God is openly and notoriously active in the world. In this news
> the Christian Church is constituted; it is this news which the
> Christian Church exists to spread. (Stringfellow, 1962k:16–17)

So, what kind of church does Stringfellow envision? What vision did he
offer American Protestantism that it might be renewed? It is upon his
answer we now focus.

THE LIFE OF THE CHURCH: ITS MISSION AND MINISTRY

The main focus of *Private and Public Faith* is twofold: to identify the
vocation of the church, and put to forward a theology of the Christian
life, and in so doing call American Protestantism to account. We have
already covered much ground with respect to Stringfellow's understanding of the church's vocation, and by 1962 his position had not shifted
substantially. However, he had developed, deepened, and distilled it
through the lens of his experience in East Harlem.

The focus of his ecclesiology (that is, the purpose of the church
and its ministry) is here concerned to balance the internal life of the
church with its external life in the world—the gathered church and the
church in dispersal, with the emphasis upon its dispersed life. Therefore,
the focus of his book and our analysis here will also be upon this aspect of his ecclesiology, namely, the Christian life in the world. In short,
through *Private and Public Faith* Stringfellow establishes the agenda for
his theology throughout the decade, within the context of the church's
own identity; he established the politics of faith.

The mission of the church had become unclear, and its form seemingly irrelevant. People were giving up on the church more than they
were giving up on God, or at least "religion" and spirituality. According to
Stringfellow, the churches were dysfunctional, debilitated, and apostate.
In response, he was committed to the "reform from within" which Ellul
had put him onto, for him and for all Christians. He encouraged everyone's dissent to be bold "lest their reluctance or timidity in acting aggra-
vate further that against which they speak" (Stringfellow, 1962k:34).[14]

14. Later, in 1970, Stringfellow's attitude towards the church had shifted somewhat.
He had not rejected the institutional church, far from it, he still understood the church

For Stringfellow, the ministry of the church is a threefold task: worship, witness, and ministry. The task of witness is the task of evangelism.[15] While evangelism was the work of the church, conversion was the work of God, and evangelism for Stringfellow constitutes simply

> the public proclamation in the world of the presence of the Word of God in the common life of the world ... fundamentally [it] is an appeal to a man to remember that which is the radical and original truth of his own being. Evangelism does not bear the Word of God to those to whom the Word is utterly unknown. The evangelist merely calls upon the one whom he addresses to recollect the One who made him and for whom he was made. The evangelist asks him to recall, as it were, his own creation in the Word of God, to remember who he truly is, to recover his very life ... Evangelism calls upon men to remember and recognize the presence and activity of God in their own particular lives. Conversion is the event of that recall and recognition. (Stringfellow, 1963e:6–7)

There is, therefore, a simplicity to evangelism, which evokes diverse and personal encounter. Evangelism and servanthood form the essence of the life of the church (the Christian life) dispersed in the world. But the character and ambition of the church's ministry must always be that of servanthood.

> The ministry of the church as the Body of Christ in the world is the same as the ministry of Christ. The ministry of Christ is the ministry of a servant in the world and for the world—a servant of the world in the name of God ... It is not ... the Church which

---

in pentecostal perspective to be the "exemplary society of reconciled humanity" or a holy nation (Stringfellow, 1970d:1346). He remained a communicant of the Episcopal church because its liturgy in some way represented the early church which emerged from the Bible. However, there was little else that compelled him to membership, and he described his "conviction as an Anglican as one of benign disaffection" (Stringfellow, 1970d:1346). It was a position brought about by a decade in which he increasingly exposed the depths of the veracity of death, and in so doing marginalized himself increasingly from most, if not all, institutions and associations. Simply, his message marginalized him.

15. With regards to evangelism, Stringfellow obviously writes amidst the rise and fall of the evangelistic work of the "so-called revival," and this is important because he is here effectively re-appropriating evangelism within a different ecclesiological and theological understanding. This "re-appropriation" is his approach to both the law and religion, and speaks of his commitment to the reality of the reconciliation of the principalities in Christ.

has introduced God to the world. God knows the world, and, indeed, the world is His own, without the Church. The Church has only the task of introducing the world to God. (Stringfellow, 1962k:77, 57)[16]

The ministry of the church, Stringfellow maintains, is a ministry of great extravagance; an extravagance through which the world might know God. As the Body of Christ it necessitates the church live a life like His, an embodiment of the "reckless, scandalous expenditure of His life for the sake of the world's life" (Stringfellow, 1962k:77).[17] Like His, the church's should also be "not a very prudential life, not a very conservative life, not a very cautious life, not—by ordinary standards—a very successful life" (Stringfellow, 1962k:77). The location of the church in Stringfellow's theology is in the world, amidst God's presence: a community, serving the world for the world, pointing always to the reality of God at work in the world—a sign, a sacrament. God does not dwell in the sanctuary, but is alive and at work in the whole world. The church is part of that world. The extravagance of the church means having freedom, unencumbered by its history, its politics, or its wealth.

To illustrate this point, Stringfellow relays a story of a clergyman who rang to ask for advice. The clergyman told of a woman who had been evicted because she couldn't pay her rent and had grievances against her landlord. He seeks Stringfellow's counsel on how to proceed and what their recourse in law might be. Stringfellow, who is running late to catch an aeroplane, answers promptly: "Well, sell one of your tapestries and pay the rent" (Stringfellow, 1962k:79). He then hung up and caught the plane. During his flight Stringfellow tells us that he began to think he had been a bit rude, and resolved to ring him and apologize. By the time the plane has landed, however, he had rejected this notion and is once again firm in his resolve. The freedom of the church, he says, is precisely that freedom to sell one of its tapestries to pay the rent, whether or not the person has a just cause. That is the extravagance of the gospel and of the church.

> If they have *that* freedom, then . . . does the tapestry have religious significance . . . The tapestry is an authentically Christian symbol only when it represents the freedom in Christ to give up

16. See also Stringfellow (1963n).

17. Note the echoes of his earlier personal note mentioned in chapter 3, under the section "Reconciliation: Emergence of Faith and Politics."

any aspect of the inherited and present life of the institutional church, including, but not limited to, possessions, for the sake of the world . . . Mission is itself the only charity which Christians have to offer the poor, the only work which Christians have to do . . . When the Church has the freedom itself to be poor among the poor, it will know how to use what riches it has. When the Church has that freedom, it will know how to minister among the rich and powerful. When the Church has that freedom, it will be a missionary people again in all the world. (Stringfellow, 1962k:79, 80, 81)

This story and Stringfellow's reflection upon it summaries his understanding of the church's vocation very well, and shows how its life of worship is now understood in more sacrificial terms. Stringfellow is emphasizing the need for the churches to move beyond serving themselves (maintenance) to serving the world (mission and ministry), and so recover their (long) forgotten identity; a process of re-membering. Doubtless his critique emerged from his experience of both the World Council of Churches and the Episcopal Church in the United States. In his critique of religion and the church Stringfellow is calling the church to account to resist the fallen powers, yet he fights shy of describing it in those terms. We can only speculate, but perhaps he is aware that to do so may obscure the very problem he wishes to illuminate at this point, and may, due to the apparent biblical illiteracy from which he claims the churches suffers, fall on deaf ears.

It seems Stringfellow is indicating to his audience the simple fact that the ministry of the church is the mission of God. Everything the church does must therefore work to that end. It is not that the church has a mission in the world, but rather that God (Word and Spirit, with and from the Father) has a mission in the world, reconciling it to himself, and this mission includes the (authentic) church. The outlook for mission and ministry (i.e., for the vocation of the church) takes place in the world, in God's Kingdom, not in the enclave of some institution or body removed from and set aside from the world. Literally, the church witnesses amidst and among the fall, for "the experience of being a Christian is one of continually encountering in the ordinary and everyday life the same Word of God which is announced and heard, remembered and dramatized, expected and fulfilled in the sanctuary of the Church" (Stringfellow, 1962k:57). Simply, the church is the servant of the Word, not vice versa.

Furthermore, the church exists to point beyond itself, not to itself—to point to the life of God in the world. It exists for God's glory, not its own. The church witnesses to the politics of God and the economy of God, as it is manifest in the world, and should not be constricted and limited by its own politics and systems which constrict the churches vision of God at work in the world. The extravagance of this life is that it will overturn our vain ambitions, our desire for stability, our desire for maintaining our own lives (order and familiarity), and deliver us as a church to the freedom of self-sacrifice, the freedom to expend its life, imitating Christ's ministry. Thus, to be the church of Christ, the church must dwell in the freedom which Christ affords, not the selfish desire of our hearts; to be able to give up the edifices, systems, politics, power, wealth, and hollow rituals that forever work together against the church being the community of believers witnessing to God in the freedom of-Christ, literally *as* Christ's body. That, it seems to me, is the essence of Stringfellow's message. The church of Christ, dispersed and gathered, dwells in the freedom of Christ in the world in God's midst and lives extravagantly for the world's sake: it is a freedom *for* humanity (Stringfellow, 1962k:68–73, 77–93).

In Stringfellow's ecclesiology, it is worth noting that great emphasis is placed upon the churches' need for unity, not God's: unity, for Stringfellow, is sacramental in that it is the outward sign of reconciliation to God. While I understand his motivation, namely that unity had become a god in itself to many organizations and churches at that time, there nevertheless seems an inconsistency here. Surely God does seek unity in the reconciliation of creation to himself, and while the act is accomplished in an act of grace through Christ, the process is ongoing through God's mission in the world. Stringfellow seems to miss this point, and it is a potentially important one.[18]

18. The notion of consistency Stringfellow describes as a "hob-goblin of faith." He has a point: consistency can be the means by which truth is eroded and ideology succeeds, as our knowledge of God becomes systematized and ordered. However, while his rhetoric is seemingly effective, it is at once undermined by the apparent inconsistency in his understanding of the church's identity and God's. I suspect that what he may have been indicating is that God in God's-self is perfect unity, rather than any negation of the mission of God and our witness to it. Furthermore, Stringfellow fully appreciated that our knowledge of God and ourselves is partial, and cannot be fully fulfilled until the eschaton. If Stringfellow was indicating this, then what we have here is a matter of polemic emphasis.

Now, it is interesting and poignant that Stringfellow's example is one concerning wealth—not, for example, the sacrifice of one's own life. This goes to the heart of the culture of wealth and success (the culture of prosperity) that abounded at that time, both in American society and the church. The church had made generous accommodation to society in this regard, and lavished the extravagance of wealth upon itself while prudence and caution were its watchwords in terms of its self-expenditure on behalf of the world. He seeks to redress this "accommodation of the churches to the world [and] the appeasement and compromises by which the churches equivocate in their witness and mission in the world" (Stringfellow, 1962k:85). The churches desire for accommodation led them to want to be culturally popular, liked, full, and to be places of unity not discord.

It was on this last issue, unity, that he had rallied against the WCC two years prior, and for the same reasons: the unity of the churches is for their own benefit, not God's; it "originates in the need of the churches of God, not the other way round" (Stringfellow, 1962k:34). Simply, God makes his own witness in the world, whether or not the churches witness to it: God is not dependent upon the churches, but the churches are dependent upon God and the world, in which God dwells.[19] God's own witness is free from the church's corruption, but that freedom should not be used as an excuse by the churches to ignore the need for reform, for "the very vocation of the churches to become and be the Church is in order to honor and praise and participate in the witness of God to Himself in the world." In other words, what Stringfellow seems to be saying is that when the church is true to its vocation, it participates in God, through participating in God's self-witness. The churches, when they are truly Christ's church, belong to God, not the world. This is in effect a refinement of his previous work on the church in his paper on worship.

Stringfellow is also clear at this point that good governance of the church (i.e., the role of the episcopate) is critical to the church's life: "The way the church is governed and who governs a church is integral to the faith which the church confesses and represents in the world" (Stringfellow, 1961a:17). However, the first and most radical change, the one which must take place before others can flow forth, begins with the

---

19. Faithful proclamation in the churches is a kind of dialogue, therefore, between the Word of God in the Bible and liturgy and the Word of God as it is seen and heard in the common lives of the congregation in the world (Stringfellow, 1962k:36).

inner life of the churches, specifically their understanding of the priest-hood and the laity, and in tones which can only be described as honoring Karl Barth's *Church and State* (Barth, 1939), he explores them through the subheadings of "service of the priesthood to the laity" and the "service of the laity to the world."

This crucial recognition of the importance of this relationship is rooted in his involvement in the ecumenical and lay-theology move-ments. He emphasizes the interdependence and difference between both laity and priesthood[20] in an attempt to address and redress the profes-sionalization of the clergy, the denigration of the laity, and the academic abuse of theology this professionalization and denigration fostered. This reordering of crucial relationships, authority, role, power, and politics is the foundation of the theology of the Christian life which he wishes to develop.

> There is no priesthood without a laity serving the world; there is no laity without a priesthood serving the laity. There is not one without the other. In many Protestant churches today there is neither. (Stringfellow, 1962k:38)

The roles of the priesthood and the laity had become disastrously con-fused: the clergy, as "professional Christians," viewed their role as repre-senting the church in the world. Ordination, rather than baptism, was viewed by many as the true seal of the Christian faith, and therapy rather than confession the primary resource of their ministry (Stringfellow, 1962k:44).

The laity, on the other hand, understood their role as worshipping in the church—sidelined to the role of spectators, and predominantly happy in their new role: "that the clergy act as substitute laity, and the laity are just observers of religion is of course consistent with and prob-ably the product of the American idea that religion has only to do with religion, but not with the cares of the world" (Stringfellow, 1962k:38). It is symptomatic of the churches' withdrawal from involvement in daily life, whereby the missionary energies of the church become internalized: evangelization, rather than worship, becomes the preoccupation of the internal life of the church. Attempts to rectify this included the profes-sionalization of laity (e.g., lay readers), but these are equally misguided,

20. Stringfellow's own footnotes explain that his use of priesthood here is aimed directly at ordained clergy, so one could, for instance, happily substitute clergy for priesthood.

for what Stringfellow has identified is the way in which the churches have come to inhabit an ideology (of professionalism and idealism). Functioning at the time was the notion that matters of religion and faith were not directly relevant to matters of the world, and some "translation" was required: this translation took the form of personal morality, which accompanied the idea of "making the gospel relevant" for modern culture. No translation was necessary, held Stringfellow—"the Body of Christ lives in the world as the unity of God and the world in Christ"— and when gathered in sacramental worship it offers "the world to God, not for His sake, not for their own sake, but for the sake of the world ... [celebrating] God's presence in the world, and on behalf of the world" (Stringfellow, 1962k:41).

Stringfellow's understanding of the role of laity and priesthood bespeaks his understanding of the vocation of the church. It can be summarized in the following manner. The ministry of the priesthood is to members of the body, and the ministry of the laity is (notoriously and visibly) to members of the world. The priesthood is a ministry devoted to the health and holiness of the members of the Body of Christ in the world, "in their relations to each other, relations consequent to their incredibly diversified ministry within the world" (Stringfellow, 1962k:44). The ministry of priesthood is primarily concerned with the internal well-being of the church. Meanwhile, the ministry of the laity is concerned with the well being of the world, proclaiming the presence of the Spirit and the work of Christ in diverse ways. Being a priest does not mean one is not also laity, but rather it means that one must be clear about one's roles. The laity's evangelistic mission is not internal but external, for it takes place in the world not the church, and a dysfunctional "anomaly emerges when evangelization rather than worship becomes characteristic of the interior life of the congregation" (Stringfellow, 1962k:39). This anomaly of which Stringfellow speaks is most characteristic of the clerical paradigm. Being laity, therefore, which by virtue of baptism all Christians are, is a radically public thing to be. The laity and the priesthood go together and require one another for the total ministry of Christ's church. However, precisely because of confusion about the identity and task of the church and its ministry, this dysfunctional missiological anomaly is the one that persists in many Protestant churches. At the heart of his concrete ideas for transformation was his idea of the seminary underground.

THE SEMINARY UNDERGROUND[21]

The ministry of the priesthood is a ministry to the members of
the Body in their relations to each other, relations consequent to
their incredibly diversified ministry within the world . . . This is
the ministry which cares for and conserves the tradition of the
Church—that is, the continuity and integrity of the Christian
mission ever since Pentecost. This is the ministry devoted to
the health and holiness of the Body of Christ in the world . . .
Candidates for seminary admission in Protestantism have not,
very often, in the first instance, been invited into such a ministry.
They have instead been invited into a community of students and
scholars examining the history of religion . . . Or they have been
induced to think of the ordained ministry as a profession and
specialty, like social work or medicine or law. They are expected
only, though sometimes necessarily, to have an academic interest
in the Christian faith and there has been much emphasis upon
the amenities of the "profession of the ministry" . . . Some semi-
narians think . . . that ordination, *rather than baptism,* is the seal
of the Christian life . . . That leads . . . to a stylized clericalism
within the Church, to the segregation of the clergy from the laity, to the assumption by the clergy of the tasks of the laity, and
to the inevitable neglect of the tasks of both clergy and laity.
(Stringfellow, 1962k:43, 44, 45)

It seems Stringfellow identified the way in which the structures at work
in the church are directly attributable to the structures imposed and
encouraged through the theological education of the clergy for their
ministry, and in turn the educational structure and rationale (secular
academic) that is adopted in the clergy's educational experience. There
is, in short, a denigration of the laity and a professionalization of the
clergy, representing an adoption of the "expert" and "amateur" distinction prevalent outside the church.

There is a structural conformity to secularism in clerical and theological education and church. And amidst this, Stringfellow is concern-

---

21. The idea of the underground seminary came from the Confessing Church.
Renaming it as the seminary underground is a more recent development and is attributable to Bill Wylie-Kellermann (Wylie-Kellermann, 1995). Stringfellow himself
referred to it in the former manner, rather than the latter. However in renaming it
Wylie-Kellermann has sought to emphasize its broad and encompassing nature, beyond
the strict confines of the "seminary." Wylie-Kellermann's own practical and significant
work in developing the Seminary Underground must also be acknowledged.

ed then with ordinary Christians whose lives are authored by God's grace not their own virtue, and the authority for such Christians to discern and live this life (Christian identity) is given in baptism: a neglected and disregarded sacrament (Stringfellow, 1994). He is concerned, in other words, with Christ's church, Christ's body in the world, and the loss of authority bestowed in baptism. Baptism, as we shall see, is the key to understanding Stringfellow's theology of the Christian life of unity (reconciliation) in Christ. This loss of authority sustains and re-enforces the clerical paradigm. However, in contrast to being defined secularly, Wylie-Kellermann indicates that Stringfellow viewed the secular vocation of both church and seminary to be nothing more or less than "the exemplary institution, the redeemed principality, disabused of its own survival" (Wylie-Kellermann,1995:66) founded upon and sustained by the Word of God.

Stringfellow is aware that any practical change to the church would need to begin with changes to theological education. It is not surprising, therefore, that Stringfellow envisioned the effects of his theology upon theological education. He described the "altered seminary" or the "anti-seminary," or the revised theological school that he envisions, as the "seminary underground" (Wylie-Kellermann, 1995): an alternative community for biblical study and reflection for resourcing the Christian life, seeking to foster the character of critical or second naiveté, seeking to foster people living the Christian life in the church of Christ.

The idea of the seminary underground came directly from Stringfellow's encounter with the Confessing Church in Germany, and in particular his encounter with the resistance seminary, founded by Dietrich Bonhoeffer (the theme of resistance was also to prove influential to Stringfellow's understanding of the life of the Christian).[22] It seeks to go beyond the seminary-taught knowledge of the Bible and its concern for the application of such knowledge (theory) to Christian and church practice. This approach treats the Bible "as a dead word and not the Living Word. Such a view of the Bible authorizing evidently a merely academic use of the Bible, if pressed to its final logic, challenges the versatility and generosity of God's revelation in history" (Stringfellow, 1967a:55–56).

His rejection of the theory-to-practice model, characterized by "making the gospel relevant," and his rejection of the therapeutic culture

22. See Stringfellow (1973a:274–76). The genesis of Stringfellow's seminary underground can be seen in Stringfellow (1967a:61–72) and Stringfellow (1962k:56–76).

of ministry which prevailed at the time,[23] is funded by a commitment to the reality of the Word of God manifest in the world, which we examined above. God, he contends, is not a stranger among us who needs expert introduction. Rather, the meaning of the incarnation is such that God's Word is addressed to all people, in the very events and relationships that constitute existence in this world. The world is where God is, where the laity are, and where the theologians should be. Knowledge of this reality comes primarily through faith.

> The seminaries have generally been so covetous of academic recognition, and so anxious for locus within the ethos and hierarchy of the university, that they have not noticed how alien and hostile those premises are to the peculiar vocation of the seminary. Thus, the seminaries succumb to disseminating ideological renditions of the faith which demean the vitality of the biblical witness by engaging in endless classifications and comparisons of ideas. All this eschews commitment and precludes a confessional study of theology . . . The seminary's manner in the preparation and qualification of those to be ordained should exemplify the church rather than imitate the university . . . . That does not imply that to be a Christian requires one to be nonsensical or to neglect to engage the intelligence in the exposition and practice of the Christian faith. It just means that the gospel is *not* essentially ideational or conceptionalistic or speculative. Theology is not the same thing as ideology. Faith is categorically different from adherence to a philosophic point of view. Faith is an event in the drama of life in this world. (Stringfellow, 1977b:13)

And, while faith encompasses the intellect, it also encompasses the whole person: mind, feelings, and the "guts of men as well" (Stringfellow, 1977b:13). Theology, Stringfellow insisted, was concerned with faith, not learning; engagement not speculation; the reality of the Word, not ideas and ideologies independently born of the human intellect. This view directly engaged and contrasted with the dominant mood amidst

---

23. For a critique and example of this, see the work of Thomas Oden. Oden's is a story of embrace and then distance in relation to modern therapeutic culture, and led to an attempt to recover the specific *theological* identity of pastoral care and counseling, grounded in the Word of God and Scripture (Oden, 1966, 1967, 1983). The similarities between Oden's pastoral theology and understanding of authentic humanity and Stringfellow's are distinct, and their common source seems to be Barth. Oden advocates a *postmodern orthodoxy*: the substance of inherited and revealed faith rather than a faith watered down by modernity (Oden, 1979).

the church, its seminaries, its clergy, and its laity, for maintaining and nurturing the various kinds of religion which we discussed above, and "applying the Bible to the modern world." What was needed was "fresh, spontaneous, unencumbered access to the Word in the Bible" (Stringfellow, 1967a:57), rather than the academicization of theology and the accompanied neglect of the Bible, which filled the seminaries and the churches.

Indeed, theology for Stringfellow is concerned with the practical reality of God's presence and action in the world and of the Christian life; theology cannot be detached from the confession of the faith and remain theology. Theology, and the theologian, cannot be separated; the life of the Christian and the subject of theology are bound together.

> Theology . . . is always in the first instance confessional. The very articulation and communication of the theological meaning of human experience and of the affairs of the world is primarily a confessional act and event—that is, an immediate and contemporary confession of the presence of the life of God in the world and a declaration and interpretation of His life in the world. To put it another way, theology is qualitatively different from the academic disciplines because it is never an abstract, theoretical, or just historical exercise, but rather an examination of the actual data of the world's existence in the faith that the Word of God is evident in that data and may be identified, discussed, studied, verified, imparted, and enjoyed. (Stringfellow, 1962k:45)[24]

Theology was a confessional act, but in so being it honors its vocation rather than denies the importance of creative and intelligent thinking. The issue is one of priorities: what is the primary and fundamental purpose of theology, and what is its subject? That is the question Stringfellow is dealing with here. His answer, inescapably, is that theology's purpose and subject is nothing other than the life of faith in the world, in the Spirit with Christ, and for this its attentions must necessarily be primarily focused upon the Bible as the witness and descriptor of that reality. Theology, as with the Christian life, is a necessarily a *confessional* act, occurring in the world as we encounter and embrace the Word. It is also, like the Christian life, a necessarily *political* act, for it reflects upon and

24. Elsewhere, later, he also describes theology in the following manner: "Thus, I would insist that all authentic theology is not only a definition and elucidation of the gospel but also indispensably a confession of the gospel for the one who speaks theologically and a proclamation of the gospel to those who hear" (Stringfellow, 1967a:57).

speaks about the reconciling activity of God in the world, and orientates people (including oneself) in relation to that divine activity. Its beginning is the reality of God's grace as the foundation of humanity—the justice of God, not human justice—and in that way at least, it usurps the law as the predicate of political action.

Therefore, the seminary underground provides an alternate perspective on knowledge of the Bible and the activity of God in the world. It represents an approach that positively lacks the expertise of a profession turned ideology. For it, the primary or first-order level of theology is altogether more "novice" or naive than that. It seeks to debunk the notion that theological knowledge exists for its own sake. The seminary underground is an approach that is egalitarian, one that requires cooperative participation in the Christian life. It exists more as an occasion or event rather than any kind of institution, appearing now here, now somewhere else. It is a charism of exemplary teaching and Bible study. It is a work of the Spirit, a form of discipleship. In the rest of this section, I shall outline some of its more salient features.

During Stringfellow's lifetime, the seminary underground had a number of manifestations.[25] Always, the concern was to pay serious attention to the Bible, to listen to it and to people, their questions, and contexts. His focus was not upon learning about the Bible, but learning about God's presence in the world, and about one's vocation in the life of God as a part of the Body of Christ.

However, the seminary underground is not anti-intellectual. Stringfellow is not here being anti-intellectual, but is rather identifying the principality of "expertise" and "professionalization" at work in the inner life of the church, and calling for change. The "experts" of modernity, which included the priesthood at that time, existed over-against non-experts, as masters of their subjects, thus rendering the subjects directly inaccessible to non-experts. They exist, furthermore, to perpetuate this; the only way to know a subject is to become an "expert," and it is this cultus in theology, and not critical and rigorous study of theology itself, which Stringfellow thinks must come to an end.

25. Early manifestations can be seen, for example, in the Ecumenical Institute of Theology and Politics, discussed above in chapter 3 under the section "Back to School." It also had later and concrete manifestation in convenings of which Wylie-Kellermann was a part (Wylie-Kellermann, 1995).

The seminary underground welcomes academic contributions (exegetical, historical, structural, literary) but envisions the role of the academic as a provider of theological "thick description"[26] which is, for example, both rigorous and critical, but itself no substitute for direct study of the Bible itself by all Christians. This, of course, is how he understood and used the movement of existentialism. The issue for him was one of priorities: there was no substitute for ordinary people engaging in simple reading, silence, and discussion.

> I am no biblical scholar; I have neither competence nor temperament to be one. The ordinary Christian, layperson or clergy, does not need to be a scholar to have recourse to the Bible and, indeed, to live within the Word of God in the Bible in this world. What the ordinary Christian is called to do is open the Bible and listen to the Word. Listening is a rare happening among human beings. (Stringfellow, 1967a:16)

Listening, Stringfellow insists, makes one vulnerable and accessible to that which is listened to. This characteristically pastoral and practical emphasis is paramount to the seminary underground and the theology Stringfellow envisages.

This was an era in which the churches looked to American culture for guidance on how they might be a church. Their desire and reliance upon secular models of growth, development and organizational understanding for their life grew at an alarming rate. This is reflected in the way it equated its survival in the modern world with the increase in the numbers of professional clergy and therapists, a desire for more mass-evangelism and programs of "lay-education," and more money, and social initiatives, etc. Amidst this clamor, Stringfellow's dissenting voice rung out in a message of clarity and simplicity—a simplicity, he realized, which went to the heart of the Christian faith.

> The only thing the church needs, the only credential for faithful ministry, is the gospel. If the church has the freedom to go into the world with merely the gospel to offer the world, then it will know how to use whatever other things it has, like money and

26. This notion of "thick description" is taken from Hans Frei's use of Clifford Geertz's view of ethnography (Frei, 1993:100). In our use here, academic and doctrinal theology remains the servant of "confessional" theology, rather than its foundation, giving it "epistemological width" as confessional theology describes reality and as the believer (theologically) seeks to orientate oneself in the world.

talent ... Then it will know how to use things as sacraments of the
gift of the gospel to the world. (Stringfellow, 1963n:5)

Therefore, the attention of the church to the world, rather than the internal gaze upon itself, is the basis for its existence, and it is founded in
and reliant upon the freedom of the gospel. It is in the world, not the
church, that God is to be found: the church is literally and simply a sign
and witness to the reality of God's presence and action (God's mission)
in the world. For Stringfellow the Bible narrates the world; it describes
the world and its order before God. And at the heart of this biblical politics is the reality of Christ's life, death, and resurrection, known in and
through pentecostal perspective (the saga of salvation). This is what the
Bible makes known, and why it is of central significance to the life of the
church and Christians. The Bible narrates the presence of the Word of
God and provides the language of discernment for enabling us to more
appreciate and be engaged by the Word at work in the world—in us, and
in all other life, reconciling and restoring all of creation. The unfolding
character and shape of these politics, and the life it fosters, is the journey
that took place for Stringfellow in his lifework.

When the Christian is freed to listen, and the Word is freed to
speak, diverse, ad-hoc, and spontaneous are the results. When it comes
into being, the character of the seminary underground fosters this environment, through the people who are gathered for the purpose of open,
faithful, and attentive study of the Bible. And in its occasional formation,
the seminary underground echoes the Word of God in another way, for
the vitality and paradox of the Word of God is that it is also free, ad-hoc,
and spontaneous. Thus the seminary underground could never become
programmatic, nor could it become a planned course of study authorized, marketed, and delivered by the institutional church. Its character
is a witness to that which it teaches.

Through listening openly, attentively, and spontaneously, the education of the seminary underground provides a context for people to learn
and discover the Word and their vocation. Ultimately, the seminary underground gives rise to ethics. Such practical knowledge is derived by
virtue of both the resurrection and the incarnation, or in other words, by
virtue of the Risen Lord experienced and encountered in the world by
the power of the Holy Spirit. The seminary underground begins its life
where we encounter Word and world simultaneously. This is the context
of work and worship, which raises the questions to which the seminary

underground responds. Thus, the focus of the education towards which the seminary underground is directed returns full circle to the Word of God, the Bible, and biography. In other words, we are biblical persons, and the seminary underground Stringfellow envisages teaches us the ethical meaning of this reality as we encounter the Word and the world.

The best way to sum up the meaning or purpose of the seminary underground is to say that it seeks to nurture and promote diverse forms of radical Christian discipleship, which are unified by the reality of the militant presence of the Word of God in the world, to which the Bible and our Christian lives witness. It restores theology to the life of the Christian—restoring faith and obedience. It returns the Bible to the center of the Christian life as the witness to God's reality in the world. Therefore, through the seminary underground, reality might be unmasked, vocation discerned, and obedient disciples made: disciples who are open and responsive to the ad-hoc, creative, authoritative, and diverse work of God's Spirit in the world. In short, it is a form of theological education for the Christian life, calling participants to listen, to hear, to respond in obedience to the biblical witness to the Word, as witnesses resisting the power of death.

The seminary underground represents an attempt to create an alternative community for biblical study and theological reflection—a kind of para-church "organization" or better yet, movement.[27] It is a "lay" or Christian community, promoting the primacy of theology as the basis for working out the Christian life in the world. But it is also an open community and seeks secondary input (thickening) from academic theology and, in turn, other disciplines also. But in all of this, the place of the Bible is unequivocally foundational and singularly authoritative.

The Adventure of Biblical Politics

The unity between faith and politics is central to Stringfellow's biblical hermeneutic. One of the tensions he highlighted in the early 1950s was their disunity, and that disunity was even more apparent amidst a political climate of the 1960s. Predominantly, faith continued to be seen as having no part in politics, and politics no part in faith. The public pursuit of one invariably meant the abandonment of the other to a personal and

27. It's ad-hoc "organization," its almost itinerant nature, is not dissimilar to the nature of the circus. We shall examine the importance of the circus to Stringfellow, and the way in which he understood it as a parable of the Kingdom, shortly.

private belief. This separation goes to the heart of American identity, allegiance to which was in great demand in the Cold-War turmoil of post-war America. Yet as we have discussed, throughout the 1950s (and beyond) Stringfellow's lifework focused upon demonstrating the unity of faith and politics. He was not alone; there was resistance, and there was protest. Another attempt to unite faith and politics coincided with his own and was to become hugely influential in the formation of the political radicalism of the New Left—a moment in history when authenticity became politicized.[28] The New Left played a crucial role in American political history, as Alan Brinkley has indicated.

> For a brief moment in the 1960s, a small group of student radicals managed to do what the American left had largely failed to achieve in almost a century of trying: create a genuine mass movement. ... Its history is important ... not only for how student radicalism ultimately went wrong, but also for how that radicalism emerged and briefly flourished. It is important above all, perhaps, for what it says about a generation—the largest generation in the nation's history—that produces, and always dominated, the New Left. (Brinkley, 1998:222)[29]

While the likes of Kennedy and Johnson were introducing legislative changes, most of these initiatives were predominantly liberal responses to the more radical energies and unrest that were apparent at the grass-roots. The New Left was perhaps the leading agent of such political radicalism throughout this decade.

According to Rossinow (1998), the New Left built upon the foundations of the Christian Faith and Life Community.[30] Stringfellow was

28. This is significant because there was (and perhaps still is) a temptation to read Stringfellow as though he were a New Left radical, however in reality his dissent from these young political activists was just the same as it was towards, for example, the Death of God movement. Despite this, there was a "niche" for Stringfellow within this newly emerged radical movement, and Stringfellow took every opportunity to speak to these groups, predominantly on college campuses around America. This association, along with the apparent similarity of their message of resistance, probably accounts for this over-identification. On the New Left, see Rossinow (1998) and Brinkley (1998:222–36).

29. It seems to me not inconceivable that one of the contributing factors to the implosion may well have been simply that those who were students at the time moved on to the next episode of their life.

30. The CFLC was located at the University of Texas by Jack Lewis, who then went on to be chaplain at Cornell University where he remained until his retirement. This is

well acquainted with this community, and had affinities with its found-er.[31] Their connections focused upon a shared concern and esteem for the Christian life in the world. But where the CFLC used existentialism foundationally, Stringfellow's use of it was more functional: the foun-dation of Stringfellow's ministry was the Word of God, witnessed to in the Bible and manifest in the world.[32] Owing to the CFLC's influence, Christian existentialism was formative to the New Left. However, this genesis serves only to further distance Stringfellow's own radicalism from the New Left radicalism and its movements of resistance which emerged at this time. Their foundations and aims and ends were sim-ply not the same, although they often looked similar. While he was no cultural radical, the culture of resistance provided Stringfellow with an environment in which he flourished and was warmly received; his politi-cal motivation was driven by the politics of the Bible.

> My esteem for the biblical witness and my approach to the Bible
> should be enough to disclose my skepticism about current efforts
> to construct political theology according to some ideological
> model . . . Biblical politics are alienated from the politics of this
> age . . . The Bible makes a political statement of the reign of Christ
> preempting all the rulers, and all pretenders to thrones and do-
> minions, subjecting incumbents and revolutionaries, surpassing
> the doctrines and promises of the ideologies of this world . . .
> The exemplification of redeemed humanity in the lordship of
> Jesus Christ in this age means a resilient and tireless witness to
> confound, rebuke and undo every regime, and every potential
> regime. (Stringfellow, 1976a:6–7)

Reading and listening to the Bible was, for Stringfellow, one of the great-est adventures of his life, and one which occupied most of his time: when not writing or speaking, his time was taken reading the Bible, the Book of Common Prayer, and the *New York Times*, in that order. The adven-ture determined the shape of his life and work. Over time the adventure absorbed his life, whereby even his more

the same chaplaincy team on which Daniel Berrigan worked. The many biographical connections between Lewis and Stringfellow are beyond the immediate scope of this study.

31. He had been offered a job with them, but turned it down (Lewis,1959).

32. The concerns of existentialism attuned Stringfellow to the way in which the gos-pel is concerned with the whole of life—the practical life of the Christian (Stringfellow, 1962i).

mundane involvements—practicing law, being attentive to the news of the moment, lecturing around the country, free lance pastoral counseling, writing, activity in church politics, maintaining my medical regime, doing chores around my home ...—[became] more and more intertwined with this major preoccupation of mine, so that I can no longer readily separate the one from the others. This merging for me of almost everything into a biblical scheme of living occurs because the data of the Bible and one's existence in common history is characteristically similar. One comes, after awhile, to live in a continuing biblical context and so is spared both an artificial compartmentalization of one's person and a false pietism in living. (Stringfellow, 1976c:4)

The Bible is central to Stringfellow's theological and political outlook because it testifies to the living reality of the Word of God in the world. It narrates the presence of the politics of reconciliation and resurrection, and teaches how one might inhabit that world. The Bible does not so much absorb reality as describe reality, and its world is the world which Stringfellow believed the Christian must inhabit. The Bible is the means by which we discern who we are; it is the means by which we discern how to be most truly human.

For Stringfellow, the Bible witnesses to authenticity in its account of the radically political nature of the incarnation, crucifixion, and resurrection; this is *authentic politics*. The politics of the Bible are the politics of the Incarnation; thus God's politics are at the heart of *vocation* or biography. Christian life is political life, determined by the politics of the Kingdom, exposing the fall and proclaiming the resurrection.

And in terms of hermeneutics, Stringfellow emphasizes the need to read the Bible as it was written: not in isolation, but in engagement with the world, with the Bible in one hand, and the newspaper or Sears catalogue in the other.[33] But its significance extends further, for the Bible and its politics encompass the whole of creation and our action in it. There is nothing which escapes the political claim of the incarnation upon our lives.

Therefore, the Bible and its politics are authoritative for our vocation: our political life of witness and worship in the world. Throughout

33. "The Psalms, with their terrible esteem for the godliness of God, and Sears, with its infinite attention to the creatureliness of human beings and its nice detail of American culture, make apt companions for the Christian as a common reader" (Stringfellow, 1970e:51).

his lifework Stringfellow calls us to join the biblical adventure, to be co-witnesses with the disciples, the apostles, and those in the early church, as we confront the principalities and powers which reign in *our* time. Our life is congruous with theirs: it is the same adventure, the same faith, the same witness, the same church. In our involvement, as we saw in our discussion of his dispute with the EHPP, social work and social action cannot replace the gospel and the need for an open Bible, but should be a consequence of it.

> The involvement of the church in public controversy, most notably in the present time in the racial crisis and in questioning the American military involvement in Vietnam, provokes great concern among many conscientious church members. They feel that social issues are not the concern of the church and that the church will somehow be defiled by open intervention in public policy. Perhaps the first thing for both clergy and laity to keep in mind is that in this world no such thing as neutrality about any public issue exists. (Stringfellow, 1966a:396)

Listening to the Bible, discerning its politics, and articulating its ethic occupied the horizons of Stringfellow's lifework. The stance he took was an uncomfortable one, and as predicted so many years ago, it cut short his life by years. To proclaim the good news and resist the power of death: this, it would appear, was his vocation, his ordinary life.

LIVING ORDINARY LIFE IN THE WORD OF GOD

Stringfellow had a penchant for the ordinary; that is where his heart and his life were located. Meanwhile the belief which so beleaguered American Protestantism at that time was that the Christian life had "to do with something other than ordinary life, with something external and abstract—disconnected from all the awful, petty, terrific, sad, lusty, terrible, intriguing, trivial, fearful, ambiguous, momentous things of anybody's existence" (Stringfellow, 1962i:2). While Stringfellow sought to recall American Protestantism to the ordinary, paradoxically his penchant contributed to his being viewed as somehow extra-ordinary ("a remarkable prophet," "an extraordinary social-critic"); it was a view he disliked intensely.[34]

---

34. While at times through his life his ego may have enjoyed the attention, he passionately disliked the lack of understanding which such a perception betrayed. However, that is not to say he was not especially pleased with having published his first book and having a wider audience; he was (Stringfellow, 1962e). His notoriety was further

Tired of the labels, Stringfellow declared his vocational calling in simple, powerful, passionate tones: "I am called in the Word of God to be William Stringfellow, nothing more and nothing less" (cited in Wylie-Kellermann,1995:71). The Christian life is concerned with each of us living our vocation—biblical people authored by biblical politics. It is a life which Stringfellow was to spend the rest of the decade pursuing, seeking clarity, and a way of embracing the dynamic and transformative power of the Word of God and the radical reality of biblical politics in the world.

In *A Private and Public Faith* he addresses the Christian life in terms of the church's ministry: the task of the laity, as opposed to the task of the priesthood. It is a political engagement with the church, rather than society, and is an important and significant starting point. Even though it may be less radical in appearance compared to later writing, it establishes an internal coherence to his later thought in its relationship to the role and purpose of the church, which is essential for more fully understanding the unity and diversity of his lifework, and a real sense of what he was trying to achieve. It provides, in other words, the ecclesial and faith-full foundations.

Stringfellow's understanding of the Christian life is inherently theological for it encounters God in the world. It is this understanding which we shall now examine. To begin with, it is worth noting that Stringfellow uses the term "God" most often, and implicit in this is the Trinity, or what he actually terms "the life of God" (Stringfellow, 1962o:7).[35] For example, previously we saw how considerable emphasis was placed upon creation and reconciliation; here it has shifted towards reconciliation and sanctification. It is furthermore an understanding of God alive in the world in Word and Spirit. The Christian's is a life lived as co-workers with Christ, living life in the Spirit, embraced by the Father in all our difference. At its very core it is a thoroughly trinitarian theology, therefore, which focuses increasingly upon the interplay between Word and Spirit in our lives and in the world. Our life is a repetition of Christ's self-sacrifice as worship, not atonement—self-sacrifice which includes the incarnation, death, descent, and resurrection. It is self-sacrifice, simply, as advocacy and embrace.

enhanced when Karl Barth came to America, as we shall see shortly.

35. This paper makes explicit this trinitarian understanding of God, naming the Trinity in this way.

The first thing to note is that when Stringfellow speaks about the Christian life he understands it as primarily a corporate and political life of witness and worship in which all Christians are implicated (Stringfellow, 1962k:49). He is eager to rectify the misconstrual of the relationship of the church and the world, and the understanding of the church as the sanctuary: the place where God is to be found. The church is not the place people come to seek God, but where they come to declare that God has taken the initiative in seeking them—where they come to worship Him. In this way his understanding of the Christian life is grounded in both the immanence and transcendence of God, through its emphasis on the union of the Christian life in the world with the worship of the gathered church. The church is never cut off from the affairs of the world, but always and everywhere deeply implicated in them; it is a stranger and an alien in a strange land, and it is as much the church in dispersal as when it is gathered (if not more so).

The Word of God is in the ordinariness of the world, and it, rather than the church, is at the center of the Christian life; it holds that life in unity and in fullness. As Stringfellow puts it:

> The simplicity—not ease—but simplicity of the Christian life is founded upon the fact of the presence of the Word of God already in the common life of the world. The practice of the Christian life consists of the discernment (the seeing and hearing), and the reliance upon (the reckless and uncalculating dependence), and the celebration (the ready and spontaneous enjoyment) of the presence of the Word of God in the common life of the world. (Stringfellow, 1962k:56)

Therefore, essential to the Christian life is the ability to hear and discern the Word of God, the freedom to live the resurrected life, and the response of adoration and worship. Indeed, the ability to discern the Word of God (active in the world) is the defining mark of the Christian, essential to everything else a Christian says or does. God's presence and our discernment provides for a freedom which is both radical and all-pervasive: "There is no place in which that freedom may not be exercised, there is no place in which the Word of God is absent. There is no time in which that freedom is restricted since the One the world awaits has already come" (Stringfellow, 1962k:68). Underlying this discernment, reliance and celebration is the fourfold duty or task of the laity in the world, what Stringfellow describes as the "stewardship of the gospel" and the "service of the laity to the world" (Stringfellow, 1962k:50–55). This task consists of prophecy, apologetics, moral theology, and evangelism—characteristics it would be worthwhile bearing in mind as we assess Stringfellow's own lifework. This fourfold task, which we shall examine shortly, is in essence the ministry and mission of the Christian life, and echoes the elements of Stringfellow's own journey of vocational self-discernment. First, we need to consider further this power of discernment.

> God witnesses to Himself in history whether or not there are Christians engaged in any witness to Him. The possibility of the witness of Christians as the Body of Christ and as members of the Body of Christ to the Word of God in the world depends upon the power given to Christians to discern the presence of the Word in the world. Further, and in the same fashion, there can be no worship, unless the power to discern the Word of God in the world is present. For how shall men worship that which they do not know? (Stringfellow, 1962k:62–63)

Always and everywhere, this power to discern the Word of God is the imperative of the life of faith. Notice here the separation between being the Body, and being *members* of the Body, pointing to the fact that in dispersion the Christian is practically and effectively the church in "common life." This power of discernment is the knowledge of the resurrection (Stringfellow, 1962k:63); it is saving knowledge, it is apprehension of the essential and radical truth of the way in which the Word of God "surpasses the dominion of death over the world's existence" (Stringfellow, 1962k:63).

Christ's descent into hell is essential to Stringfellow's understanding here: there is nothing, not even death, known or unknown to a person that God does not know. Everything in this life is but a foretaste of death, not an end in itself. The power of the resurrection means they end in Christ:

> Christ has already lived my life. Christ has already died my death. Christ is risen from death for me . . . By that event . . . no man confronts and surrenders to the powers of death—any anxieties—any crisis—without beholding the power and the truth of the Resurrection. (Stringfellow, 1962k:64)

The confrontation and confession of death in one's own biography is, says Stringfellow, the event of becoming a Christian, and in and through that event the power of discernment is given. While he does not identify it himself in these terms at this stage, it is clear that discernment is here a gift of the spirit—glossolalia. It points to the way in which a theology of the Holy Spirit is always lingering in Stringfellow's work, only later receiving attention and deliberate articulation.[36]

Conversion is an event of the resurrection, not as some "mere imaginative interpretation of the Truth: it is the Truth at work in my own existence" (Stringfellow, 1962k:65), and fully implicated in discernment, for on conversion we witness our death. It is a concrete disclosure of God's life and action in the world, an act of revelation, not a speculative proposition or positive thought. It is not special knowledge, but is the event which unifies all humanity: "the unequivocal assurance that I am loved by One who loves all others which enables me to love myself and frees me to love another, any other, every other" (Stringfellow, 1962k:65). This was the radical veracity of the resurrection, and the subsequent self-acceptance for which it provided, which was exposed to Stringfellow so significantly in Harlem.[37] The Christian life is a life of living the resurrection—and, to preempt his later description, of living a life of freedom in obedience.[38]

In East Harlem he realized that death was "no longer an abstraction confined to the usual funeral connotations . . . The grandiose terms in which the Bible describes the power of death had begun to have a concrete significance for me" (Stringfellow, 1976c:5). Harlem prepared him for the turmoil and tribulation that was to befall him in the coming years. We can see the emergence of this realization in his writing here, and it illustrates clearly how his theological understanding and his own process of conversion are intrinsically linked, and how they are also

36. Stringfellow points to conversion as the act of God, and as tending to be an ongoing process of one's life being implicated in the Word of God (Stringfellow, 1963e). He does not, however, rule out the notion that conversion might be instantaneous (it is God's work, not ours, after all), but this does not appear to be the norm in history. The classic text on conversion, which Stringfellow may well have had recourse to during his studies, is Nock (1933). It is not until *An Ethic for Christians and Other Aliens in a Strange Land* (1973b) that we see Stringfellow develop much more fully his theology of the gifts of the spirit.

37. See, for example, Stringfellow (1970d).

38. As we shall see in a moment, this idea of freedom in obedience crystallized with his meeting Barth. However, I use the phrase here to draw attention to the fact that while the phrase was not yet clear, that which theologically underpinned it (i.e., the resurrection) was dominant in his understanding of the Christian life at this point.

linked to his time in Harlem. His own theology, his own faith, is at once private and public.

Confession is the basis of the Christian life (Stringfellow, 1962k: 49–50), and this undergirds the fourfold task of the Christian life mentioned above. This fourfold task can be understood as follows.

Firstly, it is *prophetic*. Stringfellow believed that he understood what the church did not seem to: that the task of the laity and the priesthood differ. Where the priesthood is concerned with the internal life of the church and its order, the laity are concerned with the world. Their tasks clearly differ, and whereas the task of the priesthood in relation to the Word of God is summed up as preaching, that of the laity is prophecy: the task of the laity is to expose the Word of God at work in the world. In the congregation the utterance of the Word of God is the task of the priest through preaching; in the world, it is the prophetic task of the laity. Simply, one of the duties of the laity is to call the world to account.

> His task is to represent and expose the Word of God in the world, and particularly in the posture of the Word which stands over against the world's existence and the world's disregard of and arrogance toward the Word of God. And sometimes his task is to declare and convey the Word of God as it stands over against the worldliness of the church . . . prophetism is identified with the clash between the existence of the world and the presence of the Word of God in the world and, as well, with the tension between the life of the Church at any given point and the Word of God whose presence in the world the Church exists to hear, herald and expose. (Stringfellow, 1962k:52)

While it is the task of the laity, the very existence of a congregation does have prophetic impact, for the "congregation represents to the world the life to which the world is called" and in so doing "prophesies the world which is to come in God's patience, judgment and mercy" (Stringfellow, 1962k:52–53).

Similarly and secondly, amidst the world's hostility to the Word of God the laity defend and explicate the gospel through the task of *apologetics*: a task which goes hand-in-hand with their normal day-to-day involvement in the world in work, politics, business, and culture. To be silent amidst the world's hostility is, says Stringfellow, to be an accomplice; there is no grey area here in his thinking. While he seems to acknowledge the difficulty of this very public task, he also insists that it is the task of each Christian to defend the faith in the marketplace; we cannot offload our responsibility to the ecclesial authorities, bishops, or other clergy. We cannot, in other words, look to those in authority to speak for us: "each layman must be his own apologist, responsible for his stewardship of the gospel in his daily life and work" (Stringfellow, 1962k:53). In Stringfellow's vision of the church, all are created equal in the sight of God; and adjunct to that equality is the sharing of the burden of faith.

Moral theology, the third task of the laity, is concerned with the ad-hoc interpretation and articulation of "the significance of the Word of God in social conflict and chance" (Stringfellow,1962k:53). When American Protestantism spoke on such matters, it was predominantly through its various departments and agencies, which tended to be staffed by clergy. Obviously, Stringfellow insisted, in such a situation the clergy would need to act as laity, not priests. But his most significant criticism was that these programs actually served to divert the faithful from their mission in the world, instead demanding more involvement by them in (institutional) churchly matters and *discussion* about involvement in the world. Stringfellow had encountered and rebuked this dominance of discussion over action (often usurping action) for a long time—the endless committees of the WCC, SCM, EHPP, and other agencies he encountered—not because he felt reflection had no place in the Christian faith, clearly this was not the case, but because it constantly and persistently diverted attentions away from the essence of the Christian life: action (Stringfellow, 1962a). For Stringfellow, action, not reflection, is the starting point of the Christian faith—Christ's action for us, and our response—and the key to honoring the gift of life of our vocation. As Christians, therefore, we are implicated in the life of society. It is only our action, experience, or encounter with the world, the Bible, and God at work in the World in God's Spirit, that useful reflection might follow. His lifework testifies to this commitment.

> The Christian social witness is achieved only insofar as Christians are deeply implicated in the real life of society—in unions and political clubs and citizen groups and the like; it is not made by Christian people gathering off by themselves in a parish house to study and discuss social issues. Witness becomes possible only when the Christian is on the actual scene where the conflict is

taking place, the decision is being made, the legislation being enacted. (Stringfellow, 1962k:54)

At this time he considers that in dispersal the witness of the Body of Christ is done in secret, known only to those who are involved or reached by the witness, or by other Christians. The only time he thought that the explicit witness of the church is openly recognized, is when the church gathers for worship.

Fourthly, the Christian life is "candidly evangelistic" (Stringfellow, 1962k:54), but the *evangelism* which takes place in the marketplace echoes the concern for the uniqueness of the individual which his understanding of witness seemed to suggest. In contrast with the Revivalists, Stringfellow is clear: there can be no fanfare in evangelism, no great show or spectacle "lest the uniqueness with which the gospel addresses each man in his own life be vitiated. Nor is there some stereotyped scheme of evangelization" (Stringfellow, 1962k:54). Rather than being essentially verbal, evangelism is in fact an intimate act of love. Evangelism is not a matter of technique; it is a matter of living and acting in the love that unites us to each other and to God. In a sense, there is no greater task than evangelism, and no task more costly to the Body of Christ, for evangelism requires one's whole being and body. Indeed, it requires Christ's whole body.[39] "Evangelism consists of loving another human being in a way which represents to him the care of God for his particular life. Evangelism rests upon the appeal to another man to remember his own creation—to remember Who made him and for Whom he was made. Evangelism is the event in which a Christian confronts another man in a way which assures the other man that the new life which he observes in the Christian is vouchsafed for him also" (Stringfellow, 1962k:54–55). Evangelism is not, therefore, brash, remote, or impersonal. It is the *most* personal, engaged, and loving act of the Christian for another person.

The authentic Christian life can never offer a single "Christian" answer to any issue or problem, but rather all are ad hoc, reflecting the discernment of the Word by the Body in dispersal in the world.

---

39. My implicit suggestion of the significance of church unity here is intentional. Stringfellow was at this time continuing his work in this area, especially in relation to church-state relations, and the unity which he believed to be so central to the Body of Christ (the congregation) is also at the heart of evangelism: it is the same reconciling act, the same work of Christ, the same Word at work.

What a Christian looks like is a man who knows that the secret of his own life in this world is found within the life of God in this world and that this sets him free from any demand or trial or power or threat known in this world. That is to say, the discovery and gift of his own life, within and by the life of God, is the gift of his own salvation from death and from all the threats, the littler threats that exist to a man's existence, integrity, and life which are somehow less than the power of death but which are also angels of the power of death, and from the major threat of the power of death itself . . . The sacramental meaning of his action from day to day and from moment to moment will be the drama of his radical, and in a sense uncritical, unprudential, expenditure of his own life for the life of the world, that is, for the life of anybody, or in principle, anything at all, thereby representing again and remembering again in the world the one who died for the whole world and for all men, even though none of us are worthy. If you want to know what a Christian looks like, a Christian looks like a man on a cross. That's the problem of religion. There is nothing hypothetical about it at all. (Stringfellow, 1962o:7–8)

The mission and ministry of the Christian life is united by the way in which the religious and secular lives of all Christians are one: there is no compartmentalization between life in the marketplace and life in the sanctuary. The integrity of the Christian life is found in the unity of its apprehension by, comprehension of, and obedience to the Word of God militant in the world. To be a Christian is to experience constantly and persistently the presence and work of God in the ordinary everyday events of life.[40] The same God that we meet in the church as we enact our hope in sacramental worship is at work in the world. Therefore the whole of Christian life is sacramental, because it focuses upon the everyday events of life through which God's activity is discerned. The mark of the Christian, Stringfellow insists, is not observable through the externals, like what one wears, personal morality, diet, or how one speaks. For this reason, he insists he knows "nothing about God in a speculative or hypothetical sense, and I am able to speak of Him only out of my own experience of His presence" in the world and in the church (Stringfellow, 1962k:58–59).

40. The seriousness with which he took God's involvement in the ordinariness of life is witnessed, for example, in the way in which Stringfellow did not say grace before meal times. He apparently felt that the food had already been adequately blessed by God in the making of the meal—in the ordinariness of life.

Stringfellow spent his lifework committed to the task of discerning and describing the shape of this Christian life, orientated in the Word of God and rooted in the world. It was a biblical adventure. Even here in 1962 we get a sense of what is to come: a Christian lives in radical freedom, ready to give up his own life (literally) for the sake of the gospel.[41] It is a freedom born of the militant and redeeming presence of God in the world. This God is at once immanent and transcendent, similar and yet other, near and yet far, and in this God is the unity and the truth of our humanity: our authentic vocation.

Utilizing his own model, this book is a work of proclamation rather than prophecy. *A Private and Public Faith* provides a crucial foundation for helping us to grasp his undestanding of the church and the world and the Christian's role therein, that he was to go on to develop. However, we need to resist any attempt to systematize his writing and his thought; his published material conveys very clearly the ad hoc nature of his theology. This is essentially a book concerned with ecclesial self-understanding and orientation, and in that sense we must recognize the central significance of the church at work, often implicitly, in Stringfellow's writing. It is essential also for the orientation it provides: it accounts for why and how the Christian should live in the world, from an ecclesial perspective.

His book received much acclaim, and indeed, when published it rode on the back of one of the most significant and positive encounters Stringfellow was to have in his life. It was an encounter which was to launch him onto the American scene in a way other theologians could do little to rival. Along with two other episodes, it was an empirical event which further radicalized his lifework.[42] It is to these encounters that we now cast our attention.

---

41. This would have had profound implications in the context in which he wrote, which was dominated by civil rights riots and protest, and many people getting killed as a result, as we read previously.

42. These episodes are therefore empirical events which radicalized his life and work. As empirical agents of change and movement, they function in a similar way to his beloved East Harlem (see chapter 3).

6

Radicalizing Agency

Encounters Pro and Con

IN 1963 STRINGFELLOW WROTE a letter to one of his publishers expressing the desire to write a moral theology (Stringfellow, 1963j).
There were, he said, three things which contributed to his desire. The
first, which we are about to encounter for ourselves, was Karl Barth's
advocacy of Stringfellow, the second was Ellul's prompting when they
met in 1960,[1] and the third was the ongoing discussions he had with
Markus Barth.[2] He summarized:

> There seems to be a place for a new and original work in this field
> [theology and ethics], written by an American out of the experi-
> ence of American life and society. Some of the specific issues to
> deal with; racism, poverty, employment and work, patriotism, war
> and arms control, the meaning of money, space, sex, urbanization.
> The relationship of church and state, significance of ecumenical
> unity, the problems of the individual vs society, the meaning of
> vocation, sacraments and ethics.(Stringfellow, 1963j)[3]

Eager that it be adopted as a text book in seminary and university ethics courses, he asserted that he would be writing it in a more formal,
academic style. In the end, this was not to be the case: events were to

1. "He felt that Protestant moral theology in Western Europe had pretty much exhausted its vitality since the war, and looked for some contemporary contribution from
America" (Stringfellow, 1963j:1–2).

2. They had "been discussing over the years the void in American theological ethics
understanding of what the New Testament calls the principalities and powers, and we
agree that some serious treatment of these realities is essential to transcend the naiveté
of the individualistic ethics so common in American Protestant thought" (Stringfellow,
1963j:2).

3. Out of this project, the trip to see Barth and others emerged for 1964.

determine the text otherwise. This project for a moral theology was to become the self-stated aim of Stringfellow's lifework, and its concrete emergence is the focus of the remaining chapters. In seeking this moral theology, Stringfellow continues to build upon the themes and concerns which have occupied his lifework to date, and as we shall see, the empirical commitment to life remains firmly center-stage: his life and his work informing (and radicalizing) one another, leading to the vocationally immersed articulation of his moral theology most fully orientated in and derived from the politics of the Bible.

Stringfellow's lifework at this time around 1962–1963 was formed amidst "academic accolade," the cauldron of the racial crisis, and significant developments in his personal life. The impact of these three events upon the continued movement and development of Stringfellow's lifework was profound, and they require our close attention. One of the primary issues at stake in all of these encounters is the overcoming of loneliness, and the theological impact this had upon his lifework: this was a period dominated by movement—in both his own life and thought, and in the sociopolitical life of the nation.

THE ADVOCACY OF KARL BARTH

In 1962 Karl Barth visited America.[4] To many American theologians Barth was something of a demigod, the father of modern theology. To others he was anathema.[5] To Stringfellow, the usual academic games appeared prevalent: some theologians sought "to be confirmed in their systems . . . some searching for some inconsistency with which to confound him, some eager to hear and learn, some ready to question, some waiting to attack, some envious and ridiculously proud, some over-awed and uncritical, some smart, irrelevant, and academic" (Stringfellow, 1962b:4). But whether one agreed with Barth or not, one thing was certain—you wanted to be seen with him. To them, his visit

4. It lasted from April 7 to May 26, and was a mixture of lectures, tourism, and photo-opportunities. During the visit, he celebrated his seventy-sixth birthday. When referring in this section to Barth, I am referring to Karl Barth. All references to Markus Barth will be by his first name.

5. Dissenters from Barth in America included significantly Reinhold Niebuhr, considered by many Americans to be the father of modern liberal (social ethics) theology at that time. Niebuhr dismissed Barth as "irresponsible" and "irrelevant" to America (Stringfellow, 1962h:5). Stringfellow was later to consider his own theology to be a "new social ethic" for America, designed to replace Niebuhr's.

signified advocacy of their endeavors, and indicated American theology had essentially come of age.

> Karl Barth did not come to America, at last, as a critic, nor as a prophet, nor as a definitive and authentic theologian, although he is such, nor even as a teacher, although he has something to teach us and we need in America some good teachers. Karl Barth came to America to preach. (Stringfellow, 1962b:1)

Essentially, Barth came to speak to the church, not the world, and this he did faithfully. Unfortunately, he was treated less as a preacher and more like a celebrity and academic (Stringfellow, 1962b:2). Of course, Barth *was* both of these, and he expected to meet such a response, but he looked for more and sought to ensure that nothing supplanted the message he preached.

He sought to put the matter straight and convey to his eager audience that he was "a normal human being" who was "considerably involved in all sorts of human affairs" distinguished only by his devotion to the question of "proper theology": a question to which he would be glad if others would also devote themselves (Barth, 1979:x).[6] It was thus "humanness" which helped Barth and Stringfellow to connect during his visit (University of Chicago, 1962).[7] Barth also went to great lengths to emphasize the distinctive and important work which American theology needed to articulate: a "theology of freedom" (Barth, 1979:xii).

Given what almost amounted to a prevailing mystique amongst academic theologians, the notoriety of his reputation, and the high regard in which Barth's attentions were held, it is significant then that in his foreword to *Evangelical Theology*[8] Barth describes Stringfellow as the "conscientious and thoughtful New York attorney . . . who caught my attention more than any other person" (K. Barth, 1979:ix). This section examines the nature of the affinity Barth and Stringfellow shared, Barth's famed advocacy of Stringfellow, and the impact this had upon Stringfellow's own theology.[9]

---

6. See also Barth (1963a).

7. Barth also met Billy Graham, and while he found him personable enough, he was critical of his approach to evangelism.

8. See Barth (1979). An account of his visit and the lectures he delivered are presented in Busch (1976:457–60).

9. Stringfellow first met Barth in 1960, during a WSCF conference in Geneva. As mentioned above, another important influence which emerged from this WSCF con-

Stringfellow had done much to get Barth's *Gospel and Law* pub-lished, and was clearly interested and influenced by his work.[10] When Karl Barth decided to come and visit America, Stringfellow's good rela-tionship with Markus Barth turned out to be something of a blessing.[11] There were three significant events involving Karl Barth and Stringfellow during his visit: not only was Stringfellow invited to take part in a panel of highly regarded "young theologians" at Chicago University for a ques-

ference was Joseph Hromadka; see Stringfellow (1960c) for an account of this. See Stringfellow (1959b) for details of some of the preparation Stringfellow put into this conference. Following this conference in Geneva, Stringfellow left for Edinburgh where he gave a paper to the Faith and Order Commission of the WCC, which later became Stringfellow (1961a). See also Adams (1960), which praises Stringfellow for this paper and introduces him to the work of John Figgis. Another important relationship which began to be more visible at this time was with Stephen Neill (Neill, 1960). Neill and Stringfellow entered into correspondence over many years, and he would often offer critique of Stringfellow's work (Neill, 1960, 1961, 1963, 1968; Stringfellow, 1959c, a, 1963m).

10. At the request of the publishers, Doubleday, Stringfellow proofread the galleys of Barth's *Community State and Church* (Barth, 1960), in which the essay "Gospel and Law" appeared in 1960 (Cavendish, 1960), and he appears to have had a hand in its publication. He also ensured the publication of Ellul's *Theological Foundation of Law* (Ellul, 1960b). Both were considered to be risky by one publisher (University of Chicago Press), and Ellul was described by them as "too fundamentalist": Stringfellow withdrew both manuscripts from them and sought publication elsewhere (Stringfellow, 1959e).

11. Their friendship began when Stringfellow extended an invitation to Markus to speak at the conference on Christian Faith and the Legal Profession, Sept 7–10, 1958, at University of Chicago Law School. This was the conference to which Ellul had also been invited and out of which his *Theological Foundation of the Law* (Ellul, 1960b) was published in the United States (Stringfellow, 1958e) Markus described Stringfellow as "a good friend," "beloved Bill," and a "yoke fellow," and they supported each other's projects. Markus also sought Stringfellow's advice when a call was extended to him from Basel in 1972 (M. Barth, 1972). In 1962 Markus had asked for Stringfellow's comments on a paper he had prepared on the principalities and powers, and observed that he was "very thankful for knowing that we bother and work on similar problems" (M. Barth, 1962a, 1963b)—that of letting the Bible speak today. See also Barth (1963c) in which Markus makes arrangements to meet up with Stringfellow for their long overdue discussions about the principalities and powers: the letter indicates it was a shared interest, but also that Stringfellow was indebted to Markus' commentary on Ephesians (M. Barth, 1959) and its treatment of the principalities and powers (Stringfellow, 1959j). Markus declared that the division of personal faith and social engagement which beleaguered American theology "smells and stinks," and added further that what he believed united him and Stringfellow was that "God's word is living, that the Bible is relevant of itself (without the tricks applied to it by cunning magicians), and that there is no reason to despair at the sight of the power of death" (M. Barth, 1970). The affinity and bond between Markus and Stringfellow was, therefore, strong.

tion and answer session with Barth,[12] but following this Stringfellow also took the opportunity of arranging for others to meet Barth, and he them, at an informal meal, and he furthermore arranged[13] for Barth to visit East Harlem and meet various people and officials, being also instrumental in his visiting Rikers Island.

Documentary evidence in the archives about this visit takes a variety of forms. Essentially it appears that on May 8, during Barth's visit to the US and after the Chicago panel, Stringfellow contacted Markus Barth; the letter was a lament, and an invitation. He was concerned at the way in which *Time* magazine had used Barth's appeal that America might forswear its inferiority complex in order to articulate a theology of freedom. *Time* magazine had turned it into "propaganda for the American political and ideological cause" (Stringfellow, 1962c). As we shall see shortly, this was quite contrary to Barth's intended meaning, and Stringfellow wanted Barth to come and "glimpse that side of life in this country which, in my view, empirically measures what American Christians have to say. Whatever we may have to say or be able somehow to say is profoundly related to the presence and persistence and incongruity and even absurdity of poverty in American urban society" (Stringfellow, 1962c).[14] Stringfellow invited Barth to New York, and Barth accepted; he then went to great lengths to arrange people for Barth to meet in Harlem and beyond, including Anna Kross from the New York City administration, who facilitated his visit to Rikers Island (Sontag, 1962).[15] Essentially, Stringfellow gave Barth a guided tour. Barth warmed to Stringfellow, and in their outlook and manner (humanity)

12. The questions and answers were held at 8:00PM on April 25 and April 26, 1962, in the Rockefeller Memorial Chapel, The University of Chicago.

13. Correspondence surrounding this event, which took place on April 23, 1962 at Markus' home, can be found in the archives, for example (Barth, 1962b; Freddie, 1962; Katz, 1962; Pyle, 1962).

14. The invitation had been extended by Stringfellow many months prior. Markus had responded that it was possible, and that Bath would like to meet its ordinary people, rather than the "bigshots" (Stringfellow, 1962d; Barth, 1962c). Stringfellow, eager that it should take place, followed up this previous correspondence on the back of the *Time* magazine article.

15. The invitation according to Sontag was extended by the Chaplain, The Rev. Dr. E. Frederick Proelss, and Anna Kross would have been the City's official who facilitated the visit. Most of the inmates he met were drug addicts, and doubtless some of these would have originated from East Harlem. Stringfellow, who was ultimately behind this visit, was also present, along with Barth's sons, Markus and Christoph.

they seemed to share many things in common—this, Barth said, was no coincidence but simply the outcome of the fact that they "read the same Bible" (Stringfellow, 1970e:152). This appreciation emerged from the panel in Chicago, which for Stringfellow was both a "stimulation and a pleasure" (Stringfellow, 1962c), and clearly an affirmation. We need now to look at this conference.

The questions for the conference were submitted to Barth well in advance, and, to many, Stringfellow's place on the panel appeared something of an oddity for he was the only nonacademic theologian.[16] Stringfellow's two questions, in which we are especially interested here, focused upon the relationship of the churches to the state, and the principalities and powers. Both echo Stringfellow's concerns in *A Private and Public Faith*.[17] Both were very lengthy (far more so than those of the other members on the panel), and seemed to be more statements followed by a series of related questions upon which he sought Barth's comment; here we have a man who has been provided an opportunity to present, verify, and most importantly extend his own thinking in these areas. Without question Barth understood this, and it accounts partly for why he responded as he did towards Stringfellow; they were kindred spirits amidst an array of many would-be "Barthians." He also gave Stringfellow a chance to speak at length on a question from Hans Frei, thus himself making comment on America while not asserting it

16. Other members of the panel were, in the order in which they were originally listed: Professor Jarsolav Pelikan (Moderator); Professor Edward Carnell (Fuller); Professor Hans Frei (Yale); Professor Jakob Peutuchowski (Hebrew Union College); Professor Bernard Cooke S.J. (Marquette University); Professor Schubert Ogden (Southern Methodist University). Stringfellow came last (University of Chicago Divinity School, 1963). Stringfellow sat next to Hans Frei, whom he had first encountered in 1959 during some lengthy and involved work they both undertook as part of a group looking at the relationship between the church and the university for the Church Society for College Work (Church Society for College Work,1958a, b). They appear, from those papers, to have disagreed strongly: Stringfellow wanted to raise fundamental issues grounded in real life of faith, Frei wanted to work within existing epistemological assumptions and address things academically

17. Although as we have already seen, that book does not make explicit use of the principalities and powers, either because Stringfellow was unsure about introducing them because he did not have a sufficient grasp on the issues, or perhaps because he felt uneasy—concerned their mention might alienate his readers. There is also, of course, the main issue and reason: this was a work of proclamation, not prophetism.

directly. Barth seemed to use Stringfellow to speak for him, and it was an opportunity Stringfellow didn't miss.[18]

Frei's question concerned preaching, and for this reason it is worth briefly illuminating. "Unlike the Church in Nazi Germany, the Church in this country faces no clearcut political issues . . . It is difficult to preach in a society which is at once thoroughly sated and affluent and yet restless and uneasy." Frei wanted to know what exegetical principles should be applied, and whether or not the fact that the sermon points towards a gracious God might in itself make a sermon pertinent to the congregation in the context without clear-cut political issues (University of Chicago Divinity School, 1963:7). Stringfellow's response is a confident rehearsal of much of his current thinking.

> The thing that disturbs me about the question was the fact that I never saw any clear cut political issue, with the possible exception of some very erratically conservative Republicans, who thought they could see some clear cut political issues . . . I do not understand preaching as you seem to imply it here and wonder if you have not confused that task of preaching (that is to say, of exposing the Word of God—laying bare the Word of God—within the congregation—so that it may be enjoyed—so that it may be praised for itself and celebrated) with the work of prophetism . . . The Church and Christians in this country are accorded, on the whole, only two kinds of freedom—to speak publicly and to act publicly. (University of Chicago Divinity School, 1963:7)

In relation to these two freedoms, Stringfellow rehearses an argument which is central to *A Private and Public Faith*. So, with regards to the first, Stringfellow goes on to say that religion has only to do with religion, and is tolerated. With regards to the second, the church may intervene in public life only insofar as it supports and fosters national unity and the public policy at the given time; in other words, the freedoms afforded the church are freedoms in which the church has no political voice. He goes on to speak at some length, contextualizing this. It is a view Barth does not overturn, but elaborates the process of laying bare the Word of God in order to bring political issues into focus. This encounter speaks not only of Barth's fondness for the young Stringfellow's lifework, but

18. Barth turned to Frei and said "At this point I would like to ask Mr. Stringfellow to tell us something about his outlook on this question. That would be a good thing; it would help me to answer your question" (University of Chicago Divinity School, 1963:7).

also reminds us that Stringfellow's message in *A Private and Public Faith* was aimed directly at people such as these, and the distinction between preaching and prophetism is crucial, for it provides a horizon for biblically fostered political engagement with the world.

Now let us move on to Stringfellow's own two questions, both of which are rooted in his own lifework and theological agenda.

In the first question, Stringfellow asked Barth:

> to comment on how the Church and churches can maintain the freedom of the gospel to proclaim the gospel in such a society in which the churches seem to be constantly tempted to forswear the gospel in order to protect our freedom as external institutions in society. What bearing do the words of St. Paul in the thirteenth chapter of Romans have upon churches in such a position within such a society? (University of Chicago Divinity School, 1963:22)

Behind the question lay deep and controversial criticism,[19] and the issue with which it dealt was foundational to all of Stringfellow's subsequent theology: how do the churches, and how do Christians, live in the freedom of the gospel in the light of Paul's infamous words. Foresworn to silence, Barth refuses to answer, his words causing a stir amidst the gathering:

> I am troubled. What I have read and heard are statements with which I am in sympathy. *I like to hear you speak as you do,* but statements rather than questions. I could only whisper to you: *I think we agree.* But why only whisper? Because your concern is over this country—America—and . . . I came not to America in

---

19. Stringfellow's preamble to his question read as follows: "In the United States, the many and divided churches live in a society which constitutionally professes the freedom of public worship and the public practice of religion in a formal sense. That is, attendance at services, public preaching, representation of the religious and ecclesiastical authorities and institutions in public life and the like. It increasingly appears, however, that the use of that freedom . . . is confined to either the mere formalities of religious observance and the preservation of some religious causes, or the use of religion to rationalize, to serve, or to sanctify the national self-interest—the use of religion and of jargon and images of religion for the preservation, perhaps aggrandizement of the nation. Consequently, the churches do not commonly exercise a vitally critical attitude toward politics, public policy, or the nations actual life and culture" (University of Chicago Divinity School, 1963:21–22) It echoes not only his published material, but also his comments made earlier to Frei.

> order to criticize you. *Listen to this man.* (University of Chicago
> Divinity School, 1963:22, emphasis mine)[20]

His words were dramatic, and by his close Barth was standing, pointing squarely at Stringfellow. His meaning was clear: Barth advocated Stringfellow to America and urged it to listen. Stringfellow himself laughed, perhaps in jubilation. The gathering was stunned.[21]

The substance of Barth's answer is as important as his advocacy, and a discussion concerning "being subject" (as in, being subject to the state) ensued. Barth's exegesis of the term renders its meaning as conveying a notion of *responsibility*. He went on: "The Christian has to bear the task of the State, and that is what is lacking within many Christian circles; we are only spectators of political life" (University of Chicago Divinity School, 1963:23). The responsibility of the Christian is to participate in political life as a Christian—that is Barth's point. In submission to an order, we "go within the realm of this order—we take our place, and as human beings become responsible for what is done in this order" (University of Chicago Divinity School, 1963:23). This is not, as Stringfellow sought to clarify, automatic obedience, for as Barth said "there is no true obedience where there is not *free obedience*" (my emphasis, University of Chicago Divinity School, 1963:23). "Our freedom riders," responded Stringfellow, referring to the Freedom Ride protests of the civil rights movement of whom he was supportive, "must remember this" (University of Chicago Divinity School, 1963:23); contextually immersed, he urged them to remember that the Feedom Riders were acting legitimately, in free obedience to authentic politics.

Essentially, Barth insisted that Romans 13 means that the Christian life demands political action. Being subject to the state is an act of responsibility: we are responsible for the political order, responsible for

---

20. The transcript and recording diverge here: I owe this insight to a conversation with Bill Wylie-Kellermann. This quotation is taken from the transcript with the omissions restored (the latter two sets of text in italics). The editing itself was a political act, and one which no doubt would have been deeply disappointing to Stringfellow when they were published in 1963.

21. While the recording shows much noise in the gathering, the omission of this advocacy in the final edit suggests very clearly something of the feeling amongst the other panelists and the theological academy at large to Barth's advocacy. It was not what they expected and was not especially welcome. I suspect it did much to contribute to the walls of division which Stringfellow already felt existed between himself and the academy, rather than do anything at all to remove them.

seeking authentic politics. Our action is that of free obedience; an act born of the freedom of the resurrection, in obedience to God. We have seen this understanding already in Stringfellow's writing, but this particular phrasing of it by Barth was to prove so important to Stringfellow that it became the title of his next book, in which he developed many of the thoughts and ideas he had encountered here with Barth (Stringfellow, 1964b).[22]

The second question is closely related to the first and is comprehensive in scope. It showed an as yet unpublished direction in Stringfellow's own lifework, along with his existing criticism of the various forms of pietism. In this question he brings the angelic powers into the discussion in a manner which, with hindsight, provides a clear indication of the future direction of his own lifework.

> It appears to be widely believed, both within and, for that matter, outside the churches of the United States, that the history of redemption is encompassed merely by the saga of relationships in history between God and man. At the same time, it is in American Protestantism at least commonplace to distinguish as nothing more than archaic imagery, the biblical identification and discussion of the angelic powers present in the world. What there is of Protestant moral theology in America almost utterly ignores the attempt to account for, explicate, and relate one's self to the principalities and powers. Yet empirically, more and more, the principalities and powers seem to have an aggressive, indeed, possessive, ascendancy in American life—including, alas, the life of the American churches. (University of Chicago Divinity School, 1963:23)[23]

22. In the archives there is a handwritten note, undated, but filed in box 5. This box contained material related to the period 1960–1961. The note clearly makes reference to Romans 13, and explores themes of resistance, love, the Holy Spirit, and legitimate authority, angelic powers, and demonic possession. It is not clear if this note has been mis-filed, but there is no other reference to such themes explicitly at this time. If it has not been mis-filed, then it would suggest Stringfellow's own understanding of Romans 13 and the principalities and powers dated back to 1960–1961; such a date is perfectly possible, given the influence of Markus Barth and Jacques Ellul in the late 1950s in this area. It does not suggest, however, that Stringfellow had thought through the real implications of such ideas at this time. In my view this is supported by the meeting with Barth. Romans 13 was later to become central, both implicitly and explicitly (Stringfellow, 1977a).

23. Mention of "moral theology" is significant: over time Stringfellow began to understand his own task as that of articulating an American moral theology. At the time of writing, such mention of moral theology should be seen as an implicit reference

Stringfellow goes on to ask a comprehensive range of questions about the principalities and powers: Who are they? What is their significance to creation, the fall, and human sin? How do they relate to the claim of Christ's lordship over history? What is the relationship of the presence of the power of death to the principalities and powers, and therefore what (practical) freedom does the Christian have from their domin- ion? Stringfellow knows the issues; what he is seeking is their public declaration.[24]

The wording of this question and Stringfellow's later wording (Stringfellow, 1964b:51) are virtually identical, indicating the influence of this encounter upon later work; Barth's influence can be traced to the heart of Stringfellow's thinking on the principalities and powers at this point. These principalities and powers are fundamental to biblical poli- tics, for the politics of the fall and redemption are concerned with their ordering. In the world of the politics of the Bible, what is at stake is the principalities and powers, the world of possibilities and the use to which they are put, or to which they put us.

It is, as Barth says, a large question, and his response, comprehen- sive. What is interesting is the way in which Stringfellow's journey into principalities and powers made so soon after this encounter, and em- bracing so clearly the notion of freedom in obedience which Barth elu- cidates here, is something like a commentary and explication on Barth's own response; it seems to suggest that Stringfellow felt both affirmed and instructed by Barth's words.[25] In fact, at various points Stringfellow

---

to Reinhold Niebuhr, who was considered America's moral theologian *par excellence.* Niebuhr and Barth did not see eye to eye on politics, and Niebuhr was especially criti- cal of Barth (Niebuhr, 1959:141–96) and saw his "theological framework as defective for wise political decisions" (Niebuhr, 1959:186); he was too eschatological and too pragmatic. It seems to me that the same eschatological "pragmatic" (or, more precisely, practical and orientational) theology can be seen in Stringfellow; the dynamic reality of the Word of God in history, not principle and ideology, held sway. Niebuhr, being a liberal, seemed oblivious to this. Stringfellow's aligning of himself with Barth over the biblical politics of the principalities and powers is therefore a decision *against* Niebuhr, and a decisive step on the road to his explication of a new American moral theology.

24. Significantly, it is a series of questions which later form the basis of Stringfellow's own dealings with the principalities and powers (Stringfellow, 1964b:51–73) and it marks a turning point for him; a turning point which originated in his *practice* in Harlem.

25. That journey is his book *Free in Obedience* (Stringfellow, 1964b). Walter Wink's own exploration of the principalities and powers (Wink, 1984, 1986, 1992) began when he reviewed this book: "Chapter three of *Free in Obedience* changed my life" (Wink,

could almost be quoting Barth. For example, quoting Barth first, then Stringfellow:

> Everywhere that an ideology is ruling there such a power: a communist or anticommunist ideology; money is such a power . . . Sport is such a power . . . Traditions of all kinds are such angelic powers. Fashion for men and for women is also a power. What we call religion . . . is also a world of powers . . . reason is such a power. And let us not forget sex. (University of Chicago Divinity School, 1963:23)

> Ideology is perhaps the most self-evident principality in the world at the present time. Communism, fascism, racism, nationalism . . . humanism, capitalism, democracy, rationalism . . . Money is such a power . . . Sex, fashion, and sports are all among the angelic powers. (Stringfellow, 1964b:57, 59)

Barth went on to explain that all represent certain possibilities, none are good or bad, but man has separated himself from God and in so doing is alienated from God and his neighbor, and thus he has become alienated also from himself—from a person's authentic identity. Instead of being Lord of our possibilities and powers, they have become lord of him. In the Kingdom which is Jesus Christ, we are restored—our identity, our self, our being, is reconciled to its source of authenticity: "sinning man is replaced by a new man; what binds him in these powers is driven away and in the coming of the Kingdom he becomes free over against these powers. In Christ's death, man as sinner, man as alienated from himself, man as prey to death, is done in, finished" (University of Chicago Divinity School, 1963:23–24). This is virtually identical to Stringfellow's argument in relation to the church and the law, religion, and authenticity. It is also echoed later in his dealings with the principalities and powers and the power of death. In the following quotation from Stringfellow, the affinity and convergence between them is clear.

> In the biblical understanding of creation, the principalities or angelic powers, together with all other forms of life, are given by God into the dominion of men and are means through which men rejoice in the gift of life by acknowledging and honoring God, who gives life to all men and to the whole of creation . . .

1995:25). Stringfellow's own understanding of the principalities and powers in life and in print obviously predated his encounter with Barth, but his understanding was also transformed by their meeting.

> In the fall, every man, every principality, every thing exists in a
> condition of estrangement from his or its own life, as well as from
> the lives of all other men, powers, and things. In the fall the whole
> of creation is consigned to death ... [In principalities] men look
> to justify their existence, to find and define the lost meaning of
> their lives ... The idolatry of the demonic powers by men turns
> out always to be a worship of death ... The principalities claim,
> in other words, sovereignty over human life and history ... When
> a principality claims moral pre-eminence in history over a man's
> life it represents an aspiration for salvation from death and a hope
> that service to the idol will give existence a meaning somehow
> transcending death ... Death is greater than the principalities
> and powers, and none of them prevail against it. The whole of
> creation exists under the reign of death ... [Christ's] resurrection
> means the possibility of living in this life, in the very midst of
> death's works, safe and free from death. Christ's resurrection is for
> men and for the whole of creation, including the principalities of
> this world ... The reign of death ... is brought to an end in Christ's
> resurrection. (Stringfellow, 1964b:52, 62, 63, 64, 72, 73)

The reality of the power of death as reigning in the structures of
society through the principalities and powers was an important emphasis because of the prior popularity of the "Revival," and the emphasis it
placed upon equating death with personal sin: a common characteristic
of pietism. Stringfellow's is an attempt to orientate us out of that misconception. And Barth again had some interesting things to say about the
power of death or evil, in particular, the following:

> The ontological being of evil can be described in purely nega-
> tive terms, as for example, sin and evil and the devil himself are
> impossible possibilities. Or if you prefer, unreal realities. It can't
> be helped, that's her nature, because sin means life is a lie. You can
> describe a lie only in terms of a lie.... The devil whose possibility
> and reality I don't deny, can only be dealt with with horror, with
> contempt, with resistance, and even with humor ... God certainly
> laughs at him. (University of Chicago Divinity School, 1963:18)

The notion that you can describe a lie only in terms of a lie is an interesting one. Is he suggesting that resort to overstating your case against
evil, and describing evil in terms that are themselves not true, is in fact a
necessary part of speaking the truth to evil? And in so doing, evil is dealt
with by contempt, resistance, and humor?

Let us return to Stringfellow's question about the principalities and powers. Barth explained that the practical freedom which the Christian has lies in Christ's death and resurrection, and "in Him and through Him we have the freedom to look back to His first and look forward to His last coming and to look upon Him as present and as He will come. That is freedom. That is life ... Looking to Him means to be concrete with ... that one true spirit that is potent and mighty. In order to stand to fight these gods, we need His power" (University of Chicago Divinity School, 1963:24). Therefore, the practical freedom the Christian has is to be outside the power of the fall; to live in the power of life. That is, in essence, the freedom of the Christian life is implicated *now* in the *eschaton*. It is a theme we have seen already in Stringfellow, and one which will continue in prominence as he develops his understanding of the power of death and the principalities and powers following this encounter.

For now I would like to pay attention to the fact that similarities between them are so readily apparent. In Stringfellow's reception of Barth's responses (and indeed Stringfellow's statement of the questions), there is a mix of inspiration and affirmation going on. The significance of their encounter was profound and far reaching, and although it clearly tapped into thought and experience which Stringfellow was already working through in his lifework, Barth clearly helped Stringfellow to verbalize that which he had realized: to connect and move forward, and to do so with authority.

Stringfellow's resort to the use of the biblical theology of the principalities and powers is not an attempt to obscure or obfuscate the reality which faced American Protestantism—quite the opposite. His use of the principalities and powers was an attempt to bring clarity to that which seemed to so confuse and confound the churches: the spiritual nature of reality, which had been lost under the mountain of modern thinking. Moreover, it is the adoption of, or surrender to, the politics of the Bible. He wanted the churches, and Christians to allow themselves to be reconciled to their authenticity—to be reconciled to God, in Christ through the Spirit in the world. He felt the churches' ignorance of the Bible and their failure to take it seriously and authoritatively lay at the root of the problem; an ignorance of reality and the relevance of the principalities and powers in the modern world made this plain. So, in his questions to Barth it seems Stringfellow sought to get this reality on the public agenda of American's churches and its theologians; he sought to use Barth as an instrument of change within America, despite Barth's declaration of non-involvement. At one point, Barth says self-effacingly: "I don't like to speak here for Americans. That's what Americans must tell to Americans and not something that a poor man coming from Switzerland can tell you" (University of Chicago Divinity School, 1963:22). I suspect it was exactly what Stringfellow had been hoping for, for he also sought public validation of his own lifework. Therefore Barth's advocacy of Stringfellow was deeply significant both personally and publicly, for it served to authorize his theology, his radicalism, and also his emerging understanding of the reality of the authority of death, and the principalities and powers. In conclusion of this section, we need to pay attention to this act of advocacy.

Barth's declaration preceded Stringfellow's first and very political question, leading one to wonder if this was almost intentional. It is almost as if this conversation is led by some unseen hand to a seemingly inevitable, and yet entirely unpredictable, piece of advocacy: that America should "listen to this man." We can say but one thing with certainty—looking at the transcript and listening to the recording, it was a moment that the exchanges between Barth and Stringfellow had been building to and moving towards. And it wasn't over yet, for Barth concluded the conference with the following words.

> If I myself were an American citizen and a Christian and a theologian, then I would try to elaborate a theology of freedom—a theology of freedom from . . . good old Europe . . . freedom from a superiority complex . . . freedom from fear of communism, Russia, inevitable nuclear warfare and generally speaking from all the aforementioned principalities and powers . . . Freedom for, I like to say a single word, freedom for humanity . . . that freedom to which the Son frees us, and which as His gift, is the one real human freedom. My last question for this evening: will such a specific American theology one day arise? I hope so. (University of Chicago Divinity School, 1963:24)[26]

Barth's, like Stringfellow's, was an evangelical theology: it revealed and rejoiced, was engaged and excited by, the reality of God with us. Barth

---

26. This last mention of principalities and powers is met with amusement from the gathering—apparently not quite grasping the seriousness with which Barth uttered his response to Stringfellow's question. This only goes to support Stringfellow's thesis that Divinity schools were the last place to see truth.

and Stringfellow read the same Bible and were encountered by the same Word, and this, according to Barth, would appear to account for their congruence.[27] Having established theological affinity and sympathy with Stringfellow, and having identified already in conversation with Stringfellow that Christian freedom is freedom in obedience, and then having advocated America listen to Stringfellow, Barth has already indicated to the gathering a reality which (try as they might) is hard to ignore: what Stringfellow says is what Barth would say, if he could. Therefore, it would seem reasonable to conclude that when Barth outlines in closing what he would do if he were an American, it is also what he believes America should see and encounter in Stringfellow's own theology.

Stringfellow's encounters with Barth were both significant in themselves and also contributed to his emerging "status" as a national figure. The acceptance and recommendation which Barth gave Stringfellow was a turning point, for it marked a point of public and *theological* recognition and vindication; not only was Stringfellow right, but he was thoughtful and well regarded by a theologian that the American theological establishment so highly regarded. He and the "great-man himself" agreed over issues which seemed to simply fail to make an appearance on the theological horizons of the others on the panel. I am sure the advocacy was of Barth's doing but suspect Stringfellow had sought to orchestrate it; he was, after all, eager for approval at this time in his life.[28]

Stringfellow's encounters with Barth were therefore a dynamic affirmation, authorization, and stimulus to his lifework.[29] The fact that

27. Stringfellow explains that when he remarked to Barth that it was his experience that when Barth spoke he knew what was going to be said, Barth responded: "How could it be otherwise? We read the same Bible, don't we?" (Stringfellow, 1970e:152).

28. He was still in Harlem, and while things were changing and going well professionally, personally Stringfellow experienced his share of loneliness, isolation, and despair. There was, I suspect, a great personal need for love and acceptance around this time, and an ongoing working through of personal issues like loneliness; works like Stringfellow (1962g, 1962n) and Denham (1962) seem to point to this being the case. It was shortly after this encounter in 1962 that he met Anthony Towne.

29. Bill Wylie-Kellermann describes Barth's advocacy as "a blessing and an admonition to become notorious." Wylie-Kellermann also rightly observes that for any other of the panelists such advocacy would have been "quite literally, money in the bank" (Wylie-Kellermann,1994:1). For Stringfellow, this was true to a lesser degree: speaking engagements increased, more fees were earnt, but medical expenses were to soon devour what income he had earned, and illness to preclude earning more. For Stringfellow, the wealth was theological, not financial.

this was theological rather than legal recognition is also important, for in the Rockefeller Memorial Chapel that evening Barth addressed America's brightest theologians and told them to listen to *this* man— William Stringfellow. I suspect Stringfellow felt a combination of humility, justification, and joy, and perhaps most of all, a sense of camaraderie. But would America heed the infamous theologian's words?

STIRRING UP A STORM

In answer to that question, we turn our attentions to Chicago almost a year later, and the *National Conference on Religion and Race* at which Stringfellow spoke on January 24, 1963. This was an "unprecedented ecumenical gathering of nearly one thousand delegates including world renowned theologians such as Paul Tillich [as well as Martin Luther King and Rabbi Abraham Heschel] and the established leaders of nearly every religious body in America" (Branch, 1998:21). Did America listen to this man? What transpires from this conference is the answer, "probably not," at least not in ways which were instantly recognizable. Instead, he was met with resistance, especially amongst the theological and religious academy. Stringfellow's rhetoric seems to have been too impenetrable, his argument too uncompromising, his message too truthful, or his audience to unwilling to hear.

Stringfellow declared the assembly was "too little, too late, and too lily white" (Stringfellow, 1963b:13).[30] They were stunned (Branch, 1998:29, 31).[31] The conference was preoccupied with proclaiming practical response and commitment to civil disobedience and the churches involvement at various levels. Amidst this, he made an unexpected and unusual plea for realism about the truth of the racial crisis confronting America, in which, through his life in East Harlem, he had been immersed first hand. The real issue which confronted the delegation, ac-

---

30. One must bear in mind that his address was in the north. While southerners were perhaps used to being called racist, those from the north of America who were at involved in seeking to resolve the racial crisis had generally assumed a place of innocence in the affair; their role was in support of the African-Americans in their struggle, after all. Stringfellow here is essentially identifying the racism inherent in *all* of white America, and especially the dominant mood of white supremacy (benevolence, etc.) which he believed was their motivation for action. See Stringfellow (1963d,a).

31. It appears that the assembly's reaction stunned him too, and he was apparently found later visibly in shock, shut in a closet with a bottle of alcohol in his hand.

cording to him, was quite simply baptism. In so speaking, Stringfellow sought to recall the churches of America to their authentic vocation.[32]

This conference was the empirical manifestation of that which Stringfellow had previously been so critical, and its entire premise seemed flawed: "The truth is that this conference represents a mentality which still assumes that significant initiative in the racial crisis remains with the churches and the synagogues of the land," whereas in practice the churches and synagogues are generally just absent (Stringfellow, 1963b:13–14). Its desire to produce a "statement of conscience" was made "obsolete and absurd" by the "harsh realities which now emerge among American Negroes and which, now at last in the open, must be faced bluntly and truthfully and with some courage" (Stringfellow, 1963b:14). And betraying the white supremacy which he thought prevalent amidst religion in America, the conference was predicated on the "mentality which thinks that the initiative in the racial crisis resides with white folk. But the initiative has passed in the racial crisis in this country from white to black" (Stringfellow, 1963b:14).[33] His criticisms focused upon the fact that religion in America had little comprehension of how to act politically in the world, thus restraining itself to statements rather than action. His criticisms also extend to the racism inherent in religion, in the way it gave lip service to the racial crisis while avoiding implicating itself in the crisis, and in the way it believed that its own actions might actually bring the change black people sought. In this regard it wouldn't, and perhaps couldn't, face the fact of its own hand in the creation and maintenance of the crisis; religion was essentially a servant to the principality of racism. The evolution of his lifework is here consolidated in a single address.

The spirit which moves and acts in the racial crisis now, especially in the northern cities, is a spirit of radical hostility and of revenge. This conference will be protected from this news. This conference will not hear the voices of Malcolm X or even James Baldwin. And, the temptation is, by not in fact hearing them, the

---

32. Echoing this, at a much earlier date he had said: "The only enduring solution to our racial and nationality problem is the one which Christ himself described . . . the solution of love" (Stringfellow, 1950b).

33. This statement was issued in 1963, a number of years before the civil rights movement began to organizationally distance itself from white people. In this regard, Stringfellow's statement was ahead of its time.

conference will suppose they do not exist. This conference . . . represents a mentality which stupidly supposes that there is power and efficacy in individual action. From the point of view of either biblical religion, the monstrous American heresy is in thinking that the whole drama of history takes place between God and men. But the truth, biblically and theologically and empirically is quite otherwise: the drama of this history takes place amongst God and men and the principalities and powers, the great institutions and ideologies active in the world. It is the corruption and shallowness of humanism which beguiled Jew and Christian into believing that men are masters of institution or ideology. Or, to put it a bit differently, racism is not an evil in the hearts or minds of men, racism is a principality, a demonic power, a representative, image, and embodiment of death, over which men have little or no control, but which works its awful influence over the lives of men. This is the power with which Jesus Christ was confronted and which, at great and sufficient cost, he overcame. In other words, the issue here is not equality among men, but unity among men. The issue is not some common spiritual values, nor natural law, nor middle axioms. The issue is baptism. The issue is the unity of all mankind wrought in the life and work of Christ. Baptism is the sacrament of that unity of all men in God. (Stringfellow, 1963b:14–15)

In his address, Stringfellow was in no doubt: at the heart of the reconciliation of the races will be the reconciliation of all humanity to God, and this means the crucifixion. He was calling upon the very act which underlay the ecumenicity of the gathering for the resolution of the racial crisis—unity—but it met with hostility. Yet despite this he went on to conclude by offering practical application, but not of the kind that was anticipated: "We were supposed now to be practical: to say what could be done in the American racial crisis. If you want to do something, the most practical thing I can tell you is: weep. First of all, care enough to weep" (Stringfellow, 1963b:15).[34]

It is little wonder that his address was received with hostility, for he directly implicated his listeners in the reality they sought to confront; he critiqued and challenged their commonly held assumptions and as-

---

34. On ecumenism, he maintained that faith and order are concerned with "the everyday issues of life and death in this world [which] contain the substantive issues of faith and order in Christianity" (Stringfellow, 1963f:9). His criticism of the Faith and Order movement runs along similar lines to the *Religion and Race* conference, and revolves around baptism as the sacrament of unity.

sertions for understanding and dealing with the racial crisis. The radical
and unmistakable truth for Stringfellow was the moral and theological
implication of the churches in the racial crisis (the life of the White
Anglo-Saxon Protestants was built upon racism), and the slavery into
which it had therefore fallen; they were slaves to the institution and ideology of racism, not its masters. See here how he acknowledges that the
principalities and powers have actual, creaturely, independent life within
creation: they are not something primarily concerned with our private
personal moral conduct, but rather are independent entities requiring
allegiance. They are what Barth described above as the ontological being
of evil, manifest in the world: they are a lie.

Contrary to the dominant view of American Protestantism at the
time, Stringfellow held that the relevance of baptism was concretely political and social. "Baptism is the assurance—accepted, enacted, verified,
and represented by Christians—of the unity of *all* . . . in Christ . . . The
oneness of the Church is the foretaste and guarantee of the reconciliation
of all men to God, and of the unity of all men and all creation in the life
of God. The Church, as the baptized community, is called to be the image
of all mankind, the one and intimate community of God" (Stringfellow,
1962m). Instead of adopting worldly ideologies and attitudes towards
the racial crisis—whereby the churches' actions were consigned to writing pledges, conventions, pronouncements, holding Race Relations
Sundays, or even participating in nonviolent action which sought to
allow access to, for example, Woolworth's lunch counter—Stringfellow
called America's churches to re-appropriate that which is at the heart
of their very existence: to truly live as the church of Christ. Again let us
be clear, he did not oppose the direct action of the white campaigners,
so long as they remembered their moral implication in the racial crisis (which, he believed, they did not); in protesting against racism, they
themselves stood condemned. For such protest was, if anything, a public
act of confession and prayer, and if they cared at all, they would surely
weep for their part in it, and for all white people.[35]

He was simply advocating the exposure of the truth, and the fundamental truth was of humanity's reconciliation to God (and to each
other) in Christ, celebrated in the sacrament of baptism. He believed

---

35. Stringfellow was, conversely, a supporter of the Civil Rights Movement; his argument here is against the churches. We have already discussed the centrality of the issue
of race in Stringfellow's lifework, including his own restaurant sit-in.

this seemingly missiological statement was the only answer to disunity and the only answer to the racial crisis.[36] "The church does not model its society upon the prevailing society around it. But upon Baptism" (Stringfellow, 1962m). His emphasis upon baptism here represents the culmination of his thinking about unity, which began with his work in the ecumenical movement and finds a natural home in the social issue which so divided America.

Once again, then, this time in explicit relation to the racial crisis which dominated the social context of the time, Stringfellow is calling the churches of America to live authentically; by and large the churches simply couldn't see baptism in the way in which Stringfellow portrayed it—for them it was still very much a private and personal matter.[37] The racial crisis went to the heart of American identity. The churches response, which worked solely within the prevailing understanding of religion as a private and non-political entity, consigned it to complicity.

There are other illustrations of hostility occurring at the same time over this issue; one of these is in response to an article which he published the previous year—"Race, Religion and Revenge" (Stringfellow, 1962l). The article, in which explicit mention of the principalities and powers is absent, is otherwise similar in tone to his address in Chicago almost a year later. It provides a first hand account of life in Harlem amidst poverty and amidst the crisis of racism. It tells of the radical disenchantment of black people with the attempts of the cities' churches, and the efforts of white people to "integrate" them into their world in which "tolerance" is still offensively preached (offensive to the baptism of men into the body of Christ).[38] In this article, Stringfellow tells a story of a dream in which he is innocently standing on a street corner in Harlem and is

36. While the Civil Rights Bill was passed, and has reduced much explicit racial hatred, the racial crisis in America lingers on even today.

37. The fact that Anabaptists and Mennonites *could* see baptism in the way Stringfellow advocates is what lay partly behind his statement later that he considered himself theologically a closet Anabaptist (Wylie-Kellermann, 1994:158). Certainly, his thinking is thoroughly ecclesiological.

38. Here, and at the conference, Stringfellow identified another important reality which was being ignored by the churches. Amidst black Americans there was increasingly anti-Semitism; in their desire to identify and state their uniqueness, they sought to distance themselves from other "minorities." Identity amidst civil rights activists was increasingly becoming a matter of defining oneself over-against—emphasizing the radical difference (otherness/transcendence) rather than the coming alongside (unity/incarnation).

approached by two young men who stab him and kill him. Reflecting upon this unnerving dream, he thinks about why an innocent man such as himself might have been killed in this way, especially a man such as him, who had spent so many years living and working in Harlem and counted many of these people as his friends. Then he realized he was not innocent: he was white, and *"was murdered by the black man because he was a white man. The murder was retribution. The motive was revenge. No white man is innocent. I am not innocent."* When he realized this, he says, "I cried" (original emphasis; Stringfellow, 1962l:194). He cared enough to weep.

His article did not go without criticism. Almost a year later, shortly after the conference in Chicago, he received a letter from a clergyman. The man, who was deeply involved in the churches response to racism in New York (i.e., the drafting of resolutions), objected to the tone of his article, and stated that he knew many Episcopal churches in New York which do not exclude, but welcomed Negroes into their congregations. He accuses Stringfellow of lying. It highlighted precisely what Stringfellow was critical of, and what the churches failed to comprehend. He responded:

> Harlem's Negroes are fed up with nominal integration in the churches, education, politics, employment and the rest . . . [They] are not impressed or appeased by a little bit of integration here and there in the Episcopal Church or other churches . . . The thing that vitiates what you fondly call "tremendous progress" is that today—fifty years after the beginning of the Negro migration to the northern cities—most Negroes still live in New York and the other great cities in stinking, stifling, ghettos, segregated in every significant way from the rest of the city. In New York alone, 35% of the Negroes in the metropolitan area live in one or other of the five Negro ghettos. If that is progress, then go ahead and boast of it, but I think such boasting is vanity. (Stringfellow, 1963b)

Stringfellow seemed to preemptively identify many of the strains and stresses which were to drive some parts of the Civil Rights Movement to violence and retribution.[39] Violence, he also predicted, would be the next resort of the racial crisis, and perhaps to everyone's dismay it was:

39. His statements almost seem a refrain of both Stokley Carmichael and Malcolm X's impassioned words, and he speaks out of his profound and life-changing experience of living in Harlem. Except, of course, that Carmichael and X didn't utter these words until later in the decade.

Black Panthers and Malcolm X, for example, soon had a large following of people no longer committed to nonviolent protest.[40] Stringfellow's response is radical and a dissent from the mainstream. The further into the politics of reconciliation he is drawn, the more the reality of the powers and principalities and the power of death are made known, and the more marginalized he finds himself becoming. Yet at the same time, the more authentic is the personal and public reality he uncovers. That is the paradox of Stringfellow's work and of the journey it takes throughout this period, and that is also the reality of biblical politics.

Stringfellow had been committed to addressing the racial crisis for many years, and was not opposed to the nonviolent civil rights activism of Martin Luther King's organizing.[41] Indeed, he represented many of those arrested because of their participation in such action. Practicing nonviolence, he was eager to make clear, did not alter a persons moral responsibility for the thing which that person protests against: the white person demonstrating against racism was still morally implicated in racism, by virtue of being white. Real progress required this recognition, and that is, of course, Stringfellow's point in all of this. As Stringfellow put it: "It seems to me that the issue is largely a tactical one. Is this the way to get the results?" (Stringfellow, 1963c). In other words, he did not buy into the ideology of pacifism as a solution, nor the politically liberal agenda (of accommodation) which accompanied it, but instead turned to biblical politics.[42]

---

40. He recognized that this was not an isolated or unusual incident, for America "was born in violence," in the protest of the American Revolution, the Articles of Confederation, the abolitionist movement, and the Civil War, violence overseas through colonialism and war, labor revolution, women's suffrage, and "the veterans" rebellion during the Depression" (Stringfellow, 1965h:527). In the case of the racial crisis, it was a violence born of despair. While there were a considerable number of violent protests, Stringfellow was keen that people understand the way in which violence permeates the whole of society, indicating that, for example, those who own insurance policies participate in violence through this act because insurance companies speculate in slum real estate, or what is otherwise called urban renewal: the principalities perpetuate and participate in violence.

41. Upon King's assassination, Stringfellow said the following: "Whatever happens now, let white citizens remember that the era of black non-violence, the time of Martin Luther King, has been the only significant movement of social protest in the whole of American history . . . And let every white man know too that if non-violence is now ended it is not because it has failed nor because it was abandoned, but because black non-violence has been routed by the violence of white society" (Stringfellow, 1964a).

42. In a document dating from 1960, Stringfellow's own approach to the racial crisis

However, for Stringfellow civil disobedience as a whole was, in effect, a Christian duty. The tendency in America was for each side in a political struggle to claim confidence in knowing that their view is the will of God. Therefore, whenever a group's view came into tension with the law then the group would claim simply that it was doing God's will and disobey the law. The same battle went on between opposing parties in any civil struggle; for example, this was one of the recurring themes during the confrontations of the racial crisis between pro- and anti-segregationists. Stringfellow advocated the need to think differently, and his thought echoes Barth's own thinking in this area.[43]

> The fundamental service of the Christian to his state is his recognition of the authority of the state to make, enforce, administer, and adjudicate the law to govern the common life of society. But the Christian, at the same time, knows that the state holds and exercises this authority under God and, in a sense, in the name of God. The Christian also reminds the state of the service which it owes to God: the state is accountable to God in governing the common life. The Christian honors the authority of the state in a way which calls upon the state to honor God, in whom all authority essentially and finally resides. This means that the relationship between the Christian and the state is *never* one of uncritical allegiance or obedience. This means concretely that Christians could never accede to any demand of the state that the state itself become the object of men's worship . . . Christians do not engage in civil disobedience as anarchists . . . not in order to overthrow the rule of law, but as a means of changing the law. Christians then take upon themselves the state's hostility toward God, accept the condemnation of the law of the state, are imprisoned, executed, or exiled as a means of upholding the vocation of the state to exercise its authority in civil life as a service to God . . . they are subject to the state for the Lord's sake. (Stringfellow, 1962m)

is readily apparent. Originating out of his experience of life in Harlem, it was entitled "Surrender as Solution to the Racial Crisis," by which he indicated vocational surrender of one's race, it reads: "Maybe I am crazy. Maybe I am eccentric, and have had some particular experience which is to be treated with humor, or some kindred consideration. Maybe I am hysterical. Maybe I am too subjective. Maybe I am wrong. Maybe. William Stringfellow is a man who surrendered his race some time ago" (Stringfellow, 1960g).

43. This may owe something to Barth turning to Stringfellow during the conference in Chicago and whispering: "It's all in *Church and State.*" This anecdote transpired in conversation with Wylie-Kellermann, who also informs me that Stringfellow's copy of that book became heavily annotated.

This is the radical call of evangelical discipleship to resist the power of death as and when it makes itself known in the state through its rule of law, not in order to replace the state, for the church is not the state (it is the church). Rather, it seeks to call the state to account: to remind it of its own vocation, under God—to call it to authenticity. In so doing it reminds itself of its own vocation as the church. It is, simply, an act of faith: a free act of obedience (freedom in obedience), an act of mission, an act of prophecy. The purpose of civil disobedience is the positive and hopeful act of resistance to the power of death. This idea of resistance was to become a cornerstone to Stringfellow's lifework and his understanding of ethics, and its formulation can here be traced back essentially to the racial crisis and the Barth conference.

While Stringfellow's lifework at this time appears to resonate under Barth's influence, it would appear from the conference on Religion and Race that Barth's advocacy didn't appear to have the effect that one might ordinarily have expected, and at the center of this divergence was the tension between alienation and advocacy.

Stringfellow's lifework and especially his speech exposes the reality of this tension which he lived. Harlem, in which the marginalized were "alienated from society," exposed to him the actual alienation of society from God: it exposed the principalities and powers, the veracity of the resurrection, and the power of death, manifest in the world. This was not some theoretical theological statement, no idle piece of research; it was Stringfellow's life.

It was an existential encounter to which he made himself vulnerable, and which implicated him in this discovery, morally, theologically, and authentically. He discovered there was no place to hide from the burden of truth which was revealed to him.

Consequently, aligning himself with the truth which he beheld was a costly business. Authenticity before God required a stance of alienation from the "norms" of society. Essentially, authenticity led to cultural marginalization. Conversely, authenticity in society, which was the worldly and cultural "norm," was in fact alienation before God. Recovering authentic vocation is therefore a sacrificial political event of proclamation and prophetism.

The further on into his life we travel from this point, the more readily this tension between alienation and authenticity becomes apparent and prominent, as the real depths of the fall are exposed to Stringfellow,

and as he recovers real authenticity which looks to the world like alienation or marginalization. The Kingdom really is a world turned upside
down; perhaps that speaks to the truth of what Stringfellow had uncovered and exposed. It certainly left him exposed; it was a lonely and
isolating existence.

At a personal level, his lifestory is one in which those needs are met
in unlikely and unexpected ways. Standing before that conference and
delivering his message was an exacting task. His desire for approval from
the academy along with approval from his audience did not hold sway
over his message. This was a man who sought fervently, and often pain-
fully and sacrificially, to live authentically—to be true to authentically
inhabiting his life in Christ in the world, as determined by the politics of
redemption. It often met with silence, but more often the reactions were
more extreme: hostility or rapturous embrace. Trying to live this kind of
life placed huge demands upon Stringfellow physically and emotionally,[44]
and as we shall see, exposing the veracity and pervasiveness of the power
of death led increasingly to his own marginalization.

In the early 1960s, Stringfellow had thought that the "apostasy of
white denominationalism in America was an issue of acculturation and
secular conformity" (Stringfellow, 1970d:1347), and his work above
echoes this sentiment. This is why he stressed baptism; it was a reasser-
tion of the truth of the gospel in the hope of bringing about transformation from within. It was a desire that the churches might recall their
authentic vocation, and a faithful and confessional articulation of the
basis of that vocation. To a liberal ecumenical gathering used to politically correct rhetoric and advocacy of the policies which Martin Luther

44. Such hostility can be seen clearly, for example, in notes attached to a presentation he gave to the National Ecumenical Youth Conference in Tennessee, America's
South and the heartland of racial tension at the time: "The enclosed speech will give you
some idea of the deliberate indoctrination being given to our children in schools supported by our churches and our labor. As far as can be ascertained this 'Stringfellow' is
a New York lawyer frequently used as a lecturer by, you guessed it, the National Council
of Churches [A council presumably seen as a northern liberal outfit]. Portraying the use
of narcotics by children as a good thing should lead us to action—such as withdrawing
from the NCCA and giving out support and funds to organizations that support the
'American Way of Life'" (Stringfellow, 1963o). In the speech, Stringfellow spoke about
his work in Harlem and the addiction of many of its inhabitants. It is descriptive and
factual. The comments attached to this speech are indicative of the social tensions of the
time between black and white, and North and South. It speaks, therefore, of the very real
tensions that existed even within the church at this time; speaking the way Stringfellow
did was a costly enterprise.

King pursued, it was an utterance which would have probably been seen as just plain offensive.

Yet there was no sign of Stringfellow's rhetoric lightening up, for he had yet to fully appreciate the practical depths to which the power of death pervaded. Looking back after almost a decade of rebuttal by the church and its establishments, he decided he had gravely misunderstood the situation. By that time, he decided, "the apostasy here is not so quaint, but is, in truth, a *generic* apostasy: white Anglo-Saxon Protestantism is radically false. It represents no corruption of the gospel only, it is an aggression against the gospel. And as such its influence in this society and culture has been pervasive, infecting churches outside its nominal precincts as well as dominating the ethics of society" (Stringfellow, 1970d:1347). That was the issue at hand here: that through the perversity of religion which was American Protestantism the ethics of American society were shaped. American Protestantism, Stringfellow came to realize, was not a benign party, the proverbial "lost sheep," it was an active aggressor to the gospel. This is a startling pronouncement by Stringfellow, which indicates not least the extraordinary extent of his marginalization at this time, and the growing extremity or radicalization of his message. What brought this about? Essentially, a continuation of the journey of intensification over biblical politics and theology, through which the radical and political significance of the Easter story (the incarnation, death, and resurrection of Christ) is exposed.

With the empirical encounter and centrality of unity in mind, we move now to the third and final radicalizing encounter.

PARABLE OF LIFE: ANTHONY TOWNE

Homosexuals . . . are not respectable, according to the ethics of American society. The homosexual is, probably, the most unpopular sort of person in this society despite, perchance because of, the prevalence of homosexuality, in one form or another, in this country. I am a Christian, not a moralist, so I am not too much impressed by the mere fact that homosexuals are rejected by society. After all, the Pioneer of the faith expended His ministry to the whole world by caring for outcasts—the whores and tax collectors, the blind and the idiotic lepers and insurrectionists, the poor and those possessed by demons. If homosexuals in this society are orphans or prisoners for a Christian that is in itself enough reason to be concerned with them. (Stringfellow, 1965a:2)

The "guilt" of homosexuality to Stringfellow's generation was also one born of association.[45] Publicly, it appeared that Stringfellow's association with homosexuals was in fact association with the marginalized, no different from his association with drug addicts, civil rights activists, peace demonstrators and other politically unpopular clients; there is truth in this. Certainly, homosexuals were a marginalized group, but his association with them was more than the sacramental advocacy of his Christian life—Stringfellow himself was homosexual. It is the impact of this reality upon his lifework, and his own understanding of homosexuality, which we shall address in this section.

For Stringfellow, the person he was to fall in love with, Anthony Towne, was a parable of hope.[46] *A Simplicity of Faith* (Stringfellow, 1982b) is an autobiographical reflection upon faith and a moving and powerful account of Towne's sudden and unexpected death in January 1980, and Stringfellow's experience of mourning.[47] In it he acknowledges Towne as his "sweet companion for seventeen years" (Stringfellow, 1982b:115), a description the publishers tried to remove, but which he himself insisted on keeping.[48] Stringfellow's relationship with Anthony changed his life, to the degree that Stringfellow described Towne as "his conscience": that was his epithet for Anthony Towne (Stringfellow,1982b:23).[49]

45. This is evidenced by Stringfellow's own words: "Some of my colleagues in the legal profession and among the clergy advised me not to appear here, fearing that there is guilt imputed by association" (Stringfellow, 1965a). This address was given at Christ Church Cathedral, Hartford, Conn., but was originally delivered to the Mattachine Society in New York city. Stringfellow's formal association with it was through the *George Henry Foundation* for whom Stringfellow was legal counsel (Gross, 1964).

46. Although the archives seem notoriously devoid of any love letter from Stringfellow to Towne, there is one from Towne to Stringfellow (Towne, 1963b). See also Stringfellow's introduction to Towne's book of poems (Stringfellow,1963h).

47. Along with *My People is the Enemy* (Stringfellow, 1964d), and *Second Birthday* (Stringfellow, 1970e), it is the third in the trilogy of autobiography. It was, in a similar vein to these, a theological (biographical) reflection upon death; a matter of some vocational importance and significance to Stringfellow. Towne was a significant part of Stringfellow's life, and his account of their life together, their journey and collaboration, is moving and evocative.

48. This was, essentially, the closest Stringfellow ever came to becoming uncloseted.

49. Towne's influence upon Stringfellow's work was at once subtle and profound. He contributed explicitly with Stringfellow to a number of books (see Stringfellow and Towne [1967, 1971, 1976]), but he also provided the basis of acceptance and love which

They met at a party in 1962, organized by the General Secretary of the WCC, W. A. Visser 't Hooft. Towne was the barman for the night, Stringfellow a guest; both had been invited by the host, a mutual friend, Marvin Halverson.[50] "This happened," said Stringfellow, "at a time when I still used alcohol and, indeed, drank enthusiastically; hence, Anthony and I became well acquainted during that evening" (Stringfellow, 1982b:47). This chance meeting led to a further and decisive encounter:

> One morning, a few months later, Anthony came to my law office, reporting that he was at that very hour being evicted from his apartment in Greenwich Village. I spent most of the remainder of the day on the matter, but it was by then simply too late to frustrate or forestall the eviction. We did recover Anthony's possessions—books, mostly, and an old typewriter—from the clutches of the sheriff, and in the late afternoon I suggested to Anthony that he stay at my place pending opportunity to consider the situation. And so our acquaintance became friendship, then, eventually, community. (Stringfellow, 1982b:47–48)[51]

That same year they moved together to a penthouse apartment on West 79th Street in a rather rundown block. And so it was that Stringfellow left his beloved Harlem: a new chapter of his lifework had begun.

The archives appear to reveal at least two things about Stringfellow's homosexuality: firstly, its importance to his faith, and secondly, that while it was not public, it was by no means suppressed. Stringfellow's homosexual relationships would appear to date back at least as far as 1947 (Andy, 1947). Certainly, by 1948 as we have already noted, Stringfellow recounted the significance of an "unusually close friendship with another fellow" which led to a "conversion experience" (Stringfellow, 1948). Looking at the correspondence in the archives, I suspect this friendship was a homosexual relationship of some sort, and consequently his conversion experience appears to have been closely connected with the acceptance (of himself, and by another) of his sexuality; he discovered

---

allowed Stringfellow to flourish. Stringfellow dedicated his early work on the principalities and powers, *Free in Obedience*, to Towne (Stringfellow, 1964b).

50. Halverson headed up the *Foundation for Arts, Religion and Culture* and was a closeted homosexual (Berrigan, undated).

51. Stringfellow never really entered "gay culture"; Towne on the other hand was immersed in it in Greenwich Village, and Towne was responsible for introducing Stringfellow to a number of people from this scene, especially Ray Karras, who was initially to spend some time with them on Block Island.

the truth about his identity and sought to reconcile himself to it, and a personal acceptance of Christ's reconciliation of him to God. In this sense, homosexuality is highly significant for his lifework—at the center of his own vocation—and might indeed explain a number of otherwise inexplicable things.[52] Most notably, the strength and importance of this personal encounter with God to Stringfellow must not be undervalued; it was the driving force behind his lifework.

Although closeted, as a homosexual Stringfellow was himself marginalized, and this marginalization put him in touch with reading the gospel from "below"—from the perspective of the marginalized. Perhaps this is why he believed he could see the power and pervasiveness of death with such clarity: an apparent visionary among the blind. There is clearly a connection between his sexuality, his conversion, and his "existential" commitment to life, and it is clear that he used many means, including existentialism, to explore himself. His associations with leftist politics were common amongst homosexuals at this time, and homosexuals in turn became the victims of communist witch-hunts. This one subgroup became the embodiment of a nation's rage, in turn pushing homosexuals further underground. It is little wonder, then, that Stringfellow wanted to keep his sexuality a quiet and private matter.[53] He never publicly came out as gay, so his concern for the marginalized and his association with leftist politics may represent a sublimation of his homosexuality.

The key to his vocation and his life (including his sexuality) was that he discovered love, or more rightly, he was discovered by love. This is indicated by his "Politics as Ministry" paper and is also more distinctly indicated by an article entitled "Loneliness, Dread and Holiness" (Stringfellow, 1962f). In this paper, more than anywhere else, we can see the evidence not only of him having wrestled with loneliness himself, for it was a matter "too profoundly subjective" for him "to pretend to be objective about it" (Stringfellow, 1962f:1220). At that time he realized that the largest number moving to the city could be identified not by

52. For example, his affinity with and advocacy for the marginalized and dispossessed.

53. There were a number of relationships in Stringfellow's life before Anthony, the most notable of which was with someone called Syd, who appears to have been involved with the National Council of the Protestant Episcopal Church and was involved in the youth ecumenical movement. The correspondence is lengthy and originates from 1954, while Stringfellow was at law school and before he moved to Harlem. The letters represent only one side of the conversation, as there are none from Stringfellow to "Syd."

race or nationality, but by the fact that they were single, and it made loneliness very apparent, while offering some kind of distraction from it. Loneliness, in short, was the alienation of people from their authentic selves—a state of being subject to the power of death, which Christ frees us from by his own submission to death, and thereby reconciles us to Him and each other. Thus the relationship between authenticity and alienation, which Stringfellow pursued through "existentialism," is finally and fully exposed in his theology of both the fall and reconciliation. What is notable is Stringfellow's focus upon the way in which "erotic infatuation" was, for many, an attempt to sate the thirst of loneliness (Stringfellow, 1962f:1220). Out of this subjectivity, Stringfellow speaks of the way in which one can obtain services from prostitutes and homosexuals, and

> relieve loneliness in lust ... Here are folk, whether men or women, whether looking for the same or other sex, for whom seduction becomes a way of life ... Here are the lonely whose search for a partner is so dangerous, so stimulating, so exhausting that the search itself provides an apparent escape from loneliness ... [And] perhaps this is the most absurd fiction of them all: that one's own identity must be sought and can be found in another person ... There is no man who does not know loneliness: even Jesus Christ; but Christ himself has shown that there is no man who is alone ... Love yourself, that is the root of all other loves ... that means your final acceptance of and active participation in God's love for you ... And when you love another, tell him so, celebrate your love not only by words but by your life toward him and toward the whole world ... If you fear rejection by another you do not love that other ... The free man does not seek the love of others. (Stringfellow, 1962f:1220,1221,1222)

He seems to be speaking out of personal experience and struggle,[54] and his own ever increasing knowledge of love: God's and man's. Love, and therefore unity, understood and experienced both personally and politically, is central to his life-work. Note how one can substitute "loneliness"

54. Correspondence, especially from John Denham, a friend of Towne and Stringfellow, possibly a lover of one or other of them, would suggest this; as with all of his theology, there was here no separation of life and work (Denham, 1962). Stringfellow later acknowledges that his time in Harlem was lonely, and that he had therefore absorbed himself physically and intellectually. The establishing of the law firm, with William Ellis and Frank Patton, provided a semblance of routine which helped to keep loneliness at bay (Stringfellow, 1970e:36).

for "death," in the quotation without loss of clarity: loneliness taught Stringfellow something about the power of death in a personal and existential manner, just as the struggles of Harlem's residents with the various institutions taught him about death's public reign. But no doubt this was also a two-way learning process: both exposure to the power of death and the gospel taught him about death.

Stringfellow wrote this article at the end of his time in Harlem, and the fact that he did so, reflecting upon his own struggles, would go to confirm my thesis that he went to Harlem to lose himself, and to find himself: to find acceptance and love and a place to call home. In Harlem, that was achieved.[55] In Harlem he was surprised by God, and, for example, discovered the principalities and powers. His ability to see them came from his openness, and his openness was derived from his affinity with the marginalized: there was mutual acceptance and recognition. In Harlem, there was credibility to being marginalized—a freedom to be yourself. There, being marginalized meant that you were "normal." In Harlem, the world was not looking on; nobody looked on, except God.

Essentially, Stringfellow was liberated by Towne to live more openly and, although still closeted, was nevertheless more identifiable in gay circles. However, the eventual move to Block Island was, in some ways I suspect, an attempt by Stringfellow to create a distance, and to allow their relationship to flourish outside, beyond, and without the gay culture which loomed large in New York subculture.

Stringfellow's public association and involvement with homosexuality took essentially two guises: legal counsel and public speaking. In both he understood his role as advocate. In the first, he was especially prominent as the legal counsel for the George Henry Foundation, which represented many members of the leftist Mattachine Society.[56] From his counsel, we learn of the reality of his advocacy; from his public speaking, we begin to understand something more about this advocacy. In an address originally given to the Mattachine Society, he said:

55. As we saw earlier, in chapter 3, this was by his reckoning achieved in Harlem (Stringfellow, 1982b:141).

56. His involvement as legal counsel included, for example, giving advice to Louie Crew, founder of *Integrity* (Crew, 1976b, a), and Donald Schilling, during demonstration at the Civil Rights troubles in Selma (Newsweek, 1965); Stringfellow knew Schilling through the George Henry foundation, and he was also gay. What is clear is that amidst the advocacy and solidarity, there were many unspoken connections, and sexuality was one of these.

> The homosexual's rejection of self is responsible, I would venture, at least as much as any other factor for the rejection of the homosexual by society. That is most conspicuously the case where self-consciousness, display, or other ostentation characterizes the public conduct of homosexuals, as it does, to mention the notorious examples, with the elegant queens, the screaming faggots, and the Mattachine Society crowd. Mind you, I am no judge of any of those who so behave: the question I raise is, rather, how much such behavior both evidences radical self-rejection and, at the same time, solicits social rejection. (Stringfellow, 1965b:3–4)

While Stringfellow asserts the legal similarity of homosexuality and civil rights, for both were dealt with in terms of disorderly conduct, what we are most interested in is understanding Stringfellow's theological view of homosexuality, and, in his own words, "the more existential problems of sex and sin" (Stringfellow, 1965b:8). In this matter, he was eager to assert that he was "not bound by the mere conformities and conventions of this or any other society" (Stringfellow, 1965b:8).

Essentially, Stringfellow believed homosexuality received attention well in excess of its worth. Worse, it received this attention as a scapegoat from our various idols and institutions concerning relationships. He neither supported nor agreed with the politicization of homosexuality, either by radicals or conservatives. The question which plagued his theological horizons, as it plagues ours, is this: *Can a homosexual be a Christian?* Or, in other words, is Christianity compatible with homosexuality. However, the question itself is based upon a negative presumption regarding the status of homosexuality, and Stringfellow wanted to address this head on; and in so doing, he begins to reveal to us his own understanding of his sexuality.

> Can a Homosexual be a Christian. One might as well ask, can an insurance man be a Christian? Can a lawyer be a Christian? Can an ecclesiastical bureaucrat be a Christian? Can a rich man be a Christian? Can an infant be a Christian? Or one who is sick, or insane, or indolent or one possessed of power or status or respectability? Can anybody be a Christian? Can a human being be a Christian? All such questions are theologically absurd. To be a Christian does not have anything essentially to do with conduct or station or repute. To be a Christian does not have anything to do with the common pietisms of ritual, dogma or morals in and of themselves. To be a Christian has, rather, to do with that

peculiar state of being bestowed upon men by God. (Stringfellow, 1965b:8–9)

There is nothing *whatsoever* that we can do or be that might make us *worthy* of being a Christian. To be a Christian, simply, is a matter of grace, and it has everything to do with that, and the self-acceptance which it brings and enables, "which is the profound affirmation of one's own identity as a human being in relation to all other life" (Stringfellow, 1965b:9). We see now, perhaps more clearly, the significance of his own experience of acceptance and self-acceptance in Harlem, which began in his relationship in college. To be a Christian is to be made completely vulnerable to God's "own affirmation of one's existence as it is in relation to the whole of creation and then, as it were, to participate in God's affirmation of one's self and of all things" (Stringfellow, 1965b:9). Nothing of our human experience can deprive us of the love of God.

All that does stand as an impediment is our "idolatry of something common to human experience" (Stringfellow, 1965b:9)—in other words, being subject to the power of death and the principalities and powers, be it in money, power, status, race, religion, fashion, or sex and sexuality. "Can a homosexual be a Christian? Yes: if his sexuality is not an idol" (Stringfellow, 1965b:9). So long as his sexuality is not politicized, worshipped, and celebrated in and of itself, so long, finally but not exclusively, as it is not beheld as the defining characteristic of a person's identity: so long as it is not the image in which that person is made or remade.[57]

While this understanding is fashioned by Stringfellow within the context of his theology of the power of death, his view can be traced back as early as 1953, when Stringfellow wrote, "sexual appetite is biologically given and morally neutral. Motivation is the key in sex behavior" (Stringfellow, 1953a). It seems clear that his own thinking about homosexuality and his being homosexual, while not perhaps being singularly determinate, nevertheless had some significant bearing upon the formation of his theology and the direction it took throughout his

---

57. Clearly, there is no desire to either appease the Mattachine Society's politicization of sexuality here, nor the gay sub-culture which existed, and which Towne had himself been a part of. Nor does he support the homosexual "sects" in the churches, because of their separation from the rest of the church, especially on the basis of homophobia (although such separation could equally be race, nationality, profession, age, etc.) (Stringfellow, 1976c:13). Missiologically, this is an advanced bit of thinking, and reflects his commitment to unity which takes ecclesial identity well beyond what is referred to as the Homogeneous Unit Principle.

life. Moreover, this understanding and self-understanding, and the loving acceptance of him by God upon which it was founded, remained a constant in his lifework, both publicly and personally.

> Theologically the homosexual's position is no different from that rich young man, in the parable whose possessions had become for him an idol which hindered him from accepting himself in a way which means loving the whole world just as it is and thereby following Christ. (Stringfellow, 1965b:9)

Thus, there is a political consequence of our obedience to accept ourselves (in response to our being accepted in Christ), and that is the witness of loving the world and all of creation as it is. Only when we are free to accept ourselves for who we are in Christ can we begin to accept others: this is the basic pastoral and missiological premise operative in his thinking. And the politics of obedience are, for Stringfellow, the life of discipleship. For him, homosexuality, along with the rest of life, is a part of the process of conversion—a part of vocational obedience.

There seems an absence from any consideration of specific sexual ethics of homosexuality at this point, where perhaps one would normally expect to find such. Yet this is entirely deliberate, for "the matter of sexual proclivity and the prominence of the sexual identity of a person, are both highly overrated" by those who "seek scapegoats or need victims to persecute in order to tranquilize their anxieties or their skepticism concerning their own justification" (Stringfellow, 1979a:1). To undertake such consideration would therefore detract from the message Stringfellow is seeking to convey: namely, concern about the "exaggeration of the significance of sexuality and sexual preference" (Stringfellow, 1979a:1) which dominate discussion of homosexuality amidst the churches, and the scapegoating of which it is a part.

> There are no special ethics for heterosexuals, either in or out of marriage, and, then, another and separate ethics for homosexuals. For all varieties and forms of sex, for Christians, integrity lies in that which honors the gift of life which God has bestowed on each and every person. Sexuality is part of that gift, though it is *never* the fullness of that gift. Sex is a *mundane* symbol of that gift: a means by which the gift is proclaimed and celebrated and a way in which it is communicated and conveyed among human beings that they are called to love and affirm and help each other in the face of death and, most of all, a way in which a person

declares and confirms his own humanity despite the same threat
. . . There is, in other words, no fear in love. In fact, love casts out
fear. (Stringfellow, 1965b:13)

In his view moralizing does nothing other than divert attention
from the real problem, which is the idolatry of death by humanity.
Sexuality is but one small part of our identity and should not be blown
out of proportion, as was and is so often the case; to do so not only disaf-
fects homosexuals, but distorts the rest of reality and obscures idolatry
at work and diverts our attention. Therefore, for Stringfellow homosexuality is not the problem, idolatry is; and idolatry can be found in all
forms of relationships and sexual identities. While he does not explicitly
say so, this also seems to be how he perceives the various New Testament
warnings about homosexual acts: the warnings are against idolatry and
falling into idolatry. That, in essence, is his ethics at this time, sexual or
otherwise.

> I commend to you to consider sexuality in the context of conver-
> sion . . . But that death in Christ in which we are restored to new
> life does not involve the denial or suppression or repression of
> anything which we are as persons. It involves instead the renewal
> of our persons to the integrity of our creation in the Word of
> God . . . We have the exceptional freedom to be who we are, and
> thus, to welcome and affirm our sexuality as a gift, absolved from
> guilt or embarrassment or shame: to be liberated in our sexuality
> and self-indulgence or lust: to be freed to love with wholeness
> as persons and to recognize and celebrate, to play, to have fun in
> our own creation in relationship to the others and to the rest of
> creation. (Stringfellow, 1979a:2, 3, 4)[58]

Stringfellow's words here, far from skirting round the issue of morality,
would appear to drive it home. But he afforded sexuality no elevated
moral status, and so like the use of money, the spending of time, the
exercise of citizenship, or the practice of work, he held the view that God
was the only judge, and God is the only one fit or able to judge. Of course,
this could be no more than a liberal twist—an attempt to avoid having
to become morally explicit over such a contentious issue. Here we have

58. Conversion then should be understood as both event and process which restores
and re-presents our being in the light of authenticity: Stringfellow's is an orthodox view,
un-swayed by the evangelical conservatives emphasizing the event on the one hand,
or the religious liberals emphasizing the ongoing formation on the other. See Nock
(1933).

a homosexual theologian who wants his theology to be listened to and knows full well that any public notoriety as homosexual would obviate that desire. Likewise, any condemnation of homosexuals would be an attack of self-hatred, not self-acceptance, and would be to condemn himself. This is a valid line of questioning, for to many Stringfellow adopts this rule of divine judgment precisely at the point of personal moral culpability and responsibility. But on this occasion, Stringfellow does not leave it here, and he goes on to offer further insight about the nature of God's judgment, and in particular God's ability to discern the "ambiguity of what society labels homosexuality" (Stringfellow, 1965b:10), and to distinguish many and various forms of conduct which were lumped together. In so doing he illustrates his desire is to emphasize the futility and limit, the mortality and incompleteness, of our knowledge, and our inadequacy for judgment. Unity rather than judgment, grace not law, is the consequence of Christ's reconciliatory life, death, and resurrection.

Stringfellow goes on to explain this further. He emphasizes that sexuality pervades all relationships: to varying degrees all relationships are sexual. That is not to reduce all relationships to sexuality, but simply to indicate its presence in all encounters. We cannot divorce our sexuality from our encounters, and thus sexuality is more than some "act" or some specific form of conduct, and should not be isolated as such. Furthermore, the integrity of sexual activity is entirely dependent upon the particular circumstances and the persons involved. There are "three realms of intercourse in sex: manipulation, play, and once in awhile, love" (Stringfellow, 1965b:12). No single form of sexuality has exclusive rights on any of these forms. Manipulation is undesirable; play is acceptable as an expression and exploration of sex; love is a gift, now and again given, and in love "sex, whether homosexual or heterosexual can be one among many sacraments of . . . reconciliation" (Stringfellow, 1965b:13).[59]

Love, the unity of Christ, is once again the central theological theme and the organizing principle, and loving acts are the sacraments. Thus, whether in matters of sex or politics (if indeed the two can be separated), vocational authenticity is christologically determined and

59. With regards to Stringfellow's own sexual activity, he was, in his own words, celibate, at least from the time of his move to Block Island (see Stringfellow, 1982b:66, and also Stringfellow, 1976c:10). Prior to this there is some anecdotal suggestion that he was sexually active. His article on loneliness would point to and support a searching for self and this understanding of sexual identity would indicate its (partial) resolution, on a personal level.

experienced as reconciliation with oneself and the whole world. In sex or in politics, we are called to resist the idolatry of death, and biblical politics is at the heart of vocational authenticity as much here, in matters of sex and sexuality, as elsewhere. Consequently, while his understanding of sexuality seems to sit well with his wider theological position, this somewhat open view of homosexual acts does raise some questions regarding Stringfellow's biblical interpretation, especially concerning, for example, creation.

Creation is a significant and recurring theme in his lifework, and yet Stringfellow's thinking on homosexuality does not engage the binary biological difference between man and woman in creation, and moreover neither does it ask questions about the nature of reconciliation and love. For example, to what are we being restored? What is the image of Christ? And what about our created identity, male and female, reflecting God's image in their distinction, to be fruitful and multiply? Stringfellow ignores this aspect of "created order." He ignores the way in which God's similarity and difference (the knowable and unknowable) are reflected in the creation of humankind. On this note, one line of argument which would oppose Stringfellow suggests that in same-sex relationships, the "otherness," at least partially, becomes similarity—sexually, what the other experiences and feels is known to us; absolute mystery is lost.

On the one hand, amidst what he felt was the high-minded moralizing of Christians towards homosexuality, Stringfellow is decidedly pragmatic: homosexuals exist, and many of them are in are churches, and many of them are clergy—we need to deal with this within the framework of Christian faith, and at the heart of Christian faith is Christ's perfect love and reconciliation. To have a framework which denies their existence and has no place for it is to be a church which fails to nurture and support authentic vocation amongst homosexuals: it demands the denial of who they are in Christ—indeed, the denial of Christ. On the other hand, he points relentlessly to the way the emphasis of such moralizing is upon our action, rather than God's: e.g., can a person do or be x, y, or z, and be a Christian? That is the essential difference with his handling of the subject here, and while frustrating, it is entirely congruent with his wider lifework.[60] It prioritizes such ethical issues as the consequence of

60. Frustrating because, for many Christians, there will be a desire to ask whether specific moral action is Christian action, or not, and therefore whether homosexual sex, for example, is compatible with being a Christian. This, of course, is precisely what

honoring the gift of life and living authentically with integrity in obedience to God at a personal and corporate level. Nowhere, other than in
terms of his wider ethics of seeking the marginalized, confronting and
resisting death, welcoming the stranger, and witnessing to the reality of
Christ's presence in the world, does he spell out concretely what this
means, simply because it means nothing other than his ethics. In many
ways, the following extract sums up the realism of his approach which
acknowledges the fallenness of the world:

> And to those who still indulge in hackneyed exegesis which
> dwells upon scattered texts to argue that the Bible consigns ho-
> mosexuals to damnation, I think it only necessary to mention
> that by the same misleading interpretation the Bible consigns the
> gluttons and the rich, merchants and warmakers, and, indeed,
> all the rulers of the world. If such sanctions were honored, the
> churches of America would suddenly be drastically depleted.
> (Stringfellow, 1976c:13)

Lumping homosexuality in with what effectively are various fallen principalities and powers, which he seeks to resist and thereby witness to the
power of life, indicates either he believes that homosexuality is in fact
as fallen as the rest, but nevertheless a part of "creatureliness," or he is
making an inconsistent yet pragmatic and rhetorical argument, seeking
to highlight the plank in his accusers eye before they seek out the speck
(or scapegoat) of homosexuality. I suspect he intended both.

Stringfellow's own view on homosexual consensual sex is therefore
straightforward: in love, it can be sacramental. Whether or not it is acceptable behavior is not an impediment to life in Christ, because we are
judged by our response to God's initiative: faith is a matter of grace and
obedience, not moral status and justification. Christ justifies us all morally before God. Where our desire is for judgment, Stringfellow's is for
acceptance—not blind acceptance, but acceptance within the bounds of
biblical politics of reconciliation (love). His proclivity is to welcome all
difference, embraced in the reconciliatory unity of Christ (unity in difference). It is a powerful way of thinking and acting, which seems to

---

Stringfellow resists, because for him it is a matter of (a) grace and, therefore, (b) priorities. Ethics are a consequence of grace, not a pre-requisite to it. To pre-empt what we
shall shortly discuss, Stringfellow does not preclude good moral action, but sees it as an
absolute consequence of grace, a consequence of reconciliation, being accepted, being
reunited, and inhabiting one's restored creation, one's authentic vocation.

rub up against our preconceptions of the necessity for contingent judgment, and antagonize in the process. Perhaps, however, the radical acceptance we see Stringfellow witnessing to in his lifework, which itself is entirely congruent with his expressed views here on homosexuality and sexuality, is in fact the part of his lifework which is simultaneously most powerful, controversial, challenging, and difficult to accept or endorse. It is the paradox in his thinking, and at the center of this paradox is the reality named death.

7

Moving in Freedom amidst Death and Life

T HUS FAR WE HAVE traced the formation of Stringfellow's life-work from its origins in the 1940s and 1950s, through to the first half of the 1960s: a huge period of time which reflects the development and crystallization of his thought through the many varied experiences and encounters, both public and personal. The emergent essence to his thinking is biblical politics. We have looked at how Stringfellow's thought developed in relation to the internal structures of the church, and the external structures of the world, such as law. In all this, what he returns to as his central emphasis or focus is the Christian life in the world.

We have ventured with Stringfellow into the church and into the law; we have examined the importance of life to his thinking and the necessity of theology; we have journeyed with him to Harlem and Chicago and in so doing seen something of the single-mindedness of his thinking, the range of application, and the cost of being William Stringfellow. In the long process of Stringfellow's formation, we have explored the emergence of biblical politics through being attentive to some key and dramatic moments. One further event significant to the ongoing development of his lifework is that in July 1964 Stringfellow visited England, France, Spain, Switzerland, Czechoslovakia, and Germany, for meetings with Ellul, Barth, Hromadka, and others in relation to his work on moral theology.[1]

What happened next was not a radical departure, but more a radical reorientation in relation to the power of death. This itself had been

1. From his 1963 letter to Arthur Cohen (Stringfellow, 1963j), it is clear that one of the main reasons for visiting Barth, Ellul, and the rest was his commitment to writing a moral theology. His letter to Cohen is clear on this: "I would like to be free to go to Basel to have some further discussions about the project with our friend Karl Barth" (Stringfellow, 1963j:4).

building for sometime. His work on death (Stringfellow, 1976c), entitled *Instead of Death* (which includes much of the work we have been looking at in the last sub-section), and his major work on principalities and powers, *Free in Obedience*,[2] both show that what happens next emerges out of the cauldron of his lifework (and perhaps his European meetings), not at a tangent to it. Yet even amidst the process of formation, we need to allow for the unpredictable as the full extent of the power of death and the politics of the Bible were revealed to Stringfellow, for that also was to have a hand.

As with so much else in Stringfellow's story, this discovery had an especially personal dimension, and we shall come to that shortly. Before we do, however, we need to pay attention to movement in Stringfellow's work, and to what amounted to one of his first *prophetic* outings.[3] With his focus falling upon the power of death (the fall) in the world, by 1966 Stringfellow's prophetic sights rested squarely upon Johnson's much iconized and idolized Great Society.[4]

PROPHECY: POVERTY, RACISM, DEATH

The war on poverty was at the heart of Johnson's Great Society, and this Great Society was heralded by Johnson and those of liberal politics as the solution to America's ills. To Stringfellow, Johnson's apparent solution further exposed death's pervasiveness: the Great Society was a dangerous idol—a fraudulent myth being peddled to America and the world, and one which must be resisted. In his critique of and response to the Great Society, we see Stringfellow's propositions for the life of the Christian in the world take more solid and concrete form.

---

2. It is noteworthy that this book came out the same year as his account of his life in Harlem was published in *My People is the Enemy* (Stringfellow, 1964d). The latter provided the biographical insight into the reality which the former explored; the two books really belong together in this regard.

3. Using, once again, his own distinction of preaching and prophecy, which he developed in Stringfellow (1962k).

4. This was presented in his *Dissenter in a Great Society* (Stringfellow, 1966c). Much of the material for this book was, naturally, delivered the previous year, especially, and most notably the work on the orthodoxy of involvement, e.g. (Stringfellow, 1965f). It is noteworthy that while tensions over Cuba and the Soviet Union continued unabated, Stringfellow had remained quiet on these issues, aside from his previous work on communism and the occasional aside reference to Castro.

It is difficult to convey the enormity of passion and feeling which inflamed America to action at this time: these were crucial days of politics and protest. Passions and feelings ran high, and while support for Johnson's initiatives was strong, these were days of lingering optimism and gathering despair. With hindsight therefore, while Stringfellow's dissent from these political initiatives was somewhat isolated, it was nevertheless well timed. His criticism was fresh and was not partisan, for his politics were differently motivated: his comments "make no pretense to being either wholly consistent or utterly coherent; they embody an attempt to respond in terms of the versatility of Christ's gospel to particular aspects of the American social crisis, especially as it has been manifest since 1964" (Stringfellow, 1966c:vii).[5] Against the Great Society, Stringfellow speaks prophetically, but he did so in a language which was accessible and plain. The rhetoric of Johnson's Great Society pervaded the liberal political agenda which so appealed to socially concerned Christians at that time. The Great Society was the political hallowed ground and holy grail of mid-1960s politics, as we saw above in chapter 4, and in the face of this Stringfellow's attack on it was direct and unswerving and drew upon his lifework to date.

> President Johnson declares war on poverty and prosecutes that war by repackaging existing programs, issuing press releases, and designating appropriations so grossly disproportionate to the crisis as to be ridiculous. The war on poverty cannot be won by propaganda, nor by appeasement of the rich, nor by spending a nickel where five dollars is needed . . . The war on poverty, as of now, is more a sop to the conscience of the prosperous than a serious effort to cope with the threat which poverty is to the survival of the American nation, or than an authentic concern for the sufferings of the poor. (Stringfellow, 1964a:1–2)

In other words, Stringfellow felt Johnson's war on poverty was too much spin and too little substance, and an appeasement of the conscience of

5. In this volume there is virtually not a single social happening, from immolation to the riots in Watts and Harlem and bloodshed in Selma, from Goldwater and the Klu-Klux-Klan to Malcolm X and violent resistance, from technology to money, which misses Stringfellow's prophetic theological gaze. The book presents the state of America in those years with astonishing clarity. We do not have room here to explore it in detail, and focus instead on the one particular aspect of his criticisms, the Great Society, and his call for involvement, which brings shape and substance to what hitherto had little. We do so through *Dissenter in a Great Society* and the use of some other materials.

white, wealthy liberal Americans who had been so troubled by the crisis which shook America.

In one revision, his critique begins with Rev 18:4–8 and represents the first use of the book of Revelation in his work. His commentary is succinct and poignant: while the church spends its time demythologizing dogma and doctrine in the name of supposed relevance, why then do we spend equal amounts of time "mythologizing the secular"? (Stringfellow, 1966d:253). While the churches were busy unwrapping their traditions and words from their historical roots and recasting them for contemporary society, society itself was being hidden behind political spin and legend. It was a task in which theologians and politicians were both actively engaged.

> It is difficult to determine who is more to blame for this—Harvey Cox or Lyndon Johnson. For the present purpose, however, I will restrict my comments to the latter simply because President Johnson symbolizes a somber, immediate, empirical threat to my own existence—along with that of every other human being on earth, while Professor Cox does not jeopardize my life in any way—or anybody else's. In other words, when a button is pressed, the only thing that Cox can accomplish is to turn the electricity on or off; by a similar effort and the same skill, Johnson can incinerate mankind. By like token, Cox, conceivably, might someday acquire significant power—say, as President of the American Baptist Convention (and lift that denomination our of its doldrums) or even become editor of *Playboy* magazine (and save it from effeteness)—but there is not the slightest prospect of his ever being invested with exceptional secular office. Harvey Cox will never be President of the United States; Lyndon Johnson *is*. (Stringfellow, 1966d:253)[6]

The Great Society was an immediate problem of immense political proportions, and not one of deliberation through idealizations or abstract postulations. Looking to Johnson in order to demythologize the secular was, then, a pragmatic political decision, and in so doing he sought to get beneath the political hyperbole which had surrounded his political agenda and the society it sought to create. The Great Society furthered

6. In his rather dry and sardonic manner, Stringfellow is making implicit reference to Cox's highly regarded and well received work, *The Secular City* (Cox, 1965), which urged people to seek a non-religious interpretation of biblical concepts along with a lesser known article (Cox, 1961). His book sparked a debate and an eager theological following.

ideas which went to the heart of the American nation and its formation; ideas of individual enterprise in any pursuit which are morally justified by the seeking and attainment of the right objective. It was an ethos born of the white, Protestant, privileged classes. It is an ethos which is as dominant now as it was then, in which "God rules with the United States as His favorite surrogate, and in which what is right always triumphs and, therefore, that which triumphs must be right. Theologically, of course, such a crude view is ridiculously unbiblical and it is to the enduring credit of President Kennedy that he challenged this mythology, notably after the Bay of Pigs fiasco and during the Cuban missile crisis, though whether he questioned it on biblical grounds, one does not know" (Stringfellow, 1966d:254). However, Stringfellow maintains, the reality of this myth is lost on Johnson, for this myth is at the heart of his political agenda, and is pervasive whether as military power, ideological aggression, or economic conquest. The power and means of the state to silence dissent and non-conformity, and maintain the acquiescence of its people are legion, he insists. For Johnson, the Great Society was seen as a fast moving, cutting edge politics of generosity and unity. For Stringfellow, it was anathema, which did little more than expose the full extent of the power of death in American society. The myth of the Great Society was, simply, that it equates a society's greatness with God's agency, and that God somehow bestows greatness therefore upon this society. The two views were clearly in sharp contradiction. With remarkable foresight of what might nowadays be referred to under the rubric "democratization and globalization of civilized society," Stringfellow describes its agenda in the following manner:

> The Great Society myth foresees the indefinite, if not eternal, preeminence of American power in the world, not only among the nations, but also in the regions of outer space, while at the same time bestowing upon its own citizens full employment, better health, more leisure, the abolition of poverty, beautification of the countryside, de-pollution of air and water, modernization of transportation, renewal of the cities, and, eventually, equal rights for everyone. It contemplates the grandeur of a universal American hegemony in which *the* Great Society would be encompassed with satellite great societies secured by the deployment of American military forces overseas, the controlling investment of American capital in other countries, and the American ideological leadership of the nations. The myth presupposed both

a technical and moral capability for America to have guns and
butter—and the moon as well. (Stringfellow, 1966d:255)

Stringfellow conceded that Johnson's proposition was an attractive one,
especially when compared to the nostalgic offerings of rekindled nineteenth-century aspirations on offer by Goldwater or Reagan.[7] At least, by
comparison, the programs of the Great Society focus upon the future,
not the past. Yet despite this, he believed it remained an idol and a myth
(albeit a seductive myth), which was both too modest and too conservative in its outlook, clinging to a liberal dogma instead of embracing
radical change. The Great Society is a modest affair, he says, a "relatively
inconsequential movement of social change ... at a moment when what
is poignantly needed in the United States, and hence, in America's world
role, is change of revolutionary imagination and scope: change which
converts the fundamental ethics of society; change which liberates the
nation and her people from her myth" (Stringfellow, 1966d:255).

Every idol, Stringfellow was later to elucidate, "represents a thing
or being existing in a state of profound disorientation" (Stringfellow,
1969b:30), and consequently he confronted each of the great "temples"
(or idols) of the Great Society: it was a concrete and specific attempt at
re-orientation. Here, I would like to look briefly at three of these temples:
poverty, wealth and the *racial crisis*.[8]

Stringfellow believed the *war on poverty* simply further entrenched
poverty in the urban ghettos due to the way in which its funds were spent
on administration and bureaucracy, which served to maintain the status
quo, rather than provide actual assistance to the poor. Thus, it addressed
symptoms rather causes. It does not, according to Stringfellow, move beyond the paternalism of white racism, and moral complacency.[9]

7. Both Republicans, they offered a "Free Society" and a "Creative Society" respectively.

8. There were many others; see Stringfellow (1966c). Both here and later, his understanding of work and worship from the 1950s remains pretty much intact: "work takes
on the character of worship "in spirit and in truth," and in our worship we celebrate the
life and restoration we are working for ... the present obvious dichotomy between what
Christians do in the sanctuary and what they do in society can be done away with. [In
worship and our daily lives] we celebrate the gift of life as such by participating in God's
affirmation of life in the face of death" (Stringfellow, 1969b:126).

9. He was also well aware of the global exploitation of the poor upon which the
American economy depended (Stringfellow, 1966c:42–43), an awareness which was
unusual for this period. Work, which was an idol entangled in the worship of money
and poverty, was another idol engaged by Stringfellow.

> The moral complacency of most citizens in regard to poverty is largely due to the success this society has achieved in keeping the poor out of sight: the mind is not appalled by conditions the eyes have not seen; the conscience is not moved by what the nostrils have not inhaled. (Stringfellow, 1966c:25)

Wealth was integral to the myth and its creation at the very foundation of American culture, especially at this time. Identity, authenticity, autonomy and worth were all measured in terms of wealth and its acquisition. Money was the key to wealth and was the antithesis to poverty. Poverty was, therefore, essentially an inauthentic life in a post-war consumer-orientated culture: without money one could not participate in that which provided a sense of worth and value. Some consideration of money is therefore necessary,[10] for it is in Stringfellow's treatment of the issue of money, for example, that we see clearly his deepening articulation of the reality of the power of death, and concrete implications of biblical politics.

According to Stringfellow money is not evil, but it is fallen and therefore subject to the power of death, and the problem of money is in how it is regarded and how it is used to measure the worth of all other things, including people. Stringfellow believed money held an enormous and covert power over America and the lives of Americans. The idea that money has worth in and of itself, and that from this people themselves seek to derive their own worth, was at the heart of American culture and at the heart of the myth of the Great Society from which Stringfellow dissented. The exploitation of the poor by the wealthy, in order for the wealthy to make money, was something Stringfellow had experienced a great deal of in Harlem, from blatant corporate commercial injustice to advertising. Money is the measure of value and worth and had become an idol in the Great Society. At a time of both prosperity and protest, he seemed to identify the way in which money penetrated deep into the American psyche; in his practical identification of the principality of money, he recognizes the way in which money is sought to secure an escape from death.

Death, from the view of the Great Society, was equated to life without money: money was the means to authenticity. The social mythology implied that money, in short, provided a means of securing immortality,

---

10. See, for instance, Stringfellow (1966f, 1966c:34–48) for a full discussion of money as a principality and an idol.

and in highlighting this he further exposes the depth of the power of death at work and its reach. Amidst this, Stringfellow maintained that the gospel exposes the idols of death, and rather than play by the rules of death and be conformed by its reign, it transcends death's power. The bodily resurrection is not therefore some myth of an afterlife, but is rather bodily because it affects us here and now—here and now we are resurrected in our bodies, to action in the world, to transcend the power of death, and its idols. That, essentially, is the political significance of the freedom of Christ.

> The idolatry of money has its most grotesque form as a doctrine of immortality . . . If a man leaves a substantial estate, death is cheated of victory for a while, if not ultimately defeated, because the money he leaves will sustain the memory of the man and his fortune. The poor just die and are at once forgotten . . . Money thus becomes the measure of a man's moral excellence while he lives and a means to purchase a certain survival of death. Money makes men not only moral but immortal; that is the most profound and popular idolatry of money. To the Christian conscience, all ideas of immortality . . . are anathema. The gospel of Jesus Christ is not concerned with immortality but with the resurrection from death, not with survival of death . . . The gospel is . . . distinguished by the transcendence of the power of death here and now within the precincts of this life in this world. (Stringfellow, 1966c:43)

In Stringfellow's view the only use for money, as a Christian, was as a sacrament: a sign of God's reconciliation. In other words, when money is no longer an idol, economics becomes liberated, and it becomes a servant to politics, rather than the other way round (which was the reality in which America dwelt). Essentially, in Christ, in biblical politics, money and all things are made subject to God and his loving reign.

The last focus, the *racial crisis*, was entangled in the web of poverty and wealth, and symptomatic of it, clouding "the Great Society mythology more than any other single thing" (Stringfellow, 1966d:256), and its outcome would "determine the very survival of society, as well as any claim to greatness" (Stringfellow, 1966d:257). As we have already seen, Stringfellow was well acquainted with the anatomy of the racial crisis. At this time he makes clear the great extent of his knowledge, narrating the nature of the struggles and the context, and getting to the heart of the issue as the violence he had predicted in 1963 became a reality

(Stringfellow, 1966c:91–122). The trouble with the Great Society is that it works within the myth of white supremacy, it does not transcend it.

> Slavery is the most radical form of race supremacy imaginable, because it upholds a proposition that certain human beings are not persons, but property. Slavery was abolished, but white supremacy was legalized for nearly a century more by local option and now, even in the aftermath of the civil rights movement, remains institutionalized in apartheid and ghettoization. (Stringfellow, 1966d:257)

Stringfellow acknowledges that most of America is not explicitly and viciously racist, but even in their well meaning paternalism, or in their apathy, it is present. Furthermore, the fact that it is not predominantly explicit, but is rather underlying covert presence of white supremacy which is present in the essence of the Great Society, seems to point ever more to its widespread significance for the whole of white America, and his ongoing unearthing of the power of death. The white moderates who so supported the Great Society sought to improve the ghettos and make them better places to live, and to "integrate" them into the wider society. What, according to Stringfellow, they failed to comprehend was the fact that they could not have equality and maintain separation, for separation on the grounds of race was the practice of inequality. Amidst these days of reform, Stringfellow thought the only solution was to tear down the walls of liberalism and racism; nothing other than radical transformation would do.

> But to destroy the Harlem ghetto would require dispersion of the population elsewhere in the city and suburbs . . . No doubt that would threaten and dislocate the fabric of white society in a startling manner, but the answer to that is that the bourgeois white ghettos need to be destroyed just as much as the black ones if this is to become a society worthy of humanity. (Stringfellow, 1966d:257)

Of course, at the heart of this radical understanding of integration is Christ's reconciliation or unity. The Christian's response to the racial crisis should, he repeats, be that of the cross—the gift of love to one's own enemy, even to the point of death. Love is, as he said some three years earlier, the only solution to the racial crisis.[11] Now we see that love

---

11. There is a strong parallel between what Stringfellow sees going on in the racial crisis, and what was going on in his own personal life regarding acceptance and love.

in practical confrontation with the mythology of the Great Society, and the idols it embodied: it is a public and political confrontation with the state.

What then does Stringfellow say will free us from the fraudulence of the myth and blasphemy, enabling us "to revolt" (Stringfellow, 1966d:257) against the Great Society and the power of death inherent therein? That real concrete and political freedom is found in the politics of the Bible. For Stringfellow, justice comes not through resort to the law, which was the vehicle for Johnson's Great Society, but through faith. The involvement of the life of faith in the affairs of the world is a christological imperative of orthodoxy. It is to that involvement we now turn.

ORTHODOXY AND INVOLVEMENT:
ETHICS OF RECONCILIATION

Stringfellow claims that the response to Johnson is one of orthodoxy, but he is not speaking about doctrinal resolutions or formulations. His emphasis upon orthodoxy is an attempt to make plain that the radical nature of the Christian life is not some external ideological imposition (i.e., he is not some leftist radical) but is rather at the heart of the very faith which Christians profess; this orthodoxy is, therefore, normative.[12] He sets out by immediately putting distance between himself and the various "orthodoxies" of American religion, including those responses which while critical of Johnson and the world, recognizing the evil, condemn involvement in it in order that their religion may remain pure and undefiled. For example, he cites the case in Selma where a clergyman turned away those who had been protesting for the right to vote and "complained that their presence in worship would profane the religion of the parish" (Stringfellow, 1965e:1). Both sides in Selma laid claim to a religious orthodoxy. Not surprisingly, Stringfellow's solution is Christological, not religious. Christian orthodoxy is not doctrinal, but rather "is both historic and existential . . . The substance of Christian orthodoxy . . . is no less and none other than the very event of Christ"

---

12. Although consideration of this formed the final part of *Dissenter* (Stringfellow, 1966c), Stringfellow first delivered it in a slightly different form in 1965 at a meeting sponsored by the Laymen's Academy for Oecumenical Studies (Stringfellow, 1965e). We shall draw here upon both sources as necessary. His work is drawn from, and commentary upon, 2 Cor 5:15–17.

(Stringfellow, 1965e:3). Stringfellow explicitly emphasizes the centrality of orthodoxy for *life*.

In the ethics which unfold, therefore, we see the explication of his "existential," or incarnational, Christological ethic. It requires a revolution in the way in which Jesus Christ is conceived. He urges people to renounce the Jesus of superstition, of film, of democracy, the sentimental Jesus of our creation, along with the Christ of the church's creation, the fairy tale fragrant Christ of Sunday school, detached and dehumanized. He also urges discussion about Christ's humanity and divinity be put to one side, for while "not entirely irrelevant" such discussions "encourage dissipation, diverting attention from the actual event of Jesus Christ in this world and thus hindering the actual event of Christian witness in this world" (Stringfellow, 1966c:130). The relationship between the event of our own witness and the event of Jesus Christ is paramount, for this is nothing other than the ethics of the Body of Christ, which Stringfellow described earlier (Stringfellow, 1962k). Instead "let us behold Jesus Christ as the one whom God has shown Christ to be in this world: the new Adam—the true man—the man reconciled in God" (Stringfellow, 1966c:130).

This reconciliation is radical and far-reaching, bringing together in unity God, Christ, and humanity to live as one in the Spirit. Here, his writing offers further elucidation and clarification of his understanding of this central theme in his lifework, stated perhaps more succinctly than it had been previously.

> Encompassed in Him is at once the integrity and wholeness of both God and man, and the unity and love between them and every person and all things. The outreach of the reconciliation which is God's work extends to the whole of creation throughout all places and times. Jesus Christ is the embodiment of that reconciliation. Reconciliation, in terms of Christian orthodoxy, is not some occasional, unilateral, private happening, but, much more than that, the *transcendent, universal, and profoundly political event in all time. Reconciliation is a political event.* Reconciliation is the event, as II Corinthians testifies, of a new order of corporate life of men and institutions inaugurated in the world in Christ. (Stringfellow, 1966c:131)[13]

13. First emphasis mine, the second is Stringfellow's.

Thus, reconciliation cannot be thought of as occurring to one person outside of all other persons and institutions: that is the nature of its political character. The precursor to reconciliation to God is that one must suffer reconciliation with oneself, all other people, and with all of creation (Stringfellow, 1966c:131). Stringfellow's emphasis upon the transcendent here in relation to his ethics is of course significant, for it indicates that while incarnational, his ethics are not wholly immanent, but that the transcendent is central to the act of reconciliation which is realized in and through the immanent. In other words, while Stringfellow wishes to put aside the questions of Christ's divinity and humanity, they are strongly manifest, albeit implicitly, in his understanding of the reconciliation which is the foundation for his ethics of orthodoxy and thus also the foundation for the restoration of "one's own identity" (Stringfellow, 1966c:131). "To be a Christian, to be already reconciled, means to love the world, all the world, just as it is—*unconditionally*" (Stringfellow, 1966c:132). This last point is of course the re-expression of his theology of reconciliation as *advocacy*, which we saw expressed perhaps most clearly, and most personally, in chapter 2 under the section entitled "Threat."[14]

Here, then, in his ethics and opposition to the Great Society, we see the various elements of his lifework being brought together; for example, his existential commitment to authenticity (authentic vocation), his commitment to the political authority of the gospel over the law (biblical politics), and our embodiment of the Body of Christ as the church dispersed in the world (the Christian life), and his increasing integration of these with his theology of the principalities and powers, and the power of death. There is, therefore, an element of repetition going on in what he presents here: the journey of intensification continues. It represents a retelling of the story, a representation of the gospel message as his life (and its political engagement and encounters) interacts with his work, and vice-versa. In Christ's reconciliation of creation, politics and the whole world are transfigured.

---

14. Furthermore, its emphasis upon love here, and previously, in relation to advocacy and reconciliation of course would have echoed the emphasis upon love in contemporary society: but it is no mere echo, but a radical transfiguration of the social emphasis of love. The connection between the themes in his writing and in culture would have been strong.

> Because reconciliation is not private and personal so much as it
> is notorious and political, because reconciliation is a new estate
> in which all relationships without exception or excuse are trans-
> figured, it is celebrated and manifested as such: reconciliation is,
> simply, lived. (Stringfellow, 1965e:5)

How then do we live in a transfigured estate? What does our witness
look like? As we read earlier, and can read again here, Stringfellow understands the conflict in the world not in terms of good and evil, and the
vain attempt to discern evil in order to overcome it. Rather, it concerns
the power of death in the world, and the way in which the reconciliation
of the power of the resurrection works to transform and restore all of
creation to its authentic vocation (Stringfellow, 1966c:135–36).[15] Thus,
Stringfellow can demand that, amidst the racial crisis in Johnson's Great
Society, the Christian witness will be like no other, and embrace the
enemy. Therefore Christians, for example, engaged in "direct action for
equal rights for all citizens . . . [should] nevertheless persevere in loving
the humanity of the wide assortment of others assembled in political
and social and religious opposition to integration in American public
life" (Stringfellow, 1966c:133), and therefore that those in Selma should
seek to affirm Sheriff Clark's humanity, even though they have been
physically beaten by his men; or it means forgiving the Ku Klux Klan. In
short, Stringfellow says, it means "loving your neighbor in the truth that
each man's real neighbor is whoever is his very own enemy. The com-
mandment to love one's neighbor, and the example, in Christ, of love for
one's enemy are ultimately synonymous" (Stringfellow, 1966c:133). This
is a call to obedient discipleship, with radical practical, personal, and political consequences, and it interprets reconciliation *realistically*, engaged
in, rather than removed from, practical political life in the world. It is
incarnational theology in its most radical sense, reflecting the full reality
of Christ's own humanity, engaged in the practical political life of the
world, and demanding obedient realistic repetition in response to Jesus's
command to follow him, as the basis for discipleship.

   This is the Christological heart of Stringfellow's ethics at this time:
seeing the truth is a reality which grasps our whole life, exposes our
vulnerabilities, and lays us sacrificially before the power of death as a
witness to life; this, Stringfellow advocates, is an essentially and fun-

---

15. Stringfellow says that he rejected the "simplistic notion of decisions being mere
choices between self-evident good and evil" in his early teens (Stringfellow, 1970e:79).

damentally public and political reality which actually affects our lives, *right now*. In so doing, he draws out the present imperative of the true humanity or authentic vocation, actualized in and through the reconciliation in Jesus Christ.

However, while the emphasis is upon engagement with our present reality, he understands this in eschatological perspective, and it is here that we see perhaps his sharpest engagement so far with the moral context of reality and the power of death. As such it demonstrates the intensity with which he had come to recognize death as a fully living militant reality. He describes the reality of the world in the following terms:

> The present age is one of death, not evil ... *right now* in the midst of life, all men and all things are prisoners of death's power. Creation is fallen ... The Fall does not mean that the world is evil ... [but] that all of creation exists in bondage to death, without any power to prevail against death ... Death reigns over men and nations and ideas, and over all that is, as a living, militant, pervasive and, apparently, ultimate power—in other words, as *that* which gives moral significance to everyone and everything else. Death is the ruling idol which all other idols—race, nationalism, religion, money, sex, and all their counterparts—worship and serve, and to which men in their turn give honor and sacrifice through their idolatries. (original emphasis Stringfellow, 1966c:137)

The reality he describes here is of course the reality he identifies and confronts in the Great Society and in the racial crisis; his context verifies the truth of this reality. And it is a reality in which the fallen principalities and powers (the idols which worship and serve death) hold sway. In a somewhat circular argument, Stringfellow insists that that fact that most people do not see the reign of death is essential proof of death's success (Stringfellow, 1966c:137). "All that is wrong in this world cannot be attributed to the mere behavior of men" (Stringfellow, 1966c:137), and indeed, to do so is vanity, tantamount to self-idolization. In support of death's reality Stringfellow points to the various significant signs: for example, the reality of loneliness, illness, poverty, unemployment, technological dehumanization, war, famine, worship of money, personal estrangement, separation of society according to sex, race, nation, ideology—all these point to the militant action of the power of death holding sway in the world. These are the everyday realities of our existence, of course.

As Stringfellow continued to advance biblical politics, the archives tell us that his own thought at this time was deeply committed to elucidating the power of death as a precursor to ethics.[16] Essentially, we can summarize his view on the power of death in the following terms at this time. "The meaning of the secular is the meaning, biblically, of fallenness" (Stringfellow, 1966h:1), and amidst the fall, amidst our common history, the biblical message has been mistaken and misunderstood along simplistic distinctions of good and evil, right and wrong, sacred and secular.[17] Death is understood in many ways, including as the devil, an idol or demigod, the drama of alienation, the sanction of secular morality, and as pretended reality. Death is of a similar character to the Word of God, and is one of the greatest powers in existence. This resemblance to the Word of God is "the key to all personal and social ethics for Christians" (Stringfellow, 1966h:2), for this is the context of comprehension, transcendence, and confrontation. The contemporaneously relevant nature of the resurrection must be recovered in Christianity because it is the essential resource for ethics; the power of the resurrection is foundational to the ethics of resistance and the overcoming of death's power *right* now. Consequently, *style of life* rather than moralism is the really important issue for authentic vocation, for the life of faith: "the significance attaches to the sacramental, rather than the 'sacred.' The distinction is aesthetic more than ethical. It is enormously important who you are, it does not matter much what you do . . . The principal mark of the aesthetic is found

16. See the paper entitled *The Theology of Death as a Preliminary Ethical Insight* (Stringfellow, 1966h), which looks like an outline for a book. Many of these ideas found themselves absorbed into a variety of writing, (especially Stringfellow, 1969b), in which he deals specifically with some of the most significant idols of American culture (religion, work, money and status, race, the church), and explores how we might have freedom from them. Issued as a study book, each chapter had questions designed to encourage the reader to think beyond the text and explore connections with the Word and the world for themselves. Stringfellow saw it as a companion volume to Stringfellow (1964b, 1966c). He finally completed the manuscript amidst in 1968, for his ill health had rendered it much delayed.

17. Stringfellow is equally critical of the newly emergent situational or contextual ethics, which he felt represented "uncritical affirmation of the secular bereft of a sufficient theological comprehension of and empirical participation in the secular which furnish an operational ethics at least equally misguided as the old moralistic approach" (Stringfellow, 1966h:1).

in the human capacity to distinguish men from God, and to thereby be free to love both" (Stringfellow, 1966h:2).[18] This is a matter of priorities and emphasis for Stringfellow, amidst a culture where "being Christian" was, as we saw above in his critique of religion, interpreted as moral action and judgment. Here we see how he emphasizes the "being" of the Christian as the decisive and determining factor to a person's faith, and in so doing we see once more reiterated his concern for creatureliness, for human beings, and for life, which we have seen throughout his work, but especially in his "existentialism," in his personal life and sexuality, and in Harlem. It does not obviate good moral action, for that which is "good" will arise as a consequence of authentic vocation; authentic vocation does not arise as a consequence of doing that which is "good."[19] It is, therefore, an important restatement of the ongoing theme in his work of justification by faith, and marks a significant consciousness of ethics as *sacramental* rather than *dialectical*.

Here, then, we see the concrete articulation of aesthetics (liturgical action) as ethics (scial action), and the clearest and most unambiguous explication of his commitment to the unity and relevance of what Christians do in the sanctuary and what they do in the world, for, as he was later to put it, "worship has its most telling analogues in common life in revolution, on the one hand, and in play, on the other" (Stringfellow, 1970e:102). It also signifies, therefore, that he viewed the witness of Christian ethics to witness to *life* amidst the age of *death*, in sacramental rather than dialectical terms.[20]

While Stringfellow demands that we focus upon the present age, there is an eschatological dimension to our engagement with the world *right now* which is represented by and embodied in the vocation of the church, for the witness of the church is the unity of reconciliation, and the "unity of the Church is its authentic witness" (original emphasis Stringfellow, 1966c:144). In other words, the church is the living embodiment of what has, and is yet, to come. This unity is what God gives the church at Pentecost, something of His own which is given as a gift of the

18. "Thus, so-called situational ethics are, approximately, backwards!" (Stringfellow, 1966h:2). It should be noted that this is a matter of emphasis, of priorities. We see this commitment to "being" over "doing" throughout his thought, for example above, in relation to his view of the relationship of homosexuality and Christianity.

19. See, for example, Stringfellow (1969b:123–24).

20. Expansion upon this theme of the politics of liturgy and liturgical events can be seen, for example, in Stringfellow (1965c, 1981, 1975).

Spirit. Thus, the church confronts the world and is always saying "yes" and "no," simultaneously; "they are, in fact, the same word, for they each say that the end of the world is its maturing in Christ. It is that maturity of human life in society which the Church as the reconciled community foreshadows in this world" (Stringfellow, 1966c:142). This once again, echoes his previous published work (Stringfellow, 1962k) and his thinking during the 1950s. For Stringfellow the church lives as the new society amidst the old, "as the reconciled community when all else is broken and distorted"; the church, gathered and dispersed in the world, is a witness of authenticity amidst the reign of death. Reconciliation in and between the churches is not an matter of councils and collaborations, but is the real and present gift of the Spirit upon which the church is founded, and in which it has its being: in Christ, the church is restored to its authentic vocation (Stringfellow, 1966c:143–49).[21] Therefore, the church of Christ, Stringfellow advocates in conclusion to his book, "is the only society in this world worthily named great" (Stringfellow, 1966c:164).

Given that involvement in this world is an imperative of the incarnation and the vocation of the church, the ethics of reconciliation, that is, the Christian's *movement* in the world, especially as one confronts the Great Society, can be identified according to Stringfellow by four distinctive marks: *realism, inconsistency, radicalism, intercession,* all of which we can see demonstrated in his own lifework to date.

The mark of *realism* signifies that the Christian is realistic about the world and our existence in it, realistic about the reality that this is a fallen world. Echoing his thinking about loneliness, above, Stringfellow describes the Christian as the person who "knows that in this world in which, apart from God's work in all things, death is the only meaning, all relationships have been broken and all men suffer estrangement from one another and alienation from themselves" (Stringfellow, 1966c:161). In being realistic, one does not shelter behind the fairy tales of religion, but is free to live in the world as it is, nothing shocks or embarrasses, and there is no need for disguise or sentimentality.

21. Stringfellow highlights the political nature of liturgy (Stringfellow, 1966c:150–54), and the political authority of baptism (Stringfellow, 1966c:154–56), as the way in which the internal (gathered) and external (dispersed) life of the church are both political in nature, and both embrace the unity wrought in reconciliation. The implications of this understanding of the church are immense for contemporary church practice, and require one to revision the church and understand this as its reality *right now;* life in the midst of death.

Inconsistency is a mark of "fidelity to the gospel in [the Christian's] witness to the world" (Stringfellow, 1966c:161). Stringfellow declares that the Christian cannot be placed into a neat pigeonhole, "his stance and conduct are never easily predictable" (Stringfellow, 1966c:162). And here we recall no doubt his own desire not to be placed in a pigeonhole, not to be classified, not to be predicted, which he expressed at the outset of his writing career. Fidelity to the gospel stands over-against fidelity to the world and its principalities: its ideologies, nations, governments, etc. While a Christian will take a stance "for this or that cause, though the Christian takes a stand and speaks out specifically, he does not do so as the servant of some race or class or political system or ideology but as an expression of his freedom from just such idols" (Stringfellow, 1966c: 162). This characteristic is clearly visible in Stringfellow's engagement with the Great Society and the racial crisis, as well as in his own writing, which yields occasional inconsistencies.[22]

The third mark, that of *radicalism*, is essentially what it appears to be: the Christian's stance is one of complaint and resistance to the status quo, whatever it is. The Christian's "insight and experience of reconciliation in Christ," means that no human estate can match "the true society of which he is a citizen in Christ" (Stringfellow, 1966c:162). Anticipating work which was yet to come, and a context which had yet to fully materialise,[23] Stringfellow describes the Christian as a person who is "everywhere, in every society, an alien. He is always, in any society, in protest. Even when a cause which he has himself supported prevails, he will not be content but will be the first to complain against the 'new' status quo" (Stringfellow, 1966c:162). For the Christian, according to Stringfellow, there can be no rest. This seems a remarkably negative stance: the constant "No!" to the world's endeavors. To some extent, it is. However, we need to remember that this stance of resistance is one

22. Inconsistency of thought is to the academic establishment perhaps something akin to the worst sin imaginable, and certainly it was seen by the theological academy as a slight on Stringfellow's own thinking and stood in the way of his qualification to their circle. There was a supposition that inconsistency betrayed badly thought out ideas, and therefore a poor mind. In my opinion Stringfellow's lifework indicates precisely the opposite, and his purpose was neither to be studied nor vilified, but rather to inspire the hearts and minds and bodies of Christians to think the seemingly unthinkable and live the seemingly unlivable.

23. I am thinking here of the protests against the war in Vietnam, which didn't fully emerge as a movement until the late 1960s.

fuelled by, and a witness to, the absolute, universal, and eternal "Yes!" to life (authenticity), and it is this "Yes!" which is at the heart of his understanding of advocacy. Therefore, understood correctly, Stringfellow's resistance is, as he himself indicated above, the "Yes!" of advocacy of life (and of the marginalized), simultaneously spoken with the "No!" of resistance to the powers.

Intercession is the fourth and final mark of a Christian's *movement* in the world, and it expresses the concern of Christians for all people in the various issues and concerns of public life.

While a Christian's concern is embodied in "specific care for those who, in a given time in society, are the least in that society . . . those whom all the rest have ignored or forgotten or cast out or otherwise have abandoned to death" (Stringfellow, 1966c:163), that is by no means its limit. A Christian's "passion for the world" and "involvement in society," a Christian's very witness, also encompasses "his own enemy" or those he opposes, or those he disagrees with (Stringfellow, 1966c:163). For Stringfellow, a Christian's movement is clearly not limited by the politics of this world, as we have already seen; a Christian intercedes for all without discrimination, in the name of the gospel.

The Christian life of movement (or involvement) in the world is understood ecclesiologically by Stringfellow; indeed, it is necessarily so. The Christian witness is nothing other than embodying and inhabiting the living example of the society of the church (the reconciled society) affirming and loving the essential humanity of everyone in Christ amidst our "abdication of human life" (Stringfellow, 1966c:163) and the assaults of death upon human life, and placing our trust in the truth of the gospel as the author of true life and the exposer of reality. This, basically, is the Christian political witness: the inhabitation of biblical politics, at this time.

MORE PARABLES OF LIFE

Two brief accounts of events in Stringfellow's life serve as parables of this deepening discernment of death and biblical politics (the politics of reconciliation). The first, a parable of the church, the other of resistance. Together, they not only help us better understand Stringfellow's thoughts at this time, but also help us once again see the intrinsic connection between his life and his work, the one-ness of his engagement with the world and the Word.

Circus

> I consider the circus as a constellation or congregation of art
> forms which have a theological significance: most of the tradi-
> tional circus performing arts have to do with the human tran-
> scendence of death, which is, of course, the principal biblical
> theme . . . The circus arts, when maintained with integrity are
> edifying to the whole culture. (Stringfellow, 1979b)

In 1966, the same year in which he toured Vietnam, Australia, and New
Zealand, and in which *Dissenter in a Great Society* came out, Stringfellow
and Towne toured with the circus for the summer, and became its
resident theologians. Signs of Stringfellow's bad health were already
looming. It was a paradoxical encounter, reflecting the way in which
Stringfellow believed "that truth is never bland but lurks in contradiction" (Stringfellow, 1982b:86). Stringfellow had loved the circus since his
childhood and had come to appreciate it over the years as a pastime with
increasing theological significance. The circus was, simply, a parable of
the Kingdom, a parable of the church of Christ.[24] It was a childhood
dream come true.

> We outfitted a station wagon so that it could be used for sleeping,
> and joined the circus company en route, booked in a new city
> each day, traveling late each night in the circus convoy to the next
> day's stand . . . The experience did little to satiate my fascination
> with the circus as a society, but only whetted it. (Stringfellow,
> 1982b:87)

Of course, today the circus has undergone many changes and is no
longer as well regarded nor as popular as it was in America in 1966.[25]
For Stringfellow it symbolized the image of the eschatological realm
in a way which was accessible to ordinary society: it was a witness, it
enacted an ecumenical and historic hope that embraced the diversity
of all creation. Within the circus, there was embraced and celebrated
both oddities and curiosities, the exotic and the bizarre, and in the main
ring, acts which both defy and deny death (whether on the high wire,

24. Our account here is illustrative of the relationship between Stringfellow's life and
his work, rather than comprehensive. For a comprehensive treatment of Stringfellow's
theology of the circus, see Commins (1998). For Stringfellow's own account, see, for
example, Stringfellow (1976d) and Stringfellow (1982b:86–91).

25. For a fascinating account of the history of the circus, see Durant and Durant
(1957).

or shot from a cannon), human beings reclaiming their dominion over the animal kingdom (recalling the way in which Daniel 6 portrays the beasts as the principalities and powers) (Stringfellow, 1982b:89), and, of course, the clown, whose parody makes commentary "by presence and performance, on the absurdities inherent in what ordinary people take so seriously—themselves, their profits and loses, their successes and failures, their adjustments and compromises—their conformity to the world" (Stringfellow, 1982b:90). And all the while, the ringmaster pronounces the confrontation with and denial of death.

The circus, for Stringfellow, was an astonishing parable of life. Diverse and hopeful, it presented itself in dialectical opposition to death (it was a "death defying" performance of "life and death"), it ridiculed death in a very public manner, and in this way revealed death as the single real and constant enemy of life.[26]

> The service the circus does—more so, I regret to say, than the churches do—is to openly, dramatically, and humanly portray that death in the midst of life. The circus is eschatological parable and social parody: it signals a transcendence of the power of death, which exposes this world as it truly is while it pioneers the Kingdom. (Stringfellow, 1982b:91)

Stringfellow's lifework, forever indebted to the parable of the circus, was enriched beyond measure by his experience in the summer on 1966; his suspicions had been verified by his experience, his thinking enriched by his life. In a very real and concrete way, Stringfellow saw his hope for the church embodied in an unassuming form; its service was a portrayal and parody of the saga of biblical politics.

Following their tour, Stringfellow had planned to write a book on the theology of the circus, but sadly his impending ill health prevented that.[27]

26. "If people of other arts and occupations do not discern that, they are, as Saint Paul said, idiots (c.f. Romans 1:20–25; Ephesians 4:17–18)" (Stringfellow, 1982b:91).

27. See Stringfellow (1968b) and Stringfellow (1970e:168). He did manage an article, the manuscript for which is in the archives (Stringfellow, 1967b). One book that Stringfellow and Towne *were* able to collaborate on, however, was their account of the heresy charges which were brought against Bishop James Pike in October 1966 by the Episcopal House of Bishops (Stringfellow and Towne, 1967; Pike, 1967). Its publication was almost simultaneous with the event itself. Writing the book was an act of advocacy, and Stringfellow did not agree with Pike's theological position (Stringfellow, 1968c). It was an act which also exacted a high cost, and led, for example, to both disapproval

Death and Life: Illness, Death and Resurrection

It was the year of Martin Luther King's assassination and in which the civil rights bill was passed: 1968 was also the year in which Stringfellow encountered death, personally and dramatically. His very real and personal encounter with his own death is a parable of resistance.[28] It marks the beginning of a final twist in the tale of Stringfellow's lifework, characterized throughout by *movement*.

Stringfellow's ill health had been plaguing him for much of his adult life, and seems to have had its cause in a gallbladder deformity he had since birth, but it had been for him a private matter (Stringfellow, 1966e), and therefore to a large degree an untold story. It was exacerbated following his visit to India in 1952, where it is possible he contracted hepatitis. He then appears to have had a gall bladder operation in 1956, and with countless other health related interruptions to his life and work, by 1963 was given urgent medical counsel to cancel all his engagements and rest for a month (Stringfellow, 1963k). In 1967 Stringfellow's punishing schedule and workload caught up with him, and the illness which had for many years plagued him reared its head in a life-threatening form. The frantic tension which made up Stringfellow's life was, paradoxically, both the tension upon which he thrived, and also that which contributed so greatly to his illness.

In order to escape the hectic lifestyle which encumbered him in the city, in the autumn of 1967 Stringfellow moved with Towne from Manhattan to Block Island, and there set up home. Their penthouse in Manhattan had become "a kind of salon, to which all sorts of people came, and were welcomed, but with such abundance and frequency that it had become difficult to keep up with emptying ashtrays, much less concentrate enough to write" (Stringfellow, 1970e:18). Block Island

by close friends and colleagues (Neill, 1968; Stringfellow, 1968c), and even his removal from the Faith and Order Commission of the World Council of Churches. On this, Stringfellow wrote: "I was removed because I was (I suppose I still am) obnoxious to the Episcopalian authorities" (Stringfellow, 1970e:146). He had considered the Faith and Order Commission one of his more worthwhile ecumenical involvements. While the affair, and Stringfellow's involvement in it, might benefit from close and detailed scrutiny, this is beyond the immediate scope of our present discussion.

28. The account of this is told in the second of his autobiographical polemics, *A Second Birthday* (Stringfellow, 1970e), the frontispiece of which is a quote from Barth's conference in 1962, regarding the elaboration of a theology of freedom. It seems plain that Stringfellow is here consciously drawing the inference which we earlier acknowledged.

provided for Stringfellow a place of solitude, rest, reflection, and writing. I suspect also he envisioned it as a place at once removed from the sub-culture so familiar to Towne. The isolation of Block Island afforded privacy and security, and a chance for their relationship to develop outside of the normal cultural pressures of homosexual sub-culture at that time.[29] Together, they envisioned their home, Eschaton, as their own monastery (Stringfellow, 1970e:18).[30]

However, without doubt the most prominent reason for his departure from New York City, after being a resident there for some eleven years, was his health, and that particular assault, while no doubt slowed, continued. The move appears to repeat a pattern in Stringfellow's life of physically moving away in order to be able to gain perspective.[31] Leaving New York, far from abandoning it, may well have provided a certain critical distance from it which in the long term allowed his work to continue to flourish.

By April of 1968, he described his illness as some kind of enzyme shortage which led to an inability to absorb nutrition, and thus experience staggering weight loss (Stringfellow, 1968d).[32] Bouts of hospitalization and attention by the medical fraternity were intermingled amongst permanent medication and periods of relative well being. As the pain grew, so did the medical bills. At this point in his life, business was more or less put on hold so that life and death could be attended to.

Amidst the ordeal and agony of pain which he encountered, at the precipice of death and life, things come sharply into focus for Stringfellow. With hindsight, we see here a new development to his lifework at this time, which he was later able to reflect upon. It is a change, once more, precipitated by unity.

---

29. This suspicion is, I believe, borne out by the way in which a third person, Ray Karras, was on the deeds of Eschaton (Stringfellow et al., 1966) and lived there with them for a while. He appears to have been a (former) lover or acquaintance of Towne (Towne, 1963a), and helped with research on the Pike book (Stringfellow and Towne, 1967:viii). His presence goes unacknowledged by Stringfellow in any of his accounts of his time on Block Island, and it was short lived. The relationship between Towne and Stringfellow seemed to find its own measure.

30. Stringfellow named their home upon his return to Block Island, after this ordeal and the surgical intervention which facilitated it. The name represented the essence of what Stringfellow had learnt during this period of his lifework.

31. The same pattern can be seen in his attending the LSE and his time in the army.

32. See also Stringfellow (1970e:20).

Harlem had taught Stringfellow about the concrete reality of institutionalized death, whereby he comprehended it "theologically as a
militant, moral reality" (Stringfellow, 1976c:5), and that which the Bible
describes began to have real concrete significance for him. However,
it was only when he encountered death most privately and personally,
in "the debilitations of prolonged illness and the aggressions of pain"
(Stringfellow, 1976c:5) that he was able to realize that the two encounters
were with the same power, the same death which he had, by his own admission, only really encountered in another more public guise. In short,
Stringfellow saw death as at once both a public and a private act. There
was (no longer) a dichotomy between the two spheres: the physical death
which visits us in our own mortality is in fact at the same time the death
whose power and politics maintain the principalities and powers. "This
lack of distinction between the private and the political realms resolves
a secret of the gospel" (Stringfellow, 1976c:6). Jesus' demonstration of authority over the power of death, demonstrated for example through his
healing ministry and raising Lazarus from the dead, is a demonstration
of authority over the same power which "supplies the only moral sanction for the state and its ruling principalities" (Stringfellow, 1976c:8). And
this lack of distinction between the two points towards and confirms the
contemporary relevance and reality of the resurrection.

> The negation of the supposed distinction between the private and
> the political because of the coherence of death in diverse forms
> or appearances points to the truth that the resurrection, far from
> being the vague or ethereal immortality so commonly imagined,
> is eventful and accessible for human beings in every situation in
> which death is pervasive—in every personal or public circum-
> stance in common history. (Stringfellow, 1976c:9)[33]

In his illness Stringfellow experienced death publicly in the principality of medicine (Stringfellow, 1970e:23–34), for example,[34] as well as
in the personal and intimate confrontation with his own mortality
(Stringfellow, 1970e:45–54).

33. It is perhaps noteworthy that Stringfellow was writing this in 1976, and yet, bar
the obvious development in his thinking regarding the private and the political, it was
the same view of the resurrection, and the same bemoaning of its misconception, which
had filled his attentions some ten years earlier; such, perhaps, is the long-haul nature of
confronting the principalities and powers.

34. His reflections in *A Second Birthday* range across pretty well all his public concerns of the 1960s—including race, the church, poverty, technology, government.

> I became possessed by pain ... My experience of pain ... was a
> pervasive, totalitarian presence, a foreigner to life in our midst
> which could not be ignored ... To endure pain is to suffer an-
> ticipation of death, in both mind and body. The experience of
> pain is a foretaste of the event of death. Pain is an ambassador
> of death. Pain is one of death's disguises, though not one of the
> more subtle ones. It is the surrogate really, servant relationship
> evident between pain and death which causes me to write of pain
> in such personified terms ... *pain had become my work.* (original
> emphasis Stringfellow, 1970e:45, 53, 55)

Pain had engulfed Stringfellow's life, and while not overcome by it, it was
now his constant companion (it was a demonic possession) and increasingly grew in prominence. It became his work in the sense that it became
his occupation: his life was literally occupied by pain, its management,
the way it organized his time, demanded recognition, and exhausted his
faculties. His lifework changed dramatically, and the punishing schedule
which had perhaps contributed to his current condition was systemati-
cally abandoned while his "other work" was attended to.[35] In this personal
confrontation with the power of death, pain, death's acolyte, sought to
prevent him from being who he was called to be. Pain was a consequence
of his creatureliness.

The recognition of his pain as work was a breakthrough for
Stringfellow. Pain for him was neither judgment nor justification, although it sought recognition itself as the latter. In the face of pain's possession, the resurrection took on an increasingly radicalized significance,

---

35. Work, as he described above in chapter 3, was "a reality of fallen existence" which
describes the broken relationships between humanity and all of creation (Stringfellow,
1970e:62). It therefore represents the lost dominion of humanity over creation, which
the circus, as a parable, recovers. See also Stringfellow (1970e:55–68) for Stringfellow's
further, although essentially unchanged, treatment of work.

Stringfellow was in financial difficulties before the illness and associated medical
bills started mounting up. The cancellation of his speaking schedule had dramatic
financial consequences and left Stringfellow bankrupt (Stringfellow, 1968d,f). He re-
quested advances on books that were never written, including some that were probably
never serious considerations; anyway, at this time writing also went on hold. Eventually,
he was forced to sell off the land surrounding Eschaton in a piecemeal fashion. His
economic realities, as he put it somewhat humorously, "were turning me into the
classical Keynesian, upholding a doctrine of the viability of indefinite indebtedness"
(Stringfellow, 1970e:126–27). The irony of his own survival is not lost on him: his status
as a white Anglo-Saxon with a law degree from Harvard advantaged his access to loans
and monies. It was an unjust situation he had long resented.

for pain had become a "familiar crisis to be transcended by a grace also familiar" (Stringfellow, 1970e:68).

The options to save Stringfellow were limited to a radical surgical procedure to remove his pancreas. The chances of survival were slim. His chances of survival without it, equally so. Faced with the dilemmas of his present medical predicament, and his reflections upon his own life in the light of this, the total and absolute nature of God's reign crystallized for Stringfellow, especially in relation to judgment. In life, all decisions, he says, are moral decisions, and God is implicated in them all because the "event of decision poses the issue of judgment—concretely the judgment of God" (Stringfellow, 1970e:86), there is no hierarchy between our decisions, or those of institutions. Decisions are moral action, and God is judge of all:

> He judges all men and all things, every decision, every action, every thought, every omission; neither sparrows nor a hair on the head are neglected in his judgment. God's judgment is *His* knowledge, not to be apprehended or imitated by men or by institutions. His judgment is His secret. No man, no nation, no creature whatever has even a clue as to how he or it is judged in any matter: God's judgment is utterly secret. His judgment is in time and yet in the consummation of time; His judgment is contemporary but also transcendent; His judgment encompasses all that was, all that is, and all that is to be, as if it were a single event which, in the end, it is. (Stringfellow, 1970e:88)

Not only do we get some insight here into Stringfellow's eschatology, but we also see his clearest articulation of the place and reach of God's judgment. While God's judgment is absolutely unknown to us, what he asserts we can know, and what is revealed in biblical history, is the *character* of God's judgment: mercy and forgiveness displacing punishment, repentance counting as righteousness. This is this character in which the witness of the Christian life is grounded and to which it testifies in word and deed. In the immediacy of daily life, it is through the vocational event of decision that we honor the gift of life, for "vocation has to do with recognizing life as a gift and honoring the gift of life in living" (Stringfellow, 1970e:95). In sum, Stringfellow recognized his predicament for what it was: the everyday confrontation of death and life. Accepting his full and utter implication in this saga, that is, accepting that the death which rapidly approached did not hold sway over his authentic vocation, he was freed by God's grace to realize that any decision about his care, whether he had the operation or whether he didn't, did not alter the "vocational issue, which is to live as a human being while one lives." In coming to his decision to have the surgery, he was therefore able to write: "In the midst of death I felt free, with a surety and composure which, while not wholly novel to my experience, was more thorough and sustained than I had previously enjoyed" (Stringfellow, 1970e:99). It was one of the most important and decisive vocational events of his life, in which he was fully and absolutely implicated; amidst the reign of death, Stringfellow felt alive: "very much alive: never more alive" (Stringfellow, 1970e:99). His empirical experience did much to radicalize the resources of spirituality, and specifically worship and prayer, in confrontation with his, essentially, demonic possession by the power of death.

Although ordinarily confined to his house while awaiting surgery, Stringfellow went in October to Baltimore for the trial of the "Catonsville Nine." There, Stringfellow addressed a congregation of supporters (and a few spies) who had gathered in a nearby church. The Nine had destroyed service files at a draft board office in Catonsville, Maryland, using napalm made to a recipe from an Army instruction manual. Two of the nine were good friends: Dan and Philip Berrigan, of whom he acknowledged his "esteem for their Christianity, and my admiration for their guts" (Stringfellow, 1970e:131).[36] His involvement before the congregation at Baltimore bespeaks the power of his encounter with the powers of death and life amidst his pain: the reality of the reconciliation of the private and political. Physically exhausted and debilitated by pain, hardly able to speak or stand, yet somehow exhilarated by the occasion, Stringfellow addressed the crowd. And in a powerful voice, unbroken and clear and full of hope, he offered the following benediction:

> Remember, now, that the State has only one power it can use against human beings: death. The State can persecute you, pros-ecute you, imprison you, exile you, execute you. All of these mean the same thing. The State can consign you to death. The grace of Jesus Christ in this life is that death fails. There is nothing the State can do to you, or to me, which we need fear. (Stringfellow, 1970e:133)

36. Stringfellow dates his own support for protest against America's involvement in Vietnam to the visit he made to that country early in 1966 (Stringfellow, 1970e:130).

It was perhaps the most simple, the most powerful, the most impassioned, and the most embodied presentation of his lifework to date, bringing together the conjunction of the private and political force of the power of death, the deliverer and the words delivered.[37]

And so it was that on November 22, 1968, Stringfellow confronted death head on and underwent surgery. He said goodbye to those he loved: Anthony, his parents, Dan Berrigan, James Pike, and various friends. Bread was broken, the sacrament shared; death was considered an almost certain outcome—this was, after all, an experimentation rather than a cure. The operation was supposed to last three hours; after over ten, the surgeon emerged, smiling: "Strange as it may seem, your friend is alive" (Stringfellow, 1970e:175). Never had truer words been spoken, for in body and spirit he had experienced resurrection. The surgery had removed both his pancreas and his spleen, rendering Stringfellow a surgical diabetic wedded to a regime of medication and animal enzymes, the latter necessary for the absorption of nutrients and of some limited help. The rest of his life was spent under this regime, and he experienced many further ailments, including stroke and loss of sight, until his death in 1985. If anything, however, throughout all this his vocation was affirmed and strengthened; in his weakness, he was made strong, and it was the strength of life in the Spirit. This then was a physical and a spiritual event, for in the midst of his physical healing was also the recurring theme of dying to career, dying to self, and being raised to new and authentic life, and each time the authenticity had become more fully manifest.

It was nothing short of a miracle. Submitting himself, Stringfellow was raised from the dead.

> When all due allowances have been made for doctors and for medicine, it is when these mysteries—healing and love—are joined that, in fact, a miracle happens . . . Self-love is decisive . . . a love of self which, esteeming life itself as a gift, expects or demands no more than the life which is given, and which welcomes and embraces and affirms that much unconditionally . . . self-love which emulates, and, in the end, participates in, the love of God for life. (Stringfellow, 1970e:201–2)

37. After a silence, Stringfellow reports, "there was an ovation, which took me by surprise, until Anthony pointed out that it was the failure of death that the people applauded" (Stringfellow, 1970e:133); at least then, his ego, and his humor, were still intact.

It was a crucial and defining experience in his lifework, which was to have dramatic and radicalizing consequences. Stringfellow experienced resurrection, and then obediently returned to the incarnation.

THE CHRISTIAN VOCATION: THE SACRAMENTAL LIFE

> Theology is concerned with the implication of the Word of God in the world's common life. In this context, it must be recognized and affirmed that every man, if he reflects upon the event of his own life in this world, is a theologian . . . I am not a scholar (I have not the temperament for that) but am an empirical theologian . . . Biblical theology, especially the moral theology of the Bible, is itself empirical, a testimony wrought in experience not academic, in the sense of abstraction . . . In the biblical witness the Incarnation is the illustrious instance in point: the event of God acting in history in Jesus Christ addresses the experience of men contemporaneously. (Stringfellow, 1970e:21, 40, 41)

This is one of the most succinct summaries of Stringfellow's theological self-understanding, given in *Second Birthday*, and reflects the singularly authoritative place of the Bible in his lifework. He is at pains to point out that, contrary to popular opinion and expectation, he read at most about two dozen theological books. For the most time, he just read the Bible—he inhabited its world and our world, the world of the Word and the world of the Fall, simultaneously. The quote above shows how, in the face of the personal and political power of death, he is committed to life and to how we live, for to be a theologian, and to be a Christian, is to be empirical or incarnational. It is, of course, this incarnational imperative which stands out as one of the defining motifs of Stringfellow's lifework. In terms of the Christian life of worship and witness, it is an imperative to live the sacramental life: to be a sign of grace. This was at the heart of Stringfellow's authentic vocation, and continuously we see him immersed in his culture and his context simultaneously with his immersion in the Bible, the two worlds colliding.

Not surprisingly, then, in the years after 1968 Stringfellow's lifework was directly and *radically* affected by the event of his near death, and was also affected by the changing social context in which, as a radical agency, the peace movement was growing in strength in resistance to the draft and the war in southeast Asia.

Throughout the 1960s and beyond, we see the theme of *movement* active and at work in Stringfellow's lifework, both physically in his movement away from Harlem, to the Penthouse and then Block Island with Towne, but also movement which bears witness to intensification in his own thought regarding the explication and clarification of biblical politics and the place of biblical witness.

> The biblical witness is normative . . . in the sense that the Bible is the exemplary story of God's consistent, militant, continuing and patient involvement in the history of mankind . . . The biblical saga is, thus, the holy history of the world. And the problem of "relevance" between the holy history and our history is obviated because, by its very exemplary character, *the holy history is*, as it were, *concurrent with contemporary history* . . . It is the empirical realm which is the constant environment of the biblical witness— of the *living* Word of God. (Stringfellow, 1970e:43)

Stringfellow claimed he did not have a theology and hoped he never would (Stringfellow, 1970e:150–51). For him, to be a theologian meant witnessing to the knowledge of God made known by God (Jesus Christ), and the witness which testifies to that reality (the Bible). For him all theology must be empirically verified within the realm of the biblical witness, the holy history at work *right now* in our history. Not surprisingly, then, Stringfellow was at this time patiently and lovingly involved in the turbulent social context; he stood in resistance to the power of death, was an advocate of those resisting the war,[38] and in so being, was himself implicated both personally and politically as two worlds, quite literally, confronted one another head on.

His lifework shows a distinctive movement towards the margins and the dramatic emergence of biblical politics. Biblical politics describes Christ's reconciliation of creation to God the Father and the indwelling and empowerment of the Spirit in that life, enabling people to discern their vocation and live authenticly, personally and publicly radicalized such that those who inhabit their authentic vocation might necessarily and consequently stand in resistance to the power of death, and stand for Christ, manifest in the principalities and powers in personal and public dimension. This is the cumulative vision of Stringfellow's lifework, testifying to his esteem for the biblical witness and its politics,

---

38. Many of those in the peace movement were students, yet Stringfellow's view of students is far from wholly positive (Oregon University, 1968).

which *Ethic for Christians and Other Aliens in a Strange Land* exemplifies in a revolutionary manner (Stringfellow,1973b).[39]

THE EMERGENCE OF SEMIOTIC CREATIVITY

What makes *Ethic for Christians* especially distinctive in its presentation of biblical politics is its use of apocalyptic and the semiotic creativity it employs to do this—especially the use of the parables of Babylon and Jerusalem as they confront one another, the presence of the power of death as demonic possession, and the necessity of resistance and the reality of hope, as the means of living humanly amidst the fall. Yet while the underlying message is perhaps by now familiar to us, its radical form appears to have come out of nowhere. Therefore, in this final section, we trace its emergence by looking at developments in his lifework which led directly to his writing this book on moral theology in which we see his biblical politics most fully developed,[40] before going on briefly to see what this, the most well known of Stringfellow's books, has to say.

As we read, Stringfellow's commitment to writing a book on moral theology extends back to 1963 (Stringfellow, 1963j) and to his early realization of the need for, and commitment to, a Christian ethics that realized the political significance of the church as a Christian society which recognizes the importance of evangelism (Stringfellow, 1953c). As will be clear by now, in some ways this did become the subject of *all* his books and indeed his lifework. What makes *Ethic for Christians* significant, however, is the totalizing manner in which it embraces biblical politics and the biblical witness, and his use of apocalyptic is central to this. There seem to have been at least three radicalizing agencies at

39. The idea that this work exemplifies his esteem for the biblical witness was Stringfellow's own view, expressed in a document which formed part of a Leader's kit for study groups of *An Ethic for Christians and Other Aliens in a Strange Land* (Stringfellow, 1976b).

40. This marks neither the end of his life-work, nor the end of his work on moral theology. However, *Ethic for Christians* nevertheless marks a decisive moment in so far as it consciously and specifically articulates ethics fully immersed within, and expressive of, biblical politics, in a manner which was hitherto unseen in Stringfellow's life-work. It marked the first of what was to be a trilogy on ethics, although he died before the final volume could be completed. Drawing our discussions to a close at this point should not be taken to indicate that there is nothing more to say, far from it, developments in his life-work lay just around the corner (see, for example, Stringfellow (1982b,1984)). Rather, it indicates the simply the clearly defined boundaries and limitations of our present study.

work in his lifework from 1968 onwards, each contributing to the development of his biblical politics and the production of the distinctive character of *Ethic for Christians.*

The *first* of these is the changing social context. By the late 1960s and early 1970s, the political landscape of America had changed: the Great Society had been replaced by a society at war, both internally and externally, over race and Vietnam. It was a context of revolution and revolt, in which the desire for peace amidst a reality of violence became the defining characteristics of protest movements at this time, and most obviously, the movement of protest against America's involvement in southeast Asia. Stringfellow's own visit to southeast Asia in 1966 led him to be deeply critical of America's involvement there (Stringfellow, 1966g, i).

> Violence described all of the multifarious, inverted, broken, distorted and ruptured relationships characteristic of the present history of this world. Violence is the undoing of Creation. Violence is the moral confusion and practical chaos which, so long as time lasts, disrupts and displaces the truth and peace of Creation, which the Bible denominates as the Fall. Violence is the reign of death in this world and violence is the name of all and any of the works of death . . . The ubiquity of violence as the normative estate for all creatures . . . in the Fall should recall another elementary feature of violence: its versatility. Violence is often visible, but sometimes invisible; violence may be corporate or it may be personal. (Stringfellow, 1973b:127–28)[41]

By the time *Ethic for Christians* was published, violence had become for Stringfellow the empirical reality of the moral presence named death, and, moreover, the language he used to speak about it had gained a power and vitality which had not previously been present.[42] He was able to

41. Given their good friendship, Stringfellow's involvement in getting some of Ellul's works published in the United States, along with his advocacy of Ellul to America (Stringfellow, 1970b), it is probable that Stringfellow's understanding of violence was influenced by Ellul's work on the subject (Ellul, 1969), and he probably had sight of the page proofs before its publication (thus raising the possibility of Ellul's thought influencing papers he delivered pre-1970). Other influences would doubtless have included Thomas Merton (Merton, 1968), with whom Stringfellow established a friendship shortly after *My People is the Enemy* came out (Stringfellow, 1964d); Stringfellow regarded Merton very highly (Stringfellow, 1970e:191) and in fact dedicated *Ethic for Christians* to him. Influences upon Stringfellow's life, here and elsewhere, were more often relational rather than the consequence of reading theology (Stringfellow, 1970e:151).

42. Like his other books, *An Ethic for Christians and Other Aliens in a Strange Land*

speak about violence in a new way: it had become the lens through which the fall was viewed. This development was not a sudden transformation, but rather the consequence of a process of movement in his lifework, his commitment to life within the changing social context, and the emphasis of that context, through the actions of the state against its own people, as well as the acts of the state in southeast Asia. The context of America at the end of the 1960s seems only to have furthered his resolve to produce a book on moral theology, and inversely its production was directly related to his social context: "It would . . . be a misfortune to publish a book about the ethics of revolution *after* the revolution" (Stringfellow, 1969c). Amidst a culture thought by many to be in moral crisis, the production of a moral theology at this time was an astute move. This would indicate that for Stringfellow, the production of *Ethic for Christians* was a theological attempt to use the resources of the Bible to address the specific social conditions: to read what was going on in America in the light of the biblical text.

We can see perhaps an early sign of the emergence of Stringfellow's response to the state in relation to this issue when he addressed the crowd at the trial of the Catonsville Nine. We also see it, once again more personally, when Stringfellow is indicted for extending hospitality to Daniel Berrigan when he was on the run from the FBI.[43] In the shadow of Berrigan's fugitive status, Stringfellow reflected upon Jesus as a criminal (Stringfellow and Towne, 1971:59–68). Essentially, he came to see Berrigan's witness as an example of living as a free person in transcendence of death's power, as a resilient revolutionary; it was a concrete and specific witness to the confrontation of life and death, Word and world, Jesus and the state. It is a reflection, in other words, of the authority of Christ, and our authority, over death. The full force of the state pursued Berrigan to Block Island, covertly observed him, and then finally arrested him; essentially, it was a man-hunt for a man who peace-

materialized out of addresses and papers, so it is not surprising to see this thought expressed slightly earlier (Stringfellow, 1972).

43. The indictment was for "harboring" Berrigan, who stayed with Stringfellow and Towne, in the open, after he went on the run to avoid arrest, rather than submit himself to the authorities, following sentencing over the Catonsville Nine affair. If Stringfellow had gone to prison, he would most certainly have died. Once again then, his life was immediately threatened. The story is told fully by Stringfellow and Towne (Stringfellow and Towne, 1971), and marks a another important and distinctive point of development in his life-work at this time.

ably resisted the draft and protested against it in an act of resistance and advocacy. Stringfellow reflected on this in the following quote, and in so doing makes clear the very real struggle that resisting the principalities and powers had become, and the way in which the issue of the Vietnam war seemed to uniquely mobilize both the power of life and the power of death as they confront one another. In their confrontation, as the church of Christ[44] witnessed to the power of life and love, the state witnessed to the power of death, through violence. It seemed, in some ways, the most public empirical climax of the saga of biblical politics which Stringfellow had pursued.

> Theologically speaking, the war in Vietnam is not just an improvident, wicked or stupid venture. It epitomizes the militancy and insatiability of death as a moral power reigning in the nation— as that morality in relation to which everything and everyone is supposedly judged and justified. Thus to oppose the war becomes much more than a difference over policy. From the viewpoint of the State protest against the war undermines the *only* moral purpose the State has: the work of death. (Stringfellow, 1970c:183)

Note how Stringfellow's words echo once again that paradigmatic moment addressing the crowd at the trial of the Catonsville Nine. Violence, and its expression in America's involvement in Vietnam, is not the determinate issue: resistance is. Berrigan's resistance, certainly, but Stringfellow's also and perhaps more importantly, is the real radicalizing agent here: the church of Christ and the State confronting one another.[45] Following Berrigan's seizure by the FBI at Eschaton Stringfellow spent what time his "suddenly hectic circumstances would afford with the New Testament" (Stringfellow, 1970c:181); it was a recognition that "human history is holy history," dwelling simultaneously in the biblical world and the present moment (Stringfellow, 1970c: 181). Prior to his arrest, Stringfellow had spent the spring and summer

> engaged with the Babylon passages in the book of Revelation. That effort had influenced my participation in the conversations that were taking place with Daniel and Anthony. With the abrupt

44. That is, the congregation Stringfellow envisioned of Christians in an "underground" church or "seminary underground," rather than the institution of the American churches.

45. That is what marks the difference between his comments on Vietnam here, and those previously following his visit in 1965.

interruption of our talk on August 11 [1970], I put aside—though
not out of reach—the Babylon texts to return to the Acts of the
Apostles, and to some of the letters that are thought to be chronologically proximate to Acts, specifically James and First Peter.
(Stringfellow,1970c:181)

The authority of the biblical saga over the saga of death, in Stringfellow's
lifework, is clear. What is also interesting here, however, is his mention
of reading the Babylon texts of Revelation—the texts which were at the
heart of *Ethic for Christians* (Stringfellow,1973b). It is the first mention
of this.

This talk of Revelation's Babylon texts brings us to the *second* radicalizing agency. There is a hint of this agency in *A Second Birthday*, when
Stringfellow is reflecting upon leaving the city and moving to Block
Island (Stringfellow, 1970e:18–19). In leaving the city, he was at pains
to emphasize that he was not abandoning it, describing it as the "central theological symbol of society" (Stringfellow, 1970e:18). Of course,
there was a great deal of teaching amidst the churches by conservative
Christians[46] which took a contrary view about cities, seeing them instead
as the realm of sin and immorality. Stringfellow goes on:

> Biblically, the city is the scene of *both* doomsday and salvation.
> There is Babylon, but there is also Jerusalem. The city is the
> epitome of the Fall, yet it is the sign of the Eschaton. These con-
> notations of death and life associated with the city empirically
> and theologically mean that the city cannot be escaped and that
> the city must not be rejected by human beings, as it seems to be
> by the utopian hippies and their commune movement, for exam-
> ple, and least of all can it be repudiated by professed Christians.
> (Stringfellow, 1970e:18–19)

The city is, therefore, the image of Babylon and Jerusalem confronting
one another. Bearing in mind that this book was published in 1970, and
the manuscript worked on in the previous year, this would indicate that
the probable source of this theological insight was in fact Jacques Ellul's
The Meaning of the City (Ellul, 1970), page proofs of which Stringfellow
had in his possession.[47] This influence would also seem to fit with the

46. Stringfellow is especially critical of Billy Graham on this point (Stringfellow,
1970e:18–19).

47. I am indebted to Bill Wylie-Kellermann for this insight regarding Ellul's influence and the possession of page proofs by Stringfellow. Other prophetic imagery may

timing of Stringfellow's stated enthusiasm for exploring the Babylon passages from the book of Revelation, prior to the arrest of Berrigan and the indictment of Stringfellow and Towne.

However, there is also evidence that Stringfellow's interest in the relevance of Babylon to the contemporary situation was present in the previous year. In fact, just prior to his operation Stringfellow gave two addresses, and both indicate a fresh direction in his thinking. The first was entitled "Revelation and Revolution: The Ethics of Resistance for Christians and Other Aliens in a Strange Land" (Stringfellow, 1968e), the second was "How to Sing the Lord's Song in a Strange Land" (Stringfellow, 1968a).[48] Both titles are indicative of the eventual content and title of *Ethic for Christians* and suggest an early deployment of the Babylon theme, even though they were not explicitly related to the theme of the city.

The *third* agency occurred through his experience of illness in 1968 and is that of demonic possession. As we read, Stringfellow considered pain to be the acolyte of death and his illness as nothing other than demonic possession by death requiring exorcism. This personal experience was clearly one upon which he reflected theologically. Given the importance of the Bible to Stringfellow, he would doubtless have spent the winter of his convalescence immersed in Scripture. The result was an article published at the end of the summer in 1969, entitled "The Demonic in American Society" (Stringfellow, 1969a),[49] which explored

also have come from significantly earlier, through the WCC (Hoekendijk, 1961). He may also have drawn upon, or recognized the significance of, Arthur C. Clarke's use of such imagery, for the archives indicate Stringfellow collected a number of pamphlets and papers by him (Clarke, 1969).

48. The event, organized by the Disciples of Christ, at which the latter paper was delivered is also referred to by Stringfellow elsewhere (Stringfellow, 1970e:149–52). He makes clear that he prepared for this address by reading the Bible—further suggestion that what he was reading even at this early stage was related to the Babylon imagery.

49. He later expanded this article and its title, so that it became: "America as Jerusalem Lost: The Ascendency of the Demonic in American Society" (Stringfellow, 1970a). In it he describes the "moral crisis" in the following highly distinctive way, which suggests the influence by this time of Ellul's work: "It is universally conceded that the nation is in the midst of a crisis of breathtaking scope and profound consequence. It is acknowledged that for all the unsolved practical problems and for all the unreconciled social issues in contemporary American life, the fundamental matter has to do with the very idea of society. The sense of the nation's destiny—that somehow, America would be the promised land—is confused. America is not Jerusalem. America is Jerusalem lost" (Stringfellow, 1970a:1).

the nature of the "moral crisis" which confronted America at this time, and was effectively the breakdown of traditional norms and social and political patterns, brought about in part by the Civil Rights Movement, in part by the disaffection of the generation raised on grand expectations, and in part by the government's action in both domestic and foreign affairs.[50] Stringfellow describes the situation in the terms of the reign of the power of death, the principalities and powers, and demonic possession: language which had previously been absent.

> Today, the enemy of humanity and of human life in America (and in much the rest of the world) is the ascendancy of the demonic in the great institutions of science, commerce and the military, and their satellite institutions: the university, the labor unions and, increasingly, the church. . . . This is the moral issue as it is described biblically . . . Biblically the moral issue is *always* the versatile and seemingly inexhaustible aggression of the demonic, of the power of death claiming ultimate significance or sovereignty in history over men and nations. As for rebels—the dissenters and resisters and those who talk of revolution . . . bless them as the closest thing the nation has to conscience. And remember that Saint Paul admonished all to recognize in the vitality of conscience a sign of the Holy Spirit. (Stringfellow, 1969a:248)

We should also note that the relationship he articulates here between faith and action, and more importantly the *kind* of action which arises as a consequence of faith, in terms of the Holy Spirit as our conscience, indicates clearly once again the pneumatological character of his (incarnational) lifework.[51] Conscience, the work of the Holy Spirit, is therefore determinate of our (ethical) action. It is worthwhile noting that vocation then is authentic life lived in conscience in the world.

These influences all contributed to what became *Ethic for Christians* (Stringfellow, 1973b), a work which represents perhaps the most clearly articulated and radical incarnation of biblical politics in Stringfellow's lifework to this point. It is a work of apocalyptic, exposing reality and death amidst the drama of the book of Revelation—the reality of Babylon

50. It should be pointed out that it was still a minority who were thus affected; for most the period was contiguous with those which preceded it, and ultimately those which followed.

51. *Conscience and Obedience* (Stringfellow, 1977a) was the second of a planned trilogy on ethics; Stringfellow died before the third, projected to be on the Holy Spirit, was written.

and Jerusalem confronting one another. It is simultaneously a book of resistance and hope. It takes seriously the biblical saga, in which it is immersed, proclaiming the politics of the Bible as the means for living amidst the politics of this fallen world, and singing the Lord's song, loud, clear, and without restraint: advocating the truth amidst the violence and verbiage and assault of the power of death at work in the nation and proclaiming resistance as the means to live humanly. It extols the gifts of the Spirit as the means by which hope is realized.

Although Stringfellow's lifework continued and developed for many years,[52] *Ethic for Christians* is the culmination of a journey that took Stringfellow nearly three decades. Certainly, *Ethic for Christians* could not hold him, and further development continued. Nevertheless it marks a decisive point of the most clearly articulated and immersed expression of his lifework (an apex, perhaps). It is for many people the place at which they start with Stringfellow, yet for us it marks the end. We close, with an extract from its preface.

> My concern is to understand America biblically ... The effort is to comprehend the nation, to grasp what is happening right now to the nation and to consider the destiny of the nation within the scope and style of the ethics and ethical metaphors distinctive to the biblical witness in history. The task is to treat the nation within the tradition of biblical politics—to understand America biblically—*not* the other way round, *not* (to put it in an appropriately awkward way) to construe the Bible Americanly. There has been too much of the latter in this country's public life and religious ethos. There still is. To interpret the Bible for the convenience of America ... represents a radical violence to both the character and content of the biblical message. It fosters a fatal vanity that America is a divinely favored nation ... It arrogantly misappropriates political images from the Bible and applies them to America so that America is conceived of ... as *the* righteous nation ... In archetypal form in this century, material abundance, redundant productivity, technological facility, and military predominance are publicly cited to verify the alleged divine preference ... It is just this kind of Sadducean sophistry, distorting the biblical truth for American purposes, which, in truth, occasions the moral turmoil which the nation so manifestly suffers today ... The biblical topic *is* politics. The Bible is about the politics

52. His last book, *The Politics of Spirituality* (Stringfellow, 1984), is thought by some to represent perhaps his finest, most subtle, and most polished work.

8

Conclusion

W E HAVE EXAMINED STRINGFELLOW's lifework for a period of a little over a quarter of a century, and in so doing covered a large amount of ground. We have seen that for Stringfellow the reconciliation of creation to God in Christ (unity or love) is at the center of biblical politics and his understanding of faith and politics (our authenticity); the two cannot be separated. Thus, Stringfellow's is a story as much about his vocation as it is about the emerging understanding of biblical politics. The book has traced the development of this thinking in relation to the influences and radicalising agencies of social context and personal and public encounter, in which he sought to recover the Bible as the foundation of faith; the gospel authoring life.

Throughout this book we have examined his lifework in relation to faith and politics. We have done this biographically, bringing together both the confessional and critical strands necessary for successful examination of such an obscure and extraordinary person as William Stringfellow. His was a life, as we have seen, which was increasingly defined by the authority of the Word, not the world, and yet there was clearly a close relationship between the two. A sense of place, or a commitment to the empirical, concrete context ("right now") is a central motif of Stringfellow's lifework, and throughout the emergence and development of his biblical politics prevails. His motivation was born of a commitment to both the Bible and his context, and amidst this commitment there is a unity to his life and his work.

This commitment originated while in college, through his relationship with "another fellow," in which he discovered the beginnings of acceptance and love, both from another human and from God. These origins were themselves a paradigm of all that was to follow, for the importance of acceptance and love became central themes in his theology of reconciliation and unity, which in turn lay at the heart of his biblical politics. This was a decisive moment in his life, and the concrete beginnings of his faith (taking God seriously). Having had this experience, his visit to LSE and Europe did much to foster his faith, along with his understanding of and commitment to politics. Politics for him became not so much a matter of career as of ministry. It marked the beginnings of his inhabiting "authentic vocation."

His experiences overseas taught him the significance of *criticism, context,* and *commitment,* with the early signs of both advocacy and resistance emerging in relation to what he had seen in the bombed-out streets of Europe. Through his travels to Europe he was able to gain critical perspective upon America, an awareness of the deep significance of context, and a commitment to the marginalized and the aliens. Culturally, it was a time in which he realized that America's self-perception was not shared by other countries and in many cases was just plain wrong. Whilst America was awash with post-war prosperity, Europe suffered. The Confessing Church left a lasting theological impression: it was here, for instance, that he discovered (to varying degrees) the importance of faithful Bible study, the underground seminary, and the idea of "resistance." Ecumenism was, without a doubt, a central influence. It provided Stringfellow with both the theological resources and the platform through which he and his thinking could develop. It was the cornerstone to his thinking on faith and politics, and we saw how it facilitated the development of his thinking on vocation, for example, from ministry to authentic identity. The shift in thinking which rendered ethics as a consequence of authenticity, rather than determinant of it, was most significant in his later critique and advocacy of, for example, the church and homosexuality respectively. It originated out of his experiences with the law, which functioned as a kind of secular theology informing people how to act (thus defining of their identity); it was a medium through which political action was mediated and determined. By reconceiving of the law *theologically* (rather than vice-versa) Stringfellow was able to proclaim that the gospel is politics. Political zeal by this point had been transformed from a zeal for democracy into a zeal for the gospel.

Ecumenism's commitment to the laity also helped to put him in touch with the ordinary as the context of faith and divine action and to foster his ecclesiology. This was a commitment to *creatureliness.* We see this clearly in his faculty paper, written whilst at Harvard, and also in his experiences in East Harlem. With regards to the former, the issue was justification and justice (grace and law) and the moral reality of the fall. Engaging the discussions between faith and law, he confronted the way in which Christ, the subject of our faith, had been objectivized and abstracted: it was grace, not law, which justified us. This was a particularly important realization amidst the religious context of 1950s America, where faith was a very private matter authoring personal morality and the law determined public ethics and political action. The universal condition, as we saw, is the moral reality of the fall. The key to taking part in the reconciliation of creation to God is the *congregation*, for it is through it, in unity, that the life of Christ is lived. The work of the congregation, whether gathered or dispersed, is *worship*. The role of the gathered church is to sustain the body in dispersal in the world—where God is. Authentic life is therefore a life lived in obedient response to God's initiative, in the world; that is the world of "work"—the world of death. Stringfellow sought to witness to the reconciliation of the church to itself: for it to resist the vocational demands of the law and so avoid becoming an instrument of the state. For whilst the law could name sin, it could not overcome it; whilst it could be reconciled, it could not reconcile. That was the message of criticism and hope which Stringfellow proclaimed.

In East Harlem, we see his creaturely preoccupation come to the fore once again. For American society as a whole, it was a period of rapid and unprecedented growth and economic expansion, accompanied by and interrelated with the looming threat of the communist politics of the Soviet Union. Indeed, the relationship between prosperity and threat was symbiotic as the cultural identity of post-war America was forged. In this culture of consumerism and fear, the aggressive pursuit of prosperity and wealth was coupled by the need to scapegoat, and homosexuals and the poor found themselves the early victims of this kind of onslaught; they became the caricature of threat to America's re-located identity. Increased wealth fuelled heightened expectation, which in turn fostered optimism. In a world of opportunity and plenty, hope was on offer for those who could afford it. And yet amidst this culture, there was another reality: that of poverty, minorities, the disenfranchised, exploited, and this was the world in which Stringfellow immersed himself. At this point it is important to realize the paradoxical nature of Stringfellow's lifework. His was a tireless attempt, to the point of death, to live life as authentically and faithfully as he was humanly able. His own lifework can perhaps be summarized along the following lines: the more involved in mundane creatureliness of the ordinary world he becomes, the less worldly he becomes, for in the world (rather than the ecclesiastical, academic, or legal establishments on the one hand, or the "Disneyland world" of a culture dominated by prosperity, consumerism, and the American dream on the other) he discovers the Word of God. Stringfellow's is a story of a life of discipleship—a vocational preoccupation with learning to discern the Word and worship God.

The issue faced by Stringfellow in East Harlem was that of authenticity. Thus, whilst publicly it concerned the nature of the church, his resignation also allowed him to be free to live in Harlem. Stringfellow spent much of his life struggling with loneliness, and it was only really meeting Towne later which changed this. However, in the community of East Harlem he did find acceptance and experienced self-acceptance. This was unconditional acceptance for who he was; it was grace. Thus, he learnt empirically about God's action in the world and all of creation. Stringfellow's ecclesiology suggests that we are nowhere alone, for as Christ's body in dispersal or when gathered, we are held in unity with one another and him. He confronted disunity and apostasy in the church, for if law were his first principality, religion was his second. He advocated a return to the Bible and a recovery of the gospel and the basis for the church's ministry and mission, an understanding which once again placed *reconciliation* or *love* at the heart of vocation.

Rightly conceived, the Christian life was one of *servanthood, sacrifice,* and *sacrament* and demanded nothing other than the total personal and political immersion of Christians in the world, transforming the world through the life of worship and witness in diverse, radical, spontaneous, and empirical encounters with the Word and the world; there was nothing abstract about it.

Similarly, there was nothing at all abstract about the Bible; it was the holy history of the world, and in faith our lives are congruous with those we read about. The Bible makes reality known; it is the means for discerning who we are.

Being biblical people is a counter-cultural existence, in that it requires our allegiance to the power of life, not death. The adventure of the Christian life is, for him, the adventure of the Bible, in which reading and listening are a preoccupation as one is immersed in the ordinary everydayness of the world. What makes Stringfellow so passionate about the gospel is, perversely perhaps, his loneliness: it drives him not to despair (although there were times of this) but to hope. That, most of all, is the significance of that initial experience of conversion with his young friend: acceptance, at the deepest, personal, intimate level.

Three of the most distinctive radicalizing agencies which were at work upon his life were, as we saw, Barth, Towne, and the conference on civil rights. We do not need to rehearse their influence again here, except to recall briefly that the themes of advocacy and acceptance were significant and dominant in all (even though in the case of the latter, it was a call *from* Stringfellow, not an action done *to* Stringfellow). The themes of unity and love, advocacy, acceptance, and therefore authenticity, found new impetus in and through these encounters.

In his prophetic confrontation with the idol of Johnson's administration, we saw Stringfellow's identification of the cost of discipleship and the confrontation of the idols of the so-called Great Society. Johnson's was a deadly rhetoric of myth and was anathema to Stringfellow's ears. What he proposed in response was simple orthodoxy: nothing unusual or outrageous. In that respect, it was the complete opposite of the Great Society. Amidst a culture engulfed by radical political resistance taking place through the new left and the emerging protest movement on the one hand, and radical theological reinterpretation taking place in schools of thought like the Death of God movement on the other, Stringfellow's response was decidedly less "novel" (although to his readers and listeners, it was perhaps the most novel). Simply, he sought a return to the orthodoxy of faith. It was an orthodoxy which demanded involvement, in the form of obedient incarnational discipleship. This was the present imperative of true humanity and united aesthetics (liturgy) and ethics (social action)—or in other words, brought about the unity of the sanctuary and the world. The marks of the sacramental life are *realism, inconsistency, radicalism,* and *intercession.* Increasingly, we saw in his thinking the concrete articulation of the way in which Christian action should be determined not by secular politics, but by the politics of the Bible. We also saw the way in which he thinks the circus operates as a parable of such discipleship amidst the power of death, where the church was simply unable to.

His own personal confrontation with death through his illness shows us the radical form to which his commitment to context extends. It is here that reconciliation, work, death and life, take on new meaning in the deeply personal, and yet simultaneously political, encounter with death. Through this event, any notion that there is somehow a difference between the personal and political dimensions of death is forever banished. Whilst it had been present for many years, resistance to the power of death takes on absolute, concrete, unambiguous, and unified form at this point. Whilst reflecting upon his own near death, it is perhaps also poignant to recall something he later said about the nature of the Christian life. In it, Christians celebrate the *life* of their humanness:

> *always,* in some sense—though it may be diverse and imaginative —a witness of resistance to the status quo of politics and of economics and of everything in society. It is a witness of *resurrection* from death. Paradoxically those who embark on the biblical witness constantly risk death empirically—exile or execution, loss of employment or the praise of neighbors or peers, imprisonment or persecution, harassment or defamation—at the behest of the rulers of this age. (Stringfellow, 1976e)

For him, to acquiesce to, or fail to resist the power of, death is to fail to live life authentically, to fail to be true to one's vocation. The Christian life is a life lived in this eschatological struggle, between promise and fulfillment, between being named who we are in the sight of God and seeing God face to face. Stringfellow realized this with clarity, and he recognized the way in which the Christian life was a life lived in tension between death and life by virtue of its humanness. The call, however, was always for advocacy of life through authenticity and resistance to the power of death manifest in the world.

What is clear throughout his lifework is that context and creatureliness play a decisive role in its formation. What is also clear is that any attempt to understand his lifework and the implications of his moral theology cannot be satisfied by reading *An Ethic for Christians,* nor any of his works individually, for there is a unity and complexity to the development of his lifework which cannot be portrayed in a single polemical volume. In attempting to do so, for example, one may well miss the subtle, significant, and strong ecclesiology which is operative in his thinking, seeing instead only an emphasis upon the Christian life (indeed, his ecclesiology is often masked by his empirical imperative).

Context and creatureliness are determinant in his vocational formation, and context and authenticity were to combine dramatically at the end of our study as we see his engagement with the "revolution" that

was taking place in America at the time. His understanding of reconciliation, the principalities and powers and the power of death, and his
commitment to biblical politics found a new form of more radical, more
concrete counter-cultural expression. Should his distinction from the
new left and other radical movements of protest and resistance still be in
doubt, his decision to adopt the language of Babylon and Jerusalem—the
language of the biblical saga—should cast them aside once and for all. The
politics of the Bible had found their most immersed expression—most
fully involved in the Word and the world. This marks a theological unity
between faith and politics that was to abide in his lifework—it marks the
political incorporation of the world into the saga of the Word. In other
words, through his witness the politics of the world had been reconciled
to the politics of the Bible, and the advocacy of life and resistance to the
power of death have been proclaimed as the authentic vocation of the
church of Christ as it worships God when gathered, or when dispersed,
in the world.

In conclusion, I would like to recall the poem by Daniel Berrigan
which is in the frontispiece to this book. It reads:

> I've said to Bill uneasily:
> dreams in that house are like a hot pot
> constantly stirred, fumes intense, voices
> grandiloquent. What gives?
> Bill paused between beats, like the sea.
> Like the sea, he's no explainer, but pure depth.
> He's not on earth to unravel dreams—
> to precipitate them rather, like a slowly turned
> vintage vat. Drink then, and dream on.

Stringfellow's words were at times grandiloquent, certainly, and Berrigan
got him right: he's not on earth to unravel dreams, but to precipitate
them. Yet not dreams, I would suggest, for it was more concrete than this.
What Stringfellow unravels in his witness is nothing other than *reality*.
Stringfellow saw reality with a clarity few can muster: his sight and his
foresight were his gifts. What he perceived was the reality of the biblical
saga, the world's holy history. Stringfellow's witness was simply one of
radical, faithful, and sacrificial obedience—a life of worship which made
reality known. His life and his work were apocalyptic, in that sense.

Wink supposed that there would be many studies of Stringfellow;
McThenia supposed (rightly) why that might not have taken place.

Ultimately this book sheds light upon the way in which Stringfellow is not primarily a subject to be studied, nor an object to be quantified, but a parable to be told and heard. Stringfellow's lifework is a parable of obedient, faithful, and sacrificial encounter with the Word in the world. If anything, he is simply a man who sought to honor the gift of life of his vocation. His is a story of someone grasped by God and led, at first unwillingly, and increasingly less so, into a new life of proclamation and prophecy; as one who could hear, he became a witness to the Kingdom amidst the rule of death. It was obedience in the radical freedom of Christ which led him even to his own death. So, in conclusion, if we do anything with Stringfellow, we should listen to this man.

Death and Life of a Friend

My last death was William Stringfellow's.
Death
Rattled its begging bowl
like the drummer of Armageddon.
Sustenance! Sympathy! it drummed

Stringfellow, bethought; Death
lacking a name—
(unnameable, nameless horror
they muttered in terror)—
he named it finally, taming
once for all
the appetite that fed
on kings and clowns—
fed and fed, never satiated—
women, warriors,
the sleepy eyed unborn—
never enough!

We must break this thrall
once for all, became his mind's
holy obsession and vocation.
Like a priest's crucifix aloft
before the obscene undead,
Christ expiring for love, summoning a last
commanding cry; Down dog death!—

Thus Stringfellow. Transfixed, laid claim
years and years, a crucifix in hands
not his, miraculous he moved in the world
chasing death pitilessly
dismaying, dispelling death.

Then as the sun advances, and shadows
go underground
he stands, believe, in resplendent noon.
Taken from the cross
he ascends straight up.

And death, shadowy, starved, named
for what it is, is not
and no where to be seen.

—Daniel Berrigan

Bibliography

Adams, James, July 19, 1960. "Letter to William Stringfellow." In *The William Stringfellow Archives, No. 4438*. Division of Rare and Manuscript Collections, Cornell University Library. Box 5.

Andy, October 27, 1947. "Letter to Stringfellow." In *The William Stringfellow Archives, No. 4438*. Division of Rare and Manuscript Collections, Cornell University Library. Box 1.

Barth, Karl, 1939. *Church and State*. London: SCM.

———. 1949. *Dogmatics in Outline*. London: SCM.

———. 1960. *Community, State and Church*. New York: Doubleday.

———. May 2, 1963a. "Rememberance of America." In *The Christian Century*, 7–9.

———. 1979. *Evangelical Theology*. Edinburgh: T. & T. Clark. English Translation.

Barth, Markus, 1959. *Ephesians 1–3*. Garden City, NY: Doubleday.

———. November 25, 1962a. "Letter to Stringfellow." In *The William Stringfellow Archives, No.4438*. Division of Rare and Manuscript Collections, Cornell University Library. Box 6.

———. March 17, 1962b. "Letter to Stringfellow." In *The William Stringfellow Archives, No. 4438*. Division of Rare and Manuscript Collections, Cornell University Library. Box 6.

———. February 25, 1962c. "Letter to William Stringfellow." In *The William Stringfellow Archives, No. 4438*. Division of Rare and Manuscript Collections, Cornell University Library. Box 6.

———. April 28, 1963b. "Letter to William Stringfellow." In *The William Stringfellow Archives, No. 4438*. Division of Rare and Manuscript Collections, Cornell University Library. Box 7.

———. March 25, 1963c. "Letter to William Stringfellow." In *The William Stringfellow Archives, No. 4438*. Division of Rare and Manuscript Collections, Cornell University Library. Box 7.

———. September 1970. "Letter to William Stringfellow." In *The William Stringfellow Archives, No. 4438*. Division of Rare and Manuscript Collections, Cornell University Library. Unknown box.

———. August 8, 1972. "Letter to Stringfellow." In *The William Stringfellow Archives, No. 4438*. Division of Rare and Manuscript Collections, Cornell University Library. Unknown box.

Bates College, February 1951. "Academic Record of William Stringfellow." In *The William Stringfellow Archives, No. 4438*. Division of Rare and Manuscript Collections, Cornell University Library. Box 1.

Bennett, John, 1946. *Christian Ethics and Social Policy*. New York: Scribner.

Berrigan, Daniel, 1995. "My Friend." In *Radical Christian and Exemplary Lawyer* (edited by Andrew McThenia), 98–102. Grand Rapids: Eerdmans.

————. undated. "Letter to Bill Wylie Kellermann."

Berrigan, Jerome And Berrigan, Carol, 26 December 1985. "Eschaton Hospitality." In *Sojourners,* 14(11) 26.

Beschloss, Michael, 1991. *The Crisis Years: Kennedy and Khrushchev, 1960–1963.* New York: HarperCollins.

Bezilla, Gregory, 1999. *William Stringfellow's Theology and Ethics of Eschatological Existence.* MDiv thesis, Emory University.

Branch, Taylor, 1988. *Parting the Waters: America in the King Years 1954–1963.* New York: Simon & Schuster.

————. 1998. *Pillar of Fire: America in the King Years 1963–65.* New York: Simon & Schuster.

————. 2006. *At Canaan's Edge: America in the King Years, 1965–1968.* New York: Simon & Schuster.

Brinkley, Alan, 1998. *Liberalism and its Discontents.* Cambridge, Massachusetts: Harvard University Press.

Busch, Eberhard, 1976. *Karl Barth: His Life Letters and Autobiographical Texts.* London: SCM.

Caird, George, 1956. *Principalities and Powers: A Study in Pauline Theology.* Oxford: Clarendon.

Cavendish, Mavis, March 16, 1960. "Letter to William Stringfellow." In *The William Stringfellow Archives, No. 4438.* Division of Rare and Manuscript Collections, Cornell University Library. Box 5.

Chafe, William, 1991. *The Unfinished Journey: America Since World War II.* New York: Oxford University Press.

Church Society For College Work, The, 1958a. "The Christian Faith, The Church, and the University." In *The William Stringfellow Archives, No. 4438.* Division of Rare and Manuscript Collections, Cornell University Library.

————. 1958b. "Colloquy on the Church and the University, Cathedral of St. John the Divine, New York City, January 31–February 1." In *The William Stringfellow Archives, No. 4438.* Division of Rare and Manuscript Collections, Cornell University Library.

Clarke, Arthur C, 2–9 December 1969. "Beyond Babel: The Century of the Communications Satellite." In *The William Stringfellow Archives, No. 4438.* Paper presented at UNESCO Space Communications Conference. Box 14.

Commins, Gary, 1998. "Death and the Circus: The Theology of William Stringfellow." In *Anglican Theological Review* 79(2) 122–62.

Cory, Donald Webster, 1951. *The Homosexual in America: A Subjective Approach.* New York: Greenberg.

Cox, Harvey, 1961. "Playboy's Doctrine of Male." In *Christianity and Crisis,* 21(6) 56–58, 60.

————. 1965. *The Secular City.* New York: MacMillan.

Crew, Louie, June 1976a. "Letter to Stringfellow." In *The William Stringfellow Archives, No. 4438.* Division of Rare and Manuscript Collections, Cornell University Library. Box 19.

Crew, Louis, April 1976b. "Letter to Bishop Sims." In *The William Stringfellow Archives, No. 4438.* Division of Rare and Manuscript Collections, Cornell University Library. Box 19.

Cross, F. L., and Livingstone, E. A. (Editors), 1983. *The Oxford Dictionary of the Christian Church*. Oxford: Oxford University Press, 2nd edition.

Dalferth, Ingolf, 1988. *Theology and Philosophy*. Oxford: Blackwell.

Dancer, Anthony, 1998. *A Critical Discussion of Christian Identity with Particular Reference to the Thought of William Stringfellow*. MPhil thesis, University of Exeter.

Dancer, Anthony (Editor), 2002. *William Stringfellow: Theology in Anglo-American Perspective*. London: Ashgate.

D'emilio, John, 1983. *Sexual Politics, Sexual Communities*. Chicago: Chicago University Press.

D'emilio, John And Freedman, Estelle, 1988. *Intimate Matters: A History of Sexuality in America*. New York: Harper & Row.

Denham, John, October 1962. "Letter to William Stringfellow." In *The William Stringfellow Archives, No. 4438*. Division of Rare and Manuscript Collections, Cornell University Library. Box 6.

Diggins, John, 1988. *The Proud Decades: America in War and Peace*. New York: Norton.

Drane, John, 2000. *The McDonaldization of the Church*. London: Darton, Longman & Todd.

Durant, John And Durant, Alice, 1957. *Pictoral History of the American Circus*. New York: Barnes.

Edwards, George, 1972. *Jesus and the Politics of Violence*. New York: Harper and Row.

Ellul, Jacques, April 1960a. "Letter to Stringfellow in French." In *The William Stringfellow Archives, No. 4438*. Division of Rare and Manuscript Collections, Cornell University Library. Box 4.

———. 1960b. *The Theological Foundation of Law*. New York: Doubleday.

———. 1967. *The Presence of the Kingdom*. New York: Seabury.

———. 1969. *Violence*. New York: Seabury.

———. 1970. *The Meaning of the City*. Grand Rapids: Eerdmans.

Freddie, March 1962. "Letter to Stringfellow." In *The William Stringfellow Archives, No. 4438*. Division of Rare and Manuscript Collections, Cornell University Library. Box 6.

Frei, Hans, 1993. *Theology & Narrative: Selected Essays*. Oxford: Oxford University Press.

Friedan, Betty, 1963. *The Feminine Mystique*. New York: Dell.

Fuller, Lon, 1949. *Problems of Jurisprudence*. New York: Foundation.

Gaddis, John, 1982. *Strategies of Containment: A Critical Appraisal of Postwar American National Security Policy*. New York: Oxford University Press.

Gross, Alfred, March 1964. "Letter to William Stringfellow." In *The William Stringfellow Archives, No. 4438*. Division of Rare and Manuscript Collections, Cornell University Library. Box 27.

Hanft, Frank, January 16, 1956. "Letter to Harry Smith." In *The William Stringfellow Archives, No. 4438*. Division of Rare and Manuscript Collections, Cornell University Library. Box 2.

Hauerwas, Stanley And Powell, Jeff, 1995. "Creation as Apocalyptic: A Homage to William Stringfellow." In *Radical Christian and Exemplary Lawyer* (edited by Andrew McThenia), 31–40. Grand Rapids: Eerdmans.

Hauerwas, Stanley, and Willimon, William, 1996. *Where Resident Aliens Live: Exercises for Christian Practice*. Nashville: Abingdon.

Herberg, Will, 1955. *Protestant Catholic Jew: An Essay in American Religious Sociology*. New York: Garden City.

Hoekendijk, J., 1961. "On the Way to the World of Tomorrow." In *The William Stringfellow Archives, No. 4438*. Division of Rare and Manuscript Collections, Cornell University Library. Box 5.

Hostetler, Hugh, 1950. *A Concept of Church for the East Harlem Protestant Parish*. PhD dissertation, Union Theological Seminary.

Jackson, Kenneth, 1985. *Crabgrass Frontier: The Suburbanization of the United States*. New York: Oxford University Press.

Janowitz, Morris, 1978. *The Last Half-Century: Societal Change and Politics in America*. Chicago: University of Chicago Press.

Johnson, E. H, March 1953. "Letter to Sen. Walter Judd, Immigration Committee." In *The William Stringfellow Archives, No. 4438*. Division of Rare and Manuscript Collections, Cornell University Library. Box 2.

Karnow, Stanley, 1983. *Vietnam: A History*. New York: Viking Press.

Katz, Wilber, December 6, 1955. "Letter to William Stringfellow." In *The William Stringfellow Archives, No. 4438*. Division of Rare and Manuscript Collections, Cornell University Library. Box 2.

———. March 1962. "Letter to Stringfellow." In *The William Stringfellow Archives, No. 4438*. Division of Rare and Manuscript Collections, Cornell University Library. Box 6.

Kenrick, Bruce, October 19, 1960a. "Letter to William Stringfellow." In *The William Stringfellow Archives, No. 4438*. Division of Rare and Manuscript Collections, Cornell University Library. Box 4.

———. November 24, 1960b. "Letter to William Stringfellow." In *The William Stringfellow Archives, No. 4438*. Division of Rare and Manuscript Collections, Cornell University Library. Box 4.

———. 1963. *Come Out The Wilderness*. London: Collins.

Langkjaer, Erik, February 20, 1969. "Letter to William Stringfellow." In *The William Stringfellow Archives, No. 4438*. Division of Rare and Manuscript Collections, Cornell University Library. Box 14.

Lawrence, Appleton, July 15, 1963. "Letter to William Stringfellow." In *The William Stringfellow Archives, No. 4438*. Division of Rare and Manuscript Collections, Cornell University Library. Box 7.

Lee, Gary, 1985. "Publishing Ellul." In *Cross Currents*, 35(1) 92–95.

Leech, Kenneth, 1992. *The Eye of the Storm: Spiritual Resources for the Pursuit of Justice:* London: Darton Longman & Todd.

Lehmann, Paul, 1974. *The Transfiguration of Politics*. New York: Harper and Row.

Leuchtenburg, William, 1983. *In the Shadow of F.D.R.: From Harry Truman to Ronald Reagan*. Ithaca: Cornell University Press.

Lewis, Jack, September 9, 1959. "Letter to William Stringfellow." In *The William Stringfellow Archives, No. 4438*. Division of Rare and Manuscript Collections, Cornell University Library. Box 4.

Lossky, Nicholas, Bonino, José Míguez, Pobee, John, Stransky, Tom, Wainwright, Geoffrey And Webb, Pauline (Editors), 1991. *Dictionary of the Ecumenical Movement*. Geneva: World Council of Churches.

Marotta, Toby, 1981. *The Politics of Homosexuality*. Boston: Houghton Mifflin.

Mcthenia, Andrew (Editor), 1995a. *Radical Christian and Exemplary Lawyer*. Grand Rapids: Eerdmans.

Mcthenia, Andrew, 1995b. "An Uneasy Relationship with the Law." In *Radical Christian and Exemplary Lawyer* (edited by Andrew McThenia), 167–80. Grand Rapids: Eerdmans.

———. September 1998. "Honoring the Gift of Life." Unpublished.

Mensch, Elizabeth And Freeman, Alan, 1993. *The Politics of Virtue: Is Abortion Debatable?* Durham: Duke University Press.

Merton, Thomas, 1968. *Faith and Violence*. Notre Dame: University of Notre Dame Press.

Myrdal, Gunnar, 1944. *The American Dilemma*. New York: Harper and Bros.

Neill, Stephen, March 8, 1960. "Letter to William Stringfellow." In *The William Stringfellow Archives, No. 4438*. Division of Rare and Manuscript Collections, Cornell University Library. Box 5.

———. October 28, 1961. "Letter to William Stringfellow." In *The William Stringfellow Archives, No. 4438*. Division of Rare and Manuscript Collections, Cornell University Library. Box 5.

———. March 17, 1963. "Letter to William Stringfellow." In *The William Stringfellow Archives, No. 4438*. Division of Rare and Manuscript Collections, Cornell University Library. Box 7.

———. March 12, 1968. "Letter to William Stringfellow, regarding Bishop Pike Affair." In *The William Stringfellow Archives, No. 4438*. Division of Rare and Manuscript Collections, Cornell University Library. Box 13.

Newsweek, March 1965. "Selma, Civil Rights, and the Church Militant." In *The William Stringfellow Archives, No. 4438*. Division of Rare and Manuscript Collections, Cornell University Library. Box 10.

Niebuhr, Reinhold, 1936. *An Interpretation of Christian Ethics*. London: SCM.

———. 1959. *Essays in Applied Christianity*. New York: Meridian.

Nock, A. D., 1933. *Conversion*. Oxford: Oxford University Press.

Noll, Mark, 1992. *A History of Christianity in the United States and Canada*. London: SPCK.

Oden, Thomas, 1966. *Kerygma and Counselling*. Philadelpiha: Westminster.

———. 1967. *Contemporary Theology and Psychotherapy*. Philadelphia: Westminster.

———. 1979. *Agenda for Theology: Recovering Christian Roots*. San Francisco: Harper & Row.

———. 1983. *Pastoral Theology: Essentials of Ministry*. New York: HarperCollins.

Oregon University, October 18–20, 1968. "A Conversation with William Stringfellow: University of Oregon." In *The William Stringfellow Archives, No. 4438*. Unknown.

Patterson, James, 1996. *Grand Expectations: The United States, 1945–1974*. Oxford: Oxford University Press.

Pike, James, 1967. *If This Be Heresy*. New York: Harper & Row.

Pilgrim, Walter, 1999. *Uneasy Neighbours: Church and State in the New Testament*. Minneapolis: Fortress.

Polenberg, Richard, 1980. *One Nation Divisible: Class, Race and Ethnicity in the United States since 1938*. New York: Viking.

Princeton Study Group, February 1961a. "Minutes." In *The William Stringfellow Archives, No. 4438*. Division of Rare and Manuscript Collections, Cornell University Library. Box 6.

————. April 1961b. "Notes of the Meeting of the Princeton Study Group." In *The William Stringfellow Archives, No. 4438*. Division of Rare and Manuscript Collections, Cornell University Library. Box 6.

Pyle, John, March 1962. "Letter to Stringfellow." In *The William Stringfellow Archives, No. 4438*. Division of Rare and Manuscript Collections, Cornell University Library. Box 6.

Ritzer, George, 1998. *The McDonaldization Thesis*. London: Sage.

————. 2000. *The McDonaldization of Society*. London: Pine Forge.

Robinson, John, 1963. *Honest to God*. London: SCM.

Rossinow, Doug, 1998. *The Politics of Authenticity: Liberalism, Christianity, and the New Left in America*. New York: Columbia University Press.

Rowland, Stanley, July 28, 1956. "Surburbia Buys Religion." In *The Nation*, 78–80.

Schoonover, Melvin, December 1985. "Present and Powerful in Life and Death." In *Sojourners*, 14(11)12–15.

Slocum, Robert (Editor), 1997. *Prophet of Justice, Prophet of Life*. New York: Church Publishing Incorporated.

Sontag, Frederick, June 1962. "Karl Barth Visits Riker Island." In *The Witness*, 8–11.

Stringfellow, William, 1946. "Speech Notes." In *The William Stringfellow Archives, No. 4438*. Division of Rare and Manuscript Collections, Cornell University Library. Box 1.

————. October 1947a. "Does the World Hate America?" In *Churchman*, 10–11.

————. February 1947b. "The Relation of World Christianity to World Communism." In *The William Stringfellow Archives, No. 4438*. Division of Rare and Manuscript Collections, Cornell University Library. Box 1.

————. 1947c. "Speech Notes." In *The William Stringfellow Archives, No. 4438*. Division of Rare and Manuscript Collections, Cornell University Library. Box 1.

————. September 4, 1948. "Politics as Ministry: Manuscript of Speech/Testimony on Stringfellow's Commitment to Faith and Politics." In *The William Stringfellow Archives, No. 4438*. Division of Rare and Manuscript Collections, Cornell University Library. Box 1.

————. November 24, 1949. "Family Newsletter 1.1." In *The William Stringfellow Archives, No. 4438*. Division of Rare and Manuscript Collections, Cornell University Library. Unknown box.

————. May–June 1950a. "American Apologia." In *The Student Movement*, 52(5) 10–12.

————. April 12, 1950b. "Family Newsletter 1.4." In *The William Stringfellow Archives, No. 4438*. Division of Rare and Manuscript Collections, Cornell University Library. Box 1.

————. April 25, 1950c. "Letter to Mr Murray." In *The William Stringfellow Archives, No. 4438*. Division of Rare and Manuscript Collections, Cornell University Library. Box 1.

————. 1950d. "The Political Implications of the Ecumenical Movement." In *The William Stringfellow Archives, No. 4438*. Division of Rare and Manuscript Collections, Cornell University Library. Box 1.

————. November 20, 1950e. "Some Thoughts on the American sCm in Politics." In *The William Stringfellow Archives, No. 4438*. Division of Rare and Manuscript Collections, Cornell University Library. Box 1.

———. January 8, 1950f. "A Testament on Politics." In *The William Stringfellow Archives, No. 4438.* Division of Rare and Manuscript Collections, Cornell University Library. Box 2.

———. 1952. "Correspondence between Army and String refusing publication of article." In *The William Stringfellow Archives, No. 4438.* Division of Rare and Manuscript Collections, Cornell University Library. Unknown box.

———. 1953a. "Handwritten Notes from Notebook." In *The William Stringfellow Archives, No. 4438.*

———. March 5, 1953b. "Letter to John Kennedy." In *The William Stringfellow Archives, No. 4438.* Division of Rare and Manuscript Collections, Cornell University Library. Box 2.

———. 1953c. "Notes on Different types of Ethics." In *The William Stringfellow Archives, No. 4438.* Division of Rare and Manuscript Collections, Cornell University Library. Box 2.

———. June 1953d. "Proposal for an Institute of Theology and Politics (United Student Christian Council)." In *The William Stringfellow Archives, No. 4438.* Division of Rare and Manuscript Collections, Cornell University Library. Box 32.

———. 1953e. "Some Thoughts on the American SCM in Politics." In *The William Stringfellow Archives, No. 4438.* Division of Rare and Manuscript Collections, Cornell University Library. Box 1.

———. February 9, 1954. "Theology and Strategy in Christian Action." In *The William Stringfellow Archives, No. 4438.* Division of Rare and Manuscript Collections, Cornell University Library. Box 2.

———. December 13, 1955a. "Letter to Wilber Katz." In *The William Stringfellow Archives, No. 4438.* Division of Rare and Manuscript Collections, Cornell University Library. Box 2.

———. 1955b. "The Life of Worship and the Legal Profession." In *The William Stringfellow Archives, No. 4438.* Division of Rare and Manuscript Collections, Cornell University Library. Box 40.

———. April 30, 1956a. "Due Process as Natural Law: The Joinder of Law and Theology." In *The William Stringfellow Archives, No. 4438.* Division of Rare and Manuscript Collections, Cornell University Library. Box 2.

———. March 1, 1956b. "Letter to Harry and Anne Smith." In *The William Stringfellow Archives, No. 4438.* Division of Rare and Manuscript Collections, Cornell University Library. Box 2.

———. December 26, 1956c. "Letter to Roy Romer." In *The William Stringfellow Archives, No. 4438.* Division of Rare and Manuscript Collections, Cornell University Library. Box 2.

———. 1956d. "Love for Justice: The Influence of Christianity on the Development of Law." In *The William Stringfellow Archives, No. 4438.* Division of Rare and Manuscript Collections, Cornell University Library. Box 2.

———. December, 15 1956e. "Memorandum: A Lectureship in Theology and Law." In *The William Stringfellow Archives, No. 4438.* Division of Rare and Manuscript Collections, Cornell University Library. Box 2.

———. 1956f. "A Preliminary Note on Law and Theology." In *The William Stringfellow Archives, No. 4438.* Division of Rare and Manuscript Collections, Cornell University Library. Box 2.

———. 1956g. "A Proposal for An Educational and Conference Program Among Christian Laymen in the Legal Professions." In *The William Stringfellow Archives, No. 4438*. Division of Rare and Manuscript Collections, Cornell University Library. Box 2.

———. 1956h. "A Prospectus for an Educational and Conference Program Among Christian Laymen in the Legal Profession." In *The William Stringfellow Archives, No. 4438*. Division of Rare and Manuscript Collections, Cornell University Library. Box 2.

———. 1957a. "Christian Faith and the American Lawyer." In *WCC Staff News*, 79–81.

———. 14 May 1957b. "Comments on Personal Vocational Decision and the Group Ministry." In *The William Stringfellow Archives, No. 4438*. Division of Rare and Manuscript Collections, Cornell University Library. Box 4.

———. 1957c. "Comments on the Program on Christian Faith and the Legal Profession." In *The William Stringfellow Archives, No. 4438*. Division of Rare and Manuscript Collections, Cornell University Library. Box 3.

———. October 24, 1957d. "Letter to Jacques Ellul." In *The William Stringfellow Archives, No. 4438*. Division of Rare and Manuscript Collections, Cornell University Library. Box 3.

———. 1957e. "National Conference on Christianity and Law: Schedule." In *The William Stringfellow Archives, No. 4438*. Division of Rare and Manuscript Collections, Cornell University Library. Box 3.

———. 1957f. "Participants: Conference, Christianity and the Law." In *The William Stringfellow Archives, No. 4438*. Division of Rare and Manuscript Collections, Cornell University Library. Box 2.

———. April 12, 1957g. "Press Release: Christian Faith and the Legal Profession." In *The William Stringfellow Archives, No. 4438*. Division of Rare and Manuscript Collections, Cornell University Library. Box 3.

———. 1957h. "Report: Work in Law Schools in New York City in 1956–1957." In *The William Stringfellow Archives, No. 4438*. Division of Rare and Manuscript Collections, Cornell University Library. Box 3.

———. October 16, 1958a. "Letter to David Sass, Regarding Interseminary Course on Grace and Law." In *The William Stringfellow Archives, No. 4438*. Division of Rare and Manuscript Collections, Cornell University Library. Box 3.

———. November 10, 1958b. "Letter to David Wiley, Yale Divinity School." In *The William Stringfellow Archives, No. 4438*. Division of Rare and Manuscript Collections, Cornell University Library. Box 3.

———. December 10, 1958c. "Letter to Geoffrey Ainger." In *The William Stringfellow Archives, No. 4438*. Division of Rare and Manuscript Collections, Cornell University Library. Box 3.

———. January 22, 1958d. "Letter to Markus Barth." In *The William Stringfellow Archives, No. 4438*. Division of Rare and Manuscript Collections, Cornell University Library. Box 3.

———. July 9, 1958e. "Letter to Markus Barth." Division of Rare and Manuscript Collections, Cornell University Library. Box 3.

———. December 20, 1958f. "Letter to Old Duff." In *The William Stringfellow Archives, No. 4438*. Division of Rare and Manuscript Collections, Cornell University Library. Box 3.

———.November 15, 1958g. "Letter to Willis Reese, Bill Ellis and Richard Heaton regarding Bible Study Conference in Pennsylvania." In *The William Stringfellow Archives, No. 4438*. Division of Rare and Manuscript Collections, Cornell University Library. Box 3.

———. April 2, 1958h. "Resignation Letter to Group Ministry." In *The William Stringfellow Archives, No. 4438*. Division of Rare and Manuscript Collections, Cornell University Library.

———. 1959a. "Amherst College Embassy, Conference Agenda." In *The William Stringfellow Archives, No. 4438*. Division of Rare and Manuscript Collections, Cornell University Library. Box 4.

———. December 3, 1959b. "Bibliography for Study Preparatory to the WSCF Teaching Conference, Strasbourg, France, July 1960." In *The William Stringfellow Archives, No. 4438*. Division of Rare and Manuscript Collections, Cornell University Library. Box 4.

———. 1959c. "Christian Witness to Modern Society." In *The William Stringfellow Archives, No. 4438*. Division of Rare and Manuscript Collections, Cornell University Library. Box 4.

———. June 1959d. "Christianity, Poverty, and the Practice of the Law." In *Harvard Law School Bulletin*,10(6).

———. April 10, 1959e. "Letter to Alexander Morin, USCC." In *The William Stringfellow Archives, No. 4438*. Division of Rare and Manuscript Collections, Cornell University Library. Box 4.

———. February 3, 1959f. "Letter to James and Jeanne Breenan." In *The William Stringfellow Archives, No. 4438*. Division of Rare and Manuscript Collections, Cornell University Library. Box 4.

———. March 22, 1959g. "Letter to James and Jeanne Breenan." In *The William Stringfellow Archives, No. 4438*. Division of Rare and Manuscript Collections, Cornell University Library. Box 4.

———.May 15, 1959h. "Letter to Jones Shannon." In *The William Stringfellow Archives, No. 4438*. Division of Rare and Manuscript Collections, Cornell University Library. Box 4.

———. August 11, 1959i. "Letter to Revd. Francis House, World Council of Churches." In *The William Stringfellow Archives, No. 4438*. Division of Rare and Manuscript Collections, Cornell University Library. Box 4.

———. January 28, 1959j. "Letter to Wilber Katz." In *The William Stringfellow Archives, No. 4438*. Division of Rare and Manuscript Collections, Cornell University Library. Box 4.

———. 1959k. "Work as Mission: Secular Work and Christian Vocation." WCC, Geneva.

———. 1960a. "La Misere, Le Christianisme et Le Driot." In *Foi et Vie*, 59(2), 83–96.

———. June 29, 1960b. "Letter to Frank Patton." In *The William Stringfellow Archives, No. 4438*. Division of Rare and Manuscript Collections, Cornell University Library. Box 4.

———. July 27, 1960c. "Letter to Frank Patton." In *The William Stringfellow Archives, No. 4438*. Division of Rare and Manuscript Collections, Cornell University Library. Box 5.

————. April 1960d. "Letter to Jacques Ellul." In *The William Stringfellow Archives, No. 4438.* Division of Rare and Manuscript Collections, Cornell University Library. Box 4.

————. January 19, 1960e. "Letter to Richard." In *The William Stringfellow Archives, No. 4438.* Division of Rare and Manuscript Collections, Cornell University Library. Box 4.

————.October 26, 1960f. "Letter to William Stringfellow." In *The William Stringfellow Archives, No. 4438.* Division of Rare and Manuscript Collections, Cornell University Library. Box 4.

————. 1960g. "Surrender as Solution to the Racial Crisis." In *The William Stringfellow Archives, No. 4438.* Division of Rare and Manuscript Collections, Cornell University Library. Box 4.

————. 1961a. *Law, Polity and the Reunion of the Church.* Geneva: Fith and Order Commission, World Council of Churches.

————. April 5, 1961b. "Letter to Jones Shannon, The Church Society for College Work." In *The William Stringfellow Archives, No. 4438.* Division of Rare and Manuscript Collections, Cornell University Library. Box 5.

————. May 1961c. "Poverty, Piety, Charity and Mission." In *The Christian Century,* 78:584–86.

————. February 12, 1962a. "Action—Religion's Lost Art." In *The William Stringfellow Archives, No. 4438.* Division of Rare and Manuscript Collections, Cornell University Library. Box 6.

————. May 1962b. "A Glimpse of Karl Barth in America." In *The William Stringfellow Archives, No. 4438.* Division of Rare and Manuscript Collections, Cornell University Library. Box 6.

————. May 1962c. "Letter to Markus Barth." In *The William Stringfellow Archives, No. 4438.* Division of Rare and Manuscript Collections, Cornell University Library. Box 6.

————.February 21, 1962d. "Letter to Markus Barth." In *The William Stringfellow Archives, No. 4438.* Division of Rare and Manuscript Collections, Cornell University Library. Box 6.

————.October 27, 1962e. "Letter to Sister." In *The William Stringfellow Archives, No. 4438.* Division of Rare and Manuscript Collections, Cornell University Library. Box 6.

————. October 1962f. "Loneliness, Dread and Holiness." In *The Christian Century,* 79:1220–22.

————. 1962g. "Loneliness, Dread and Holiness." In *The William Stringfellow Archives, No. 4438.* Division of Rare and Manuscript Collections, Cornell University Library. Box 6.

————. May 1962h. "Need for Better Understanding Called for by Karl Barth." In *The Witness,* 4–5. Undated.

————. August 1962i. "Open Letter to Friends." In *The William Stringfellow Archives, No. 4438.* Division of Rare and Manuscript Collections, Cornell University Library. Box 6.

————. April 1962j. "Poverty, the Law and the Ethics of Society (Manuscript)." In *The William Stringfellow Archives, No. 4438.* Division of Rare and Manuscript Collections, Cornell University Library. Box 6.

————. 1962k. *A Private and Public Faith.* Grand Rapids: Eerdmans.

———. February 1962l. "Race, Religion, and Revenge." In *The Christian Century,*
79:192–94.

———. November 1962m. "Race, The Church, and the Law." In *The Episcopalian,*
31–34.

———. 1962n. "Sex – 3." In *The William Stringfellow Archives, No. 4438.* Division of Rare
and Manuscript Collections, Cornell University Library. Box 6.

———. February 11, 1962o. "What I Am Doing and Why I Am Doing It." In *The William
Stringfellow Archives, No. 4438.* Division of Rare and Manuscript Collections,
Cornell University Library. Box 6.

———. August 1963a. "Are Protestants Ecumenical Reactionaries?" In *The William
Stringfellow Archives, No. 4438.* Division of Rare and Manuscript Collections,
Cornell University Library. Box 31.

———. February 1963b. "Care Enough to Weep." In *The Witness,* 13–15.

———. 1963c. "The Church and Race: An Interview with William Stringfellow." In
The William Stringfellow Archives, No. 4438. Division of Rare and Manuscript
Collections, Cornell University Library. Box 7.

———. 1963d. "The Episcopal Society for Cultural and Racial Unity." In *The William
Stringfellow Archives, No. 4438.* Division of Rare and Manuscript Collections,
Cornell University Library. Box 7.

———. November 1963e. "Evangelism and Conversion." In *International Journal of
Religious Education,* 6–22.

———. August 1963f. "The Freedom of God." In *The Witness,* 8–10.

———. 1963g. *Instead of Death.* New York: Seabury Press.

———. December 29, 1963h. "Introduction to Anthony Towne's Book of Poems." In
The William Stringfellow Archives, No. 4438. Division of Rare and Manuscript
Collections, Cornell University Library. Box 7.

———. March 28, 1963i. "Letter to Anthony Towne." In *The William Stringfellow
Archives, No. 4438.* Division of Rare and Manuscript Collections, Cornell University
Library. Box 7.

———. August 4, 1963j. "Letter to Arthur Cohen, Editor of Holt Rinehart and Winston."
In *The William Stringfellow Archives, No. 4438.* Division of Rare and Manuscript
Collections, Cornell University Library. Box 7.

———. December 8, 1963k. "Letter to J. D. Reasner." In *The William Stringfellow Archives,
No. 4438.* Division of Rare and Manuscript Collections, Cornell University Library.
Box 7.

———. February 21, 1963l. "Letter to Revd. Leland Henry." In *The William Stringfellow
Archives, No. 4438.* Box 7.

———. May 17, 1963m. "Letter to Stephen Neill." In *The William Stringfellow Archives,
No. 4438.* Division of Rare and Manuscript Collections, Cornell University Library.
Box 7.

———. May 1963n. "The Ministry of the Church." In *The Pulpit,* 34(5) 4–5.

———. August 1963o. "Summary Presentation." In *National EYC Study Conference.*
Tennessee.

———. December 1964a. "Excerpts from Remarks of William Stringfellow, conference
on Poverty and Christian Response." In *The William Stringfellow Archives, No. 4438.*
Division of Rare and Manuscript Collections, Cornell University Library. Box 6.

———. 1964b. *Free In Obedience.* New York: Seabury.

————. September 1964c. "God, Guilt and Goldwater." In *The Christian Century*, 81:1079–83.

————. 1964d. *My People is the Enemy: An Autobiographical Polemic*. New York: Holt, Rinehart and Winston.

————. September 1965a. "The Humanity of Sex." In *The William Stringfellow Archives, No. 4438*. Division of Rare and Manuscript Collections, Cornell University Library. Box 31.

————. September 1965b. "The Humanity of Sex." In *The William Stringfellow Archives, No. 4438*. Division of Rare and Manuscript Collections, Cornell University Library. Box 8.

————. December 1965c. "Liturgy as Political Event." In *The Christian Century*, 82,1573–75.

————. July 1965d. "Look Up and Live "My People is the Enemy."" In *The William Stringfellow Archives, No. 4438*. Division of Rare and Manuscript Collections, Cornell University Library. Box 35.

————. October 1965e. "The Orthodoxy of Involvement." In *The William Stringfellow Archives, No. 4438*. Division of Rare and Manuscript Collections, Cornell University Library. Unknown box.

————. October 1965f. "The Orthodoxy of Radical Involvement." In *The William Stringfellow Archives, No. 4438*. Division of Rare and Manuscript Collections, Cornell University Library. Unknown box.

————. March 1965g. "Poverty, Law and the Ethics of Society." In *North Dakota Law Review*, 40(3), 6–10.

————. 1965h. "The Violence of Despair." In *Notre Dame Lawyer*, 40(5), 527–33.

————. June 14, 1966a. "Celebrating God's Presence." In *The Mennonite*, 396–97.

————. August 1966b. "Difference Between Gospel and Religion." In *The Mennonite*, page 517.

————. 1966c. *Dissenter in a Great Society*. New York: Holt, Rinehart and Winston.

————. Autumn 1966d. "The Great Society as a Myth." In *Dialog*, 5:252–57.

————. May 22, 1966e. "Letter to Revd. Richard Peterson." In *The William Stringfellow Archives, No. 4438*. Division of Rare and Manuscript Collections, Cornell University Library. Box 8.

————. January 1966f. "Money and What It Means." In *Presbyterian Survey*, 56(1) 20–22.

————. 16 March 1966g. "Reflections on Vietnam." In *The William Stringfellow Archives, No. 4438*. Division of Rare and Manuscript Collections, Cornell University Library. Unknown box.

————. July 1966h. "The Theology of Death as a preliminary ethical insight." In *The William Stringfellow Archives, No. 4438*. Division of Rare and Manuscript Collections, Cornell University Library. Unknown box.

————. November 1966i. "Vietnam and the Churches." In *The Christian Herald*.

————. 1967a. *Count it All Joy: Reflections on Faith, Doubt, and Temptation*. Grand Rapids: Eerdmans.

————. 1967b. "The Idea of Society as a Circus." In *The William Stringfellow Archives, No. 4438*. Division of Rare and Manuscript Collections, Cornell University Library. Box 30.

————. February 1967c. "Our Obsolete Religion." In *Christian Living*, page 36.

———. October 1, 1968a. "How to Sing the Lord's Song in a Strange Land." In *The William Stringfellow Archives, No. 4438*. Division of Rare and Manuscript Collections, Cornell University Library. Box 13.

———. May 6, 1968b. "Letter to Bill Eerdman." In *The William Stringfellow Archives, No. 4438*. Division of Rare and Manuscript Collections, Cornell University Library. Box 13.

———. October 15, 1968c. "Letter to Bill Eerdman." In *The William Stringfellow Archives, No. 4438*. Division of Rare and Manuscript Collections, Cornell University Library. Box 13.

———. April 26, 1968d. "Letter to Joe." In *The William Stringfellow Archives, No. 4438*. Division of Rare and Manuscript Collections, Cornell University Library. Box 13.

———. September 28, 1968e. "Letter to Leslie Carlson, suggesting title for talk: 'Revelation and Revolution: The Ethics of Resistance for Christians and Other Aliens in a Strange Land.'" In *The William Stringfellow Archives, No. 4438*. Division of Rare and Manuscript Collections, Cornell University Library. Box 13.

———. May 23, 1968f. "Letter to Mary." In *The William Stringfellow Archives, No. 4438*. Division of Rare and Manuscript Collections, Cornell University Library. Box 13.

———. September 1969a. "The Demonic in American Society." In *Christianity and Crisis*, 29: 244–48.

———. 1969b. *Imposters of God: Inquiries into Favorite Idols*. New York: Witness Books.

———. September 1, 1969c. "Letter to Bill Eerdman." In *The William Stringfellow Archives, No. 4438*. Division of Rare and Manuscript Collections, Cornell University Library. Box 14.

———. January 1969d. "The Versatility of the Holy Spirit and the Ministry of the Gospel." In *The William Stringfellow Archives, No. 4438*. Division of Rare and Manuscript Collections, Cornell University Library. Box 14.

———. March 1970a. "America as Jerusalem Lost: The Ascendency of the Demonic in American Society." In *The William Stringfellow Archives, No. 4438*. Division of Rare and Manuscript Collections, Cornell University Library. Box 35.

———. Winter 1970b. "The American Importance of Jacques Ellul." In *Katallaagete*, 2:135–138.

———. September 1970c. "An Authority over Death." In *Christianity and Crisis*, 30, 181–83.

———. November 1970d. "Harlem, Rebellion and Resurrection." In *The Christian Century*, 87(45), 1345–48.

———. 1970e. *A Second Birthday*. New York: Doubleday.

———. October 1972. "Must the Stones Cry Out?" In *Christianity and Crisis*, 32(18) 234–38.

———. 1973a. "Does America need a Barmen Declaration?" In *Christianity and Crisis*, 33(22) 274–76.

———. 1973b. *An Ethic for Christians and Other Aliens in a Strange Land*. Waco: Word.

———. December 1975. "The Politics of Advent." In *The Witness*, 9–10.

———. 1976a. "The Bible and Ideology." In *Sojourners*, 5(7) 6–7.

———. 1976b. "Farewell Word from the Author, Creative Resources Leader's Kit Notes." In *The William Stringfellow Archives, No. 4438*. Division of Rare and Manuscript Collections, Cornell University Library. Box 31.

———. 1976c. *Instead of Death*. New York: Seabury, 2nd edition.

————. April 1976d. "untitled column." In *Sojourners*, 5(4) 10.

————. February 1976e. *William Stringfellow, Prophet to America: Digest of Days with William Stringfellow February, 15–17 1976*. Fifth Avenue and Marion Street, Seattle, Washington: First United Methodist Church.

————. 1977a. *Conscience and Obedience: The Politics of Romans 13 and Revelation 13 in Light of the Second Coming*. Waco: Word.

————. 1977b. "Myths, Endless Genealogies, the Promotion of Speculations and the Vain Discussion Thereof." In *Sojourners*, 13: 12–13.

————. September 1979a. "Address given to National Convention of Integrity." In *The William Stringfellow Archives, No. 4438*. Division of Rare and Manuscript Collections, Cornell University Library. Box 22.

————. July 1979b. "Letter to Howell Conant." In *The William Stringfellow Archives, No. 4438*. Division of Rare and Manuscript Collections, Cornell University Library. Box 21.

————. December 1981. "Advent as a Penitential Season." In *The Witness*, 64(21) 10–12.

————. 1982a. "A Lawyer's Work." In *Christian Legal Society Quarterly*, 3(3) 17, 19.

————. 1982b. *A Simplicity of Faith: My Experience in Mourning*. Nashville: Abingdon.

————. 1984. *The Politics of Spirituality*. Philadelphia: Westminster Press.

————. 1994. "Authority in Baptism: The Vocation of Jesus and the Ministry of the Laity." In *A Keeper of the Word: Selected Writings of William Stringfellow* (edited by Bill Wylie-Kellermann), 156–62. Grand Rapids: Eerdmans.

————. undated. "Undated handwritten notes concerning the nature of the Church." In *The William Stringfellow Archives, No. 4438*. Division of Rare and Manuscript Collections, Cornell University Library. Box 34.

Stringfellow, William And Towne, Anthony, 1967. *The Bishop Pike Affair: Scandals of Conscience and Heresy, Relevance and Solemnity in the Contemporary Church*. New York: Harper & Row.

————. 1971. *Suspect Tenderness: The Ethics of the Berrigan Witness*. New York: Holt, Rinehart and Winston.

————. 1976. *The Death and Life of Bishop Pike*. Garden City, NY: Doubleday.

Stringfellow, William, Towne, Anthony and Karras, Ray, February 23, 1966. "Certificate of Purchase of Land, for Eschaton, Block Island." In *The William Stringfellow Archives, No. 4438*. Division of Rare and Manuscript Collections, Cornell University Library.

Temple, William, 1928. *Christianity and the State*. London: Macmillan.

Towne, Anthony, August 25, 1963a. "Letter to John." In *The William Stringfellow Archives, No. 4438*. Division of Rare and Manuscript Collections, Cornell University Library. Box 7.

————. October 1963b. "Letter to Stringfellow." In *The William Stringfellow Archives, No. 4438*. Division of Rare and Manuscript Collections, Cornell University Library. Box 7.

University Of Chicago, Office Of Public Relations, April 1962. "Information Released About Barth." In *The William Stringfellow Archives, No. 4438*. Division of Rare and Manuscript Collections, Cornell University Library. Box 6.

University Of Chicago Divinity School, 1963. "Introduction to Theology: Questions to and Discussions with Dr. Karl Barth." In *Criterion*, 2(1) 3–24.

Van Dusen, Henry P. And Ehrenstrom, Nils (Editors), 1954. *The Laity—The Christian in His Vocation*. New York: Harper.

Vidler, A. R., and W. A. Whitehouse, (Editors), 1946. *Natural Law: A Christian Reconsideration*. London: SCM.

Village Voice, July 3, 1969. "Untited." In *Village Voice*, page 18.

Wills, Garry, 1972. *Bare Ruined Choirs: Doubt, Prophecy, and Radical Religion*. Garden City, NY: Doubleday.

Wink, Walter, 1984. *Naming the Powers: The Language of Power in the New Testament*. Philadelphia: Fortress.

————. 1986. *Unmasking the Powers: The Invisible Forces that Determine Human Existence*. Philadelphia: Fortress.

————. 1992. *Engaging the Powers: Discernment and Resistance in a World of Domination*. Philadelphia: Fortress.

————. 1995. "Stringfellow on the Powers." In *Radical Christian and Exemplary Lawyer* (edited by Andrew McThenia), 17–30. Grand Rapids: Eerdmans.

Wolfe, Alan, 1991. *America at Century's End*. Berkley: University of California Press.

Wuthnow, Robert, 1988. *The Restructuring of American Religion*. Princeton: Princeton University Press.

Wylie-Kellermann, Bill, 1994. *A Keeper of the Word: Selected Writings of William Stringfellow*. Grand Rapids: Eerdmans.

————. 1995. "Bill, The Bible, and the Seminary Underground." In *Radical Christian and Exemplary Lawyer* (edited by Andrew McThenia), 56–72. Grand Rapids: Eerdmans.

————. 1997. "Listen to this Man: A Parable before the Powers." In *Prophet of Justice Prophet of Life* (edited by Robert Slocum), 4–8. New York: Church Publishing Incorporated.

————. 1999. "Not Vice Versa. Reading the Power Biblically: Stringfellow, Hermeneutics, and the Principalities." In *Anglican Theological Review*, 81(4) 665–82.

————. undated. "East Harlem Protestant Parish—Background and Notes."

Yoder, John Howard, 1972. *The Politics of Jesus*. Grand Rapids: Eerdmans.

Zeilinger, Thomas, 1999. *Zwischen-Räume: Theologie der Mächte und Gewalten*. Stuttgart: W.Kohlhammer.

Ziegler, Edward, September 1966. "Letter to William Stringfellow." In *The William Stringfellow Archives, No. 4438*. Division of Rare and Manuscript Collections, Cornell University Library. Unknown box.

Name Index

Adams, James, 169n9
Andy, 40n9, 77, 194

Baillie, John, 55n35
Baldwin, James, 183
Barrymore, Drew, 95
Barth, Christoph, 170n15
Barth, Karl, vii, xiii, 3, 5, 54–55, 58,
    58n42, 62n48, 111, 125–26,
    127n7, 128n8, 143, 147n23,
    157n34, 160n38, 166, 166n3,
    167–82, 167nn4–5, 168nn6–
    9, 169nn10–11, 170nn13–15,
    172n18, 174n21, 175n22,
    176n23, 177n25, 180n26,
    181nn27, 29, 189, 189n43,
    190, 206, 206n1, 227n28, 248
Barth, Marcus, 75, 85n81, 93, 93n95,
    166, 167n4, 169, 169n11,
    170nn13–15
Benedict, Don, 71n61
Bennett, John, 38n4
Berdyaev, Nikolai, 75
Berrigan, Daniel, vi, 4, 36, 49,
    125n11, 154n30, 194n50,
    232–33, 238–39, 238n43, 241,
    250, 252
Berrigan, Phillip, 36, 49, 232
Beschloss, Michael, 102–3
Bonhoeffer, Dietrich, 49, 146
Bormann, Martin, 38
Branch, Taylor, 4, 111–12, 111nn15–
    16, 113, 113n20, 114n22, 182

Brinkley, Alan, ix, 16n3, 28n22,
    34n29, 49, 49n24, 101, 101n3,
    102n4, 153, 153n28
Brunner, Emil, 55n35

Caird, George, 93n94
Carmichael, Stokley, 118–19,
    187n39
Carnell, Edward, 171n16
Cavendish, Mavis, 169n10
Chafe, William, 16n3
Clark, Jim, Sheriff, 114–15, 218
Clarke, Arthur C., 241n47
Clinton, Bill, 95
Cohen, Arthur, 206n1,
Cooke, Bernard, 171n16
Cory, Donald Webster, 20, 70n57
Cox, Harvey, 209
Crew, Louie, 194n56
Cross, F. L., 47n22,

D'Emilio, John, ix, 18–20, 18n5,
    19n6, 20n8, 22, 28n22, 42n13,
    120–22, 120n32
Dalferth, Ingolf, 6n7, 10
Denham, John, 77, 181n28, 196n54
Drane, John, 28
Durant, Alice, 225n25
Durant, John, 225n25

Edwards, Jonathan, 28n23
Ehrenstrom, Nils, 38n4, 39n6
Ellis, William, 53n31, 196n54

Ellul, Jacques, 55n35, 58, 58n42,
    78n75, 87n84, 93, 93n95,
    125n2, 126–27, 137, 166,
    169nn10–11, 175n22, 206,
    206n1, 237n41, 240, 240n47,
    241n49

Figgis, John, 169n9
Finney, Charles, 28n23
Flemming, Ian, 101
Fletcher, Joseph, 57
Freddie, 170n13
Freedman, Estelle, 19n6
Freeman, Alan, 27, 29, 29n24, 34,
    38n4
Frei, Hans, 126n4, 150n26, 171–72,
    171n16, 172n18, 173n19
Friedan, Betty, 123n34
Fuller, Lon, 38n4

Gandhi, 111
Geertz, Clifford, 150n26
Goldwater, Barry, 110, 110n13,
    208n5, 211
Graham, Billy, 17n4, 27, 27n21, 29,
    103, 132, 132n11, 168n7
Gross, Alfred, 33, 193n45

Halverson, Marvin, 194, 194n50
Hanft, Frank, 68n54
Hargraves, Archie, 71n61
Hartt, Julian, 53n31
Hauerwas, Stanley, 5
Henry, George, 121n33
Herberg, Will, 26
Heschel, Abraham, 182
Hoekendijk, J., 241n47
Hostetler, Hugh, 72n64
Hromadka, Joseph, 55n35, 125,
    169n9

Jackson, Kenneth, 31n26
Jackson, Michael, 95
James, William, 28

Jesus Christ, viii, xiii, 2, 10n10,
    37n3, 41, 48, 60–62, 65, 81,
    104n9, 126, 130, 137, 154,
    177, 184, 196, 213, 216,
    218–19, 232, 234–35, 238
Johnson, E. H., 46n20, 51,
Johnson, Lyndon B., xiii, 102, 104–
    10, 104n9, 105n10, 110n13,
    111n14, 112, 118–19, 118n28,
    119n29, 123, 153, 207–11,
    215, 218, 248

Karnow, Stanley, 118
Karras, Ray, 194n51, 228n29
Katz, Wilbur, 68n54, 170n13
Kennan, George, 17
Kennedy, John F., 46n20, 100–4,
    101n3, 103n7, 106, 108, 131,
    153, 210
Kenrick, Bruce, 71n61, 86n82
Khruschev, Nikita, 103
Kierkegaard, Søren, 75
King, Martin Luther, Jr., 38n4, 111–
    12, 111nn15–16, 112n19, 114,
    116, 116n25, 118, 135, 182,
    188, 188n41, 191, 227
Kinsey, Alfred, 19–20
Kraemer, Hendrik, 55n35
Kross, Anna, 170, 170n15

Langkjaer, Erik, 132n11
Lawrence, Appleton, Bishop, 89n89
Lee, Gary, 58n42,
Lewis, Jack, ix, 49n23,
    153–54nn30–31
Lincoln, Abraham, 104n9
Livingstone, E. A., 47n22
Lossky, Nicholas, 50n26

Malcolm X, 109, 111–12, 112n19,
    114–15, 114n22, 183, 187n39,
    188, 208n5
Maritain, Jacques, 54
Marotta, Toby, 18n5, 20–21, 21n12

McCarthy, Joseph, Senator, 18, 19, 20, 20n9
McThenia, Andrew, 8–10, 9n9, 49, 58nn39–40, 68, 89, 250
Mensch, Elizabeth, 27, 29, 29n24, 34, 38n4
Merton, Thomas, 237n41
Moody, Dwight, 28
Myrdal, Gunnar, 20, 70n57

Neill, Stephen, 55n35, 169n9, 227n27
Niebuhr, Reinhold, 38n4, 42n13, 54, 55n35, 111, 111n16, 167n5, 176n23
Niemoller, Martin, 42n13, 47
Nixon, Richard, 101, 103n7, 132n11
Nock, A. D., 160n36, 201n58,
Noll, Mark, 28–29

Obama, Barack, 95
Oden, Thomas, 147n23
Ogden, Schubert, 171n16

Parks, Rosa, 111n17
Patterson, James, 16nn2–3, 17n4, 22–26, 22n15, 23n16, 24n18, 26n21, 28n22, 29–30, 31n26, 32–34, 99, 101–10, 101nn1–2, 102n4, 103n7, 104n9, 105n10, 107n11, 110n12, 113–18, 118n28, 119nn29, 31, 123
Patton, Frank, 126n3, 196n54
Pelikan, Jaroslav, 171n16
Peutuchowski, Jakob, 171n16
Pike, James, Bishop, viii, 59n43, 226n27, 228n29, 233
Powell, Jeff, 5
Proelss, E. Fredrick, 170n15
Pyle, John, 170n13

Reagan, Ronald, 211
Ritzer, George, 32n28
Robinson, John, 134n12

Roosevelt, Franklin Delanor, 17, 109, 118
Rossinow, Doug, 153, 153n28
Rowland, Stanley, 31

Schilling, Donald, 97n56
Schleiermacher, Friedrich, 28n23
Schoonover, Melvin, 2
Sinatra, Frank, 101
Sittler, Joseph, 46n20
Slocum, Robert, 6n6, 9n9
Smellie, B., 47
Smith, Howard, 109
Sontag, Frederick, 170, 170n15
Swayze, Patrick, 95
Syd, 95n53

Temple, William, 38–39n5, 47–48
Tillich, Paul, 58n43, 182
Tito, Josip Broz, 15, 16n1
Todd, George, 72–74, 72n63, 73n67
Towne, Anthony, xiii, 4, 4n3, 75, 181n28, 192–94, 193nn46–47, 49, 194n49, 51, 196n54, 197, 199n57, 225, 226n27, 227–28, 228n29, 235, 238, 238n43, 241, 247–48
Truman, Harry S., 17, 28n22

Underwood, Kenneth, 53n31

Van Dusen, Henry P., 38n5, 39n6
Vidler, A. R., 38, 38n5
Visser t'Hooft, Willem Adolph, 194

Wallace, Henry, 21, 28n22, 115
Warren, Earl, Chief Justice, 119n31
Webber, George, 71n61, 83n30
Wesley, John, 28n23
Whitehouse, W. A., 38
Williams, Rowan, vii–viii
Wills, Garry, 29
Wingrin, Gustav, 55n35
Wink, Walter, 87n86, 176n25, 250

Wylie-Kellermann, Bill, ix, 5n5, 9–10n10, 77n71, 80n76, 93n94, 145n21, 146, 149n25, 157, 174n20, 181n29, 186n37, 189n43, 240n47

Ziegler, Edward, 28n23